D0073409

THE LABOR LAWYER'S GUIDE TO THE RIGHTS AND RESPONSIBILITIES OF EMPLOYEE WHISTLEBLOWERS

Recent Titles from Quorum Books

The Technology Assessment Process: A Strategic Framework for Managing
Technical Innovation
Blake L. White

The Anatomy of Industrial Decline: Productivity, Investment, and Location
in U.S. Manufacturing
John E. Ullmann

Interpersonal Communication for Technically Trained Managers: A Guide to
Skills and Techniques
Dale E. Jackson

Improved Business Planning Using Competitive Intelligence
Carolyn M. Vella and John J. McGonagle, Jr.

Retail Marketing Strategy: Planning, Implementation, and Control
A. Coskun Samli

Venturing Abroad: Innovation by U.S. Multinationals
Frank Clayton Schuller

Microcomputers, Corporate Planning, and Decision Support Systems
Edited by The WEFA Group, David J. Gianturco, and Nariman Behravesh

The Investment Side of Corporate Cash Management
Robert T. March

A Practical Approach to International Operations
Michael Gendron

Exceptional Entrepreneurial Women: Strategies for Success
Russel R. Taylor

Collective Bargaining and Impasse Resolution in the Public Sector
David A. Dilts and William J. Walsh

New Directions in MIS Management: A Guide for the 1990s
Robert J. Thierauf

THE LABOR LAWYER'S GUIDE TO THE RIGHTS AND RESPONSIBILITIES OF EMPLOYEE WHISTLEBLOWERS

Stephen M. Kohn
and
Michael D. Kohn

Everett Library
Queens College
1900 Selwyn Avenue
Charlotte, N. C.   28274

Quorum Books
NEW YORK•WESTPORT, CONNECTICUT•LONDON

5 0703 00083488 5

344.73
K827l

Library of Congress Cataloging-in-Publication Data

Kohn, Stephen M. (Stephen Martin)
    The labor lawyer's guide to the rights and
responsibilities of employee whistleblowers.

    Bibliography: p.
    Includes index.
    1. Employees, Dismissal of—Law and legislation—
United States. 2. Discrimination in employment—Law
and legislation—United States. 3. Whistle blowing—
Law and legislature—United States. I. Kohn, Michael D.
II. Title.
KF3471.K64   1988   344.73'012596   88-6017
                           347.30412596

ISBN 0-89930-207-6 (lib. bdg. : alk. paper)

British Library Cataloguing in Publication Data is available.

Copyright © 1988 by Stephen M. Kohn and Michael D. Kohn

All rights reserved. No portion of this book may be
reproduced, by any process or technique, without the
express written consent of the publisher.

Library of Congress Catalog Card Number: 88-6017
ISBN: 0-89930-207-6

First published in 1988 by Quorum Books

Greenwood Press, Inc.
88 Post Road West, Westport, Connecticut 06881

Printed in the United States of America

♾™

The paper used in this book complies with the
Permanent Paper Standard issued by the National
Information Standards Organization (Z39.48-1984).

10 9 8 7 6 5 4 3 2 1

In memory of our Father, Arthur,
who served his country gallantly,
and to our Mother, Corinne,
an inspiration to all who know her.

CONTENTS

ACKNOWLEDGMENTS

We would like to express our appreciation to everyone who helped make this book possible, especially for the support given us by our Nanny, our loving sister, our Uncle Harold Dressler, and to Leslie Rose, David Colapinto, and our many friends and colleagues who assisted us with this project. We also wish to express our special thanks to the students of the Antioch School of Law and to Thomas Gannon for his interest in the topic and push to get it into print; to Sharon Coose for her assistance in producing the manuscript; to Diana Teran for assistance with Chapter 7; to Michael Rose for proofreading; and Amy Brazill for her tireless effort that insured the manuscript's completion.

THE LABOR LAWYER'S GUIDE TO THE RIGHTS AND RESPONSIBILITIES OF EMPLOYEE WHISTLEBLOWERS

1

INTRODUCTION

An important source of information vital to honest government, the enforcement of laws, and the protection of the public health and safety are whistleblowers: employees who disclose violations of law to their management,[1] labor unions, news reporters,[2] or directly to governmental authorities.[3] Whistleblowers have significantly contributed to the enforcement of environmental and nuclear safety laws,[4] have saved American taxpayers billion of dollars,[5] and have exposed and corrected countless problems within the federal bureaucracy.[6]

Reaction against whistleblowers has been harsh. They are often subject to retaliation from their employers. They have been called "malcontents," "informants," "bag ladies," and "mental health patients."[7] A government official with the responsibility of protecting whistleblowers recently warned them to "keep quiet" or face getting "their heads blown off."[8]

Litigation in this area is often acrimonious and aggressive. It is not uncommon for employees' attorneys to raise serious ethical charges against corporate law firms.[9] Litigation can run on for years, and the costs to both sides have skyrocketed well into the hundreds of thousands of dollars. The desire of either government or corporate wrongdoers to cover up the whistleblower allegations can result in ugly and protracted legal battles.[10] In recent testimony, attorneys for a major utilities law firm that often defends employers in suits against whistleblowers, plainly admitted that the "collateral consequences" of a court ruling in support of a whistleblower can "dwarf" the actual liability the employer may face in losing a wrongful termination dispute.[11] Whistleblower cases are hard fought not just because of animosity which may arise in the course of an employment discrimination case, but also because of the economic or political impact of the actual disclosures. Unexpectedly strong backlash from their employers and the high cost of litigation have prompted many whistleblowers to advise their peers: "Forget it!"[12]

This book will focus on the legal remedies available to employee whistleblowers. Twenty years ago a landmark article in the *Columbia Law Journal* articulated the need for a new tort; a tort action based upon the wrongful discharge of an employee who testified, or who exposed corporate corruption, regarding health and safety hazards and other clear violations of public policy.[13] Prior to this article one state—California—had recognized a wrongful discharge tort for such discharges.[14] Likewise, the U.S. Supreme Court was on the verge of recognizing whistleblowing among government employees as a protected First Amendment activity.[15] In the twenty years since these developments, whistleblower law has begun to come into its own. Approximately twenty-seven federal statutes were passed explicitly protecting whistleblowers. The U.S. Constitution and the Federal Civil Service Reform Act protect whistleblowers employed by federal, state, and local government, and a majority of state jurisdictions have altered the common law to provide for a *public policy* exception designed to protect whistleblowers.[16]

Slowly, society has recognized the value of protecting employees who disclose public safety and corruption issues. The new tort of wrongful whistleblower discharge is evolving—and its parameters are maturing. Presently, there is no agreement among the various states as to what is protected activity, what type of disclosures constitute legitimate whistleblowing, what type of damages are recoverable under this new cause of action, and how overlapping statutes and laws should be interpreted. Through the maze of wrongful discharge cases and statutes, however, clear patterns and principles have emerged. The nature and scope of whistleblower protection are beginning to take on a clear and well-defined shape.

In this book we will first go backward and review the jurisprudential and constitutional roots of whistleblower protection. Second, we will outline the numerous legal remedies, under both state and federal law, which prohibit the discharge of employee whistleblowers. Third, we will present an overview of the practical issues which generally arise in all whistleblower litigation. The book will conclude with an analysis of the major controverted issues in this area of the law—specifically the scope of protected activity, the definition of public policy, and the federal preemption doctrine.

This is not a book dedicated either to advocating the virtue of whistleblowing or to explicating the significant social contributions these employees have had on society. We focus instead on basic legal principles and laws necessary to adequately understand and litigate a whistleblower case.

NOTES

1. See Stephen M. Kohn and Thomas Carpenter, "Nuclear Whistleblower Protection and the Scope of Protected Activity Under Section 210 of the Energy Reorganization Act," 4 *Antioch Law Review* 73 (Summer 1986); *Phillips v. Interior Board of Mine Op. App.*, 500 F.2d 772 (D.C. Cir. 1974); *Kansas Gas and Electric v. Brock*, 780 F.2d 1505 (10th Cir. 1985), cert. denied, 106 S.Ct. 3311 (1986).

2. *Donovan v. Peter Zimmer America, Inc.*, 557 F. Supp. 642 (D.S.C. 1982) (news media disclosure); *Wedderspoon v. Milligan*, 80—Water Pollution Control Act Case No. 1., Decision of U.S. Department of Labor Administrative Law Judge (July 11, 1980), adopted by U.S. Secretary of Labor (July 28, 1980) (contacting "environmental activist" and news media); *Consolidated Edison Co. of N.Y. v. Donovan*, 673 F.2d 61 (2nd Cir. 1982) (working with union safety committee); *Nunn v. Duke Power*, Decision and Order of the U.S. Deputy Secretary of Labor, at pp. 12–13 (July 30, 1987) (employee contacts with citizen intervenor groups with intent to provide safety information to NRC); Kohn and Carpenter, *supra*, pp. 86–89.

3. *Brown & Root, Inc. v. Donovan*, 747 F.2d 1029 (5th Cir. 1984); *Hanna v. School District of Allentown*, 79—Toxic Substances Control Act. (TSCA)–1, slip op. of Secretary of Labor at 11 (July 28, 1980), rev'd on other grounds, *School Dist. of Allentown v. Marshall*, 657 F.2d 16 (3rd Cir. 1981); *Haney v. North American Car Corp.*, 81–Solid Waste Disposal Act (SWDA)–1, slip op. of Administrative Law Judge (ALJ) at 12 (Dec. 15, 1981), adopted by Secretary of Labor (June 30, 1982).

4. See Ralph Nader, ed., *Whistleblowing* (1972); C. Peters and T. Branch, *Blowing the Whistle* (1972); A. Westin, *Whistleblowing: Loyalty and Dissent in the Corporation* (1981); Senate Comm. on Governmental Affairs, 95th Cong., 2d sess., *The Whistleblowers: A Report on Federal Employees Who Disclose Acts of Waste, Abuse, and Corruption* (Comm. Print, 1978); Stephen Kohn, *Protecting Environmental and Nuclear Whistleblowers: A Litigation Manual* (Nuclear Information and Resource Service, 1985); *McAllen v. U.S. Environmental Protection Agency*, et al., 86—Water Pollution Control Act—Case No. 1, Decision of U.S. Department of Labor Administrative Law Judge (Nov. 28, 1986); Speech by C. Kennedy, "Whistleblowing: Contribution or Catastrophe?" to the American Association for the Advancement of Science (Feb. 15, 1978); Thomas M. Devine, Donald G. Aplin," Abuse of Authority: The Office of the Special Counsel and Whistleblower Protection," 4 *Antioch Law Journal* 5, 10 (Summer 1986); U.S. Department of Agriculture, Office of Inspector General, Report of Investigation: Food Safety and Inspection Service Special Review of the Inspection Program in Southern California, File No. SF–2499–7 (Nov. 13, 1985) and reports referenced therein [hereinafter referred to as USDA OIG Report], Devine and Aplin, *supra* at 42–44; see *United States v. Garde*, 673 F. Supp. 604 (D. D.C., Oct. 27, 1987). Also see, *Rose v. Secretary of Dept. of Labor*, 800 F.2d 563, 565 (6th Cir. 1986) (concurring op. of J. Edwards).

5. Government Accounting Office, *5-Year Summary of Results of GAO Fraud Hot-Line*, GAO/AFMD–84–70 (Washington, D.C., Sept. 25, 1984); Nader, ed., *Whistleblowing* (1972); S. Kohn and T. Carpenter, "Nuclear Whistleblower Protection and the Scope of Protected Activity Under Section 210 of the Energy Reorganization Act," 4 *Antioch Law Journal* 73, 74 (Summer 1986).

6. See Thomas Devine and Donald Aplin, "Abuse of Authority: The Office of the Special Counsel and Whistleblower Protection," 4 *Antioch Law Review* 5 (Summer 1986).

7. U.S. House of Representatives, Report of the Civil Service Subcommittee of the House Post Office and Civil Service Commission, House Report 99–859, 99th Cong., 2d Sess., p. 17 (Washington, D.C.: Government Printing Office, 1986).

8. Ibid.

9. *Hasan v. N.P.S.*, 86–Energy Reorganization Act—24, U.S. Dept. of Labor Administrative Law Judge Decision on "Motion to Disqualify Respondent's Counsel, for Default Judgment and for Sanctions" (appealed 10/21/86, settlement agreement reached without concession as to legality of the ALJ's decision, joint motion to vacate pursuant to terms of settlement agreement granted 2/4/87); U.S. Department of Labor, Wage and Hour Division, Investigation Report by Herman R. Northcott, Jr. (Feb. 10, 1986) (See *Wensil v. Shaw*, 86–Energy Reorganization Act (ERA)–15, file of the U.S. Department of Labor); M. Galen, "An Ethical Furor over a Witness," *National Law Journal*, December 22, 1986; Eugene R. Fidell, *Federal Protection of Private Sector Health and Safety Whistleblowers: A Report to the Administrative Conference of the United States* (Washington, D.C., March 1987).

10. Ibid.

11. N. Reynolds, R. Walker, P. Dykema (law firm of Bishop, Cook, Purcell & Reynolds), "Comments on Preliminary Recommendations of the Administrative Conference of the United States Regarding Private Sector Health and Safety Whistleblower Statutes" (Washington, D.C., April 10, 1987).

12. Myron Glazer and Penina Glazer, "Whistleblowing," *Psychology Today*, August 1986, p. 42.

13. Blades, "*Employment at Will v. Individual Freedom:* On Limiting the Abusive Exercise of Employer Power," 67 *Columbia Law Review* 1404 (1967).

14. *Peterman vs. International Brotherhood of Teamsters*, 174 Cal. App. 184, 344 P.2d 25 (1959).

15. *Pickering v. Board of Education*, 391 U.S. 563 (1968).

16. Philip Borowsky and Lex Larson, *Unjust Dismissal* (New York: Matthew Bender, 1987).

2

CONSTITUTIONAL DEVELOPMENT OF WHISTLEBLOWER PROTECTION LAW

The constitutional roots of modern whistleblower law derive from a synthesis of two completely independent judicial developments—one in the law of contempt, and the other in the law of contract. In the late nineteenth century the employment *at-will* doctrine was well settled in American law. Essentially, the employment relationship was contractual in nature and both the employee and employer had the right to terminate the relationship for any reason or no reason. Attempts by government to interfere with this freedom to contract—by passing laws to protect employees, such as eight-hour-day laws or minimum-wage laws—were regularly found unconstitutional. The concept of employment discrimination was not recognized in law. At the same time, it was well settled in law that people could not intimidate witnesses or parties appearing in court. Such intimidation was illegal and the perpetrator was subject to contempt of court—a summary process that can result in both fines and imprisonment.

Over the years the ironclad at-will doctrine was eroded, and Congress' power to prohibit certain forms of employment discrimination was constitutionally recognized by the U.S. Supreme Court. Simultaneously, state courts slowly changed the common law at-will rule. During the 1980s a majority of state jurisdictions modified the strict at-will doctrine, and carved out a *public policy exception*. This exception protects employees from termination if the discharge is in violation of a state *public policy*. The public policy exception to the employment at-will doctrine is summarized by most courts as follows: An employer may fire an employee for any reason or no reason, but not for a reason which violates a clear mandate of public policy. Today, whistleblowers are regularly protected under both federal statutory and state statutory, or common law.

As whistleblowers began to receive protection under common law and statutory remedies, the law of contempt was altered. The historic power of a court to find persons in contempt for actions which occurred outside the geographical location of the court fell into disuse—and in 1941 the U.S. Supreme Court, interpreting the federal contempt laws, reversed a contempt citation for a person who improperly induced a litigant to drop his case.[1] The alleged impropriety occurred beyond the geographical domain of the courthouse. The Supreme Court reasoned that this type of misconduct was better adjudicated, not through summary contempt proceedings, but in formal criminal proceedings, under existing federal law.[2] The historic contempt power of the federal courts was restricted in cases concerning interference with the administration of justice. Courts stopped utilizing the contempt remedy to protect witnesses and parties to court proceedings from intimidation which occurred outside the courthouses. The prohibition on witness intimidation remained—only the remedy moved from contempt to more established litigation under federal statute, state statute, and common law. Essentially, the historic contempt power of courts to protect witnesses has now been merged with state and federal laws, which have been used effectively to protect both whistleblowers and witnesses.

WITNESS PROTECTION AND THE LAW OF CONTEMPT

The origins of whistleblower law stretch back to antiquity. Although the rights of employee whistleblowers have only recently received constitutional sanction, the contempt power of courts was used throughout history to prohibit the harassment of witnesses or parties engaged in judicial proceedings.[3] A whistleblower is a witness—an employee who obtains information of corporate or government wrongdoing. In most cases whistleblowers are fired or harassed after they either initiate a suit to vindicate their rights or after they disclose information to a government investigation, a grand jury, or at a hearing. For example, the first state to prohibit the wrongful discharge of a whistleblower was California. The facts of the case concerned an employee's discharge for refusing to commit perjury.[4] Likewise, the federal whistleblower statutes all prohibit discharge for employees who either "testify" or "commence" litigation or enforcement proceedings under federal law.[5] Even if a whistleblower is not a formal witness at the time he or she suffers from retaliation, in most cases it is clear that the employee may shortly become a witness in either a civil, administrative, or criminal proceeding.

It parties or witnesses in judicial proceedings are intimidated from testifying, the ability of a citizen to obtain justice is undermined, and eventually the very existence of a republican form of government is threatened. If people are afraid to assert their rights or testify in court, what avenues remain open for societal action against civil or criminal wrongdoers? What good is a law passed by Congress or a legislature if people are intimidated from insisting upon its enforcement?

Government has the undisputed power to protect witnesses and parties. In *Marbury v. Madison* the U.S. Supreme Court Chief Justice Marshall wrote:

[t]he very essence of civil liberty certainly consists in the right of every individual to claim the protection of the laws, whenever he receives an injury. One of the first duties of the government is to afford him that protection."[6]

The power of government to protect witnesses and parties from retaliation was historically enforced directly by courts through summary contempt proceedings.[7] In his distinguished 1884 *Treatise on Contempt*, Stewart Rapalje noted that under common law a contempt of court would lie for "any attempt to threaten or intimidate a person from instituting or defending any action." Contempt could also be found if a person acted to "threaten," "intimidate," or coerce a witness to "suppress or withhold the truth."[8]

In 1916 the Supreme Court of Arkansas in *Turk v. State*[9] summarized this rule: "It is universally held that intimidating a witness and preventing his appearance at court . . . is a contempt of court."[10] Courts in both England and the United States followed this precedent.[11] Although the early contempt cases did not arise in the context of the employer-employee relationship, the conduct courts found contemptuous was extremely similar to the problems that contemporary whistleblowers face.

The contempt power is no longer invoked to prohibit intimidation of witnesses or parties when that intimidation occurs outside of the physical domain of a court. Prior to the twentieth century, contempts of court were issued for conduct committed far from a courthouse—and sometimes even for conduct which occurred outside the jurisdiction of a court. For example, in *Turk v. State* the Supreme Court of Arkansas reasoned that contempt could be found for actions occurring far away from a courthouse. The court reasoned that the "arm" of the court was "long enough and strong enough to keep open and unobstructed the way to its door.[12]

In 1941 the U.S. Supreme Court, in *Nye v. U.S.*, struck down a federal court's use of the contempt power to punish a person who interfered with a litigant's ability to pursue his case in a federal court.[13] The Supreme Court found the conduct of the lower court "reprehensible" but was not willing to authorize federal courts to punish such obstruction by contempt. Justice Douglas, who wrote the majority opinion, held that summary contempt proceedings should be used for "misbehavior" which "obstructed the administration of justice," only when such misconduct is within the geographic location of the court itself:

The fact that in purpose and effect there was an obstruction in the administration of justice did not bring the condemned conduct within the vicinity of the court in any normal meaning of the term. It was not misbehavior in the vicinity of the court disrupting to quiet and order or actually interrupting the court in the conduct of its business.[14]

The holding in *Nye* was narrow. The power of courts to find persons who intimidate witnesses or parties in contempt was not found unconsitutional.[15] The U.S. Judicial Code was narrowly construed to limit the contempt power of federal judges. A defendant in a summary contempt proceeding risks imprisonment without the benefit of a jury trial. Because of the conflict between the right of a defendant and the necessity to protect the orderly administration of justice, Justice Douglas held that "instances where there is no right to a jury" must be "narrowly restricted."[16] Obstruction of justice (including witness intimidation) was sanctionable under other federal statutes where the defendant would have the right to a jury trial.[17] The Supreme Court reasoned that people accused of witness intimidation or interference with a person's right to file a suit should be afforded a jury trial—not imprisoned and fired in a summary proceeding.

THE RISE OF EMPLOYMENT LAW AND
WHISTLEBLOWER PROTECTION

Establishing the legal rights of whistleblowers under statutory and common law has been a slow process stretching over the last forty years. During this process Congress and the U.S. Supreme Court were initially in the forefront of protecting employees who gave negative testimony or information against an employer from job-related retaliation. Since the early 1970s, however, state courts have taken the lead and have established, in most state jurisdictions, effective remedies for wrongfully discharged whistleblowers.

In the late nineteenth and early twentieth century there was no recognized principle in employment law concerning whistleblower protection. Employers had the right to fire employees for any reason or no reason—or even an "immoral" reason. In *Payne v. Western and Atlantic Railroad Co.,* [18] the Tennessee Supreme Court summarized the at-will doctrine:

All may dismiss their employees at will, be they many or few, for good cause, for no cause or even for cause morally wrong, without being thereby guilty of legal wrong. . . . Trade is free; so is employment. The law leaves employer and employee to make their own contracts. . . . This secures to all civil and industrial liberty. A contrary rule would lead to a judicial tyranny as arbitrary, irresponsible and intolerable as that exercised by Scroggs and Jeffreys.[19]

In *Payne* the Court upheld the right of an employer to terminate an employee if that employee shopped at a store disapproved of by the employer. In doing so, the Court justified corporate use of their size and wealth to dominate their employees and society. The Court stated: "Great corporations, strong associations, and wealthy individuals may thus do great mischief and wrong" and "greatly injure individuals and the public." This conduct was allowable, however, because "power is inherent in size and strength and wealth; and the law cannot set bound for it, unless it is exercised illegally."[20]

Employees could be hired and fired at will—employers were "free" not to hire women, blacks, Jews, union members, Irish, or any class of people they did not like. Those who were hired could be discharged for any reason and compelled to work at no minimum wage, no maximum hours, and in dangerous and hazardous occupations. Employees had no basic legal rights—except those which could be obtained through private contract.

Although there has been tremendous change in the employee–employer relationship since the Tennessee Supreme Court decided *Payne*, the roots of modern labor law are grounded in the majority opinion of *Payne*. Modern labor law is still based on policies rooted in laissez-faire principles of employee and employer rights.

The majority in *Payne* did recognize that even extreme laissez-faire policies could be tempered. Although the court recognized that capital could "injure" the public and cause "great mischief and wrong," it also recognized that capital was required to act within the bounds of law and its power could not be "exercised illegally."[21] Thus the state maintained some form of legislative power to statutorily limit the freedom of capital over labor. At the time the *Payne* case was decided there were no laws limiting the monopolistic rights of corporations to require that their employees not frequent certain stores.

The dissent in *Payne* articulated a public policy exception to the unlimited power of capital to determine the working conditions of their employees. The roots of the modern public policy exception to the at-will doctrine were articulated in the hundred-year-old dissent authored by Justice Freeman:

Perfect freedom in all legitimate uses is due to capital, and should be zealously enforced; but public policy and all the best interests of society demands it shall be restrained within legitimate boundaries, and any channel by which it may escape or overleap these boundaries, should be carefully but judiciously guarded. For its legitimate uses I have perfect respect, against its illegitimate use I feel bound, for the best interests both of capital and labor, to protest.[22]

This tension between the at-will doctrine and the power of the legislature to equalize the employee-employer relationship in light of public policy issues was similarly unfolding in the U.S. Supreme Court.

In 1898 Congress passed a law which made it illegal for carriers engaged in interstate commerce to terminate an employee on the basis of union membership.[23] If an agent or an employer of an interstate carrier did terminate an employee on the basis of union membership, he was liable for a fine of "not less than one hundred dollars and not more than one thousand dollars."[24] In *Adair v. U.S.* the constitutionality of this provision was challenged.[25]

The U.S. Supreme Court used *Adair* to canonize the at-will doctrine to constitutional proportions. The Court struck down the legality of the union protection provision of the 1898 act on the basis of the Fourteenth Amendment right to contract. Relying upon its decision in *Lochner v. New York*,[26] the Court reasoned:

While, as already suggested, the right of liberty and property guaranteed by the Constitution against deprivation without due process of law, is subject to such reasonable restraints as the common good or the general welfare may require, it is not within the functions of government—at least in the absence of contract between the parties—to compel any person in the course of his business and against his will to accept or retain the personal services of another, or to compel any person, against his will, to perform personal services for another. The right of a person to sell his labor upon such terms as he deems proper is, in its essence, the same as the right of the purchaser of labor to prescribe the conditions upon which he will accept such labor from the person offering to sell it. So the right of the employe to quit the service of the employer, for whatever reason, is the same as the right of the employer, for whatever reason, to dispense with the services of such employe.[27]

The Court explicitly struck down the statute on the basis of the "equality of right" existing between labor and capital. The Court ignored the gross discrepancies between the respective strengths of an individual and a major corporation and gave constitutional status to the fiction of equality between employers and employees:

In all such particulars the employer and the employee have equality of rights, and any legislation that disturbs that equality is an arbitrary interference with the liberty of contract which no government can legally justify in a free land.[28]

The *Adair* court adopted the same principle as did the *Payne* court. *Adair* did not hold that Congress could not pass any law restricting the employee-employer relationship—but it narrowly restricted the potential scope of such intervention by reading into the Constitution laissez-faire notions of capital and labor.[29]

The majority in *Adair* did, however, at least in theory, recognize that certain areas of the public interest could justify a limitation of the right of labor and capital to "freely" contract. The Court recognized the potential right of the state to condition the "right to purchase or sell labor" through the reliance upon certain inherent police powers which the state always maintains:

There are, however, certain powers, existing in the sovereignty of each State in the Union, somewhat vaguely termed police powers, the exact description and limitation which have not been attempted by the courts. Those powers, broadly stated and without, at present, any attempt at a more specific limitation, relate to the safety, health, morals and general welfare of the public. Both property and liberty are held on such reasonable conditions as may be imposed by the governing power of the State in the exercise of those powers, and with such conditions the Fourteenth Amendment was not designed to interfere.[30]

Justice Holmes, dissenting in *Adair*, picked up on the majority recognition that issues related to "safety, health, morals and general welfare of the public" could lawfully justify abridging the at-will doctrine. Like the dissent in *Payne*, Holmes utilized the concept of public policy and reasoned that Congress was well within its right to reasonably define sound public policy exceptions to the at-will doctrine:

I confess that I think that the right to make contracts at will that has been derived from the word liberty in the amendments has been stretched to its extreme by the decisions; but they agree that sometimes the right may be restrained. Where there is, or generally is believed to be, an important ground of public policy for restraint the Constitution does not forbid it, whether this court agrees or disagrees with the policy pursued. It cannot be doubted that to prevent strikes, and, so far as possible, to foster its scheme of arbitration, might be deemed by Congress an important point of policy.[31]

As Justice Holmes pointed out, the supremacy of the at-will doctrine during the pre–New Deal era was not totally based upon a reading of constitutional or common law principles. In fact those principles recognized potential legal and public policy exceptions to the at-will doctrine. Politically, the U.S. Supreme Court was not willing to apply those exceptions to most of the cases that came before it.[32]

In the New Deal and post–New Deal era, however, Congress, legislatures, and the courts began to enforce the right of employees to be free from employer discriminations. The turning point in this constitutional history was the massive union organizing movement which occurred during the Great Depression (1929–1940). The economic hardship and social dislocation caused by the Depression set the social-economic stage for a bloody and violent confrontation between labor and capital. Strikes, including illegal occupations of factories, occurred throughout the United States. Between 1929 and 1932 over two-hundred workers were killed in strike-related violence. The Congress of Industrial Organizations (CIO) union was formed. Many in its leadership were radicals—including socialists and communists—who effectively organized millions of employees into powerful industrial unions.[33]

Congress reacted to the rise of the labor movement in the 1930s and the hardship and poverty caused by the Depression by enacting a series of laws designed to aid the poor or working person. The pinnacle of these efforts for the labor movement was the passage of the National Labor Relations Act (Wagner Act) on July 5, 1935.[34] This act went further than any other previous law designed to protect the rights of employees who desired to join labor unions. It made it unlawful to discriminate against an employee because he or she was a union member or supporter—and it set up an administrative mechanism to force employers to reinstate, with back pay, any employee discharged because of union membership.[35] The law thereby created a significant exception to the at-will doctrine. The National Labor Relations Act (NLRA) was the forerunner of all other employment discrimination laws—and the procedure and principle adopted to adjudicate NLRA unfair labor practice cases have been followed by numerous other legislative bodies in enacting laws which recognize employee rights.

The NLRA not only protected employees on the basis of union membership—it also contained a witness protection provision. Section 8(4) of the NLRA reads: "It shall be an unfair labor practice for an employer . . . [t]o discharge or otherwise discriminate against an employee because he has filed charges or given testimony under this Act."[36] Section 8(4) of the NLRA was the first federal statutory whistleblower protection law. Any employee who "offered testimony or provided information about an illegal unfair labor practice" would be protected. Section 8(4) went further than just protecting employees' right to organize—it protected employees who testified. Whistleblower protection laws are essentially witness protection laws. When an employee witnesses a potential illegal act—be it criminal fraud, an environmental violation, or an illegal antiunion activity—and then provides information to his or her supervisor, the government, or the public in an attempt to correct the problem, that is the heart of whistleblowing. A whistleblower may not envision himself or herself to be a "witness," per se. But, in fact, once a disclosure of wrongdoing is made to an authority, a whistleblower immediately has the status of a potential or actual witness.

The U.S. Supreme Court decision upholding the constitutionality of the NLRA marked the turning point in the legality of employee protection laws. Divided 5–4, the Court found that Congress, under the commerce clause, had the power to enact the NLRA. Additionally, the Court found that the requirement that management reinstate with back pay employees fired for union-related activities was constitutional.[37] The majority in the landmark decision *NLRB v. Jones & Laughlin Steel Corp,* justified the reinstatement and back pay provisions as an appropriate remedy for a violation of the statute.[38] Proceedings under the NLRA were governed by a detailed administrative procedure set out in the act, and the act did not create any common law remedies.

The dissent relied, in part, upon the holding of the *Adair* line of cases,[39] and repeated its former holding that "The right of contract is fundamental and includes the privilege of selecting those with whom one is willing to assume contractual relations."[40] The holding of the *Adair* line of cases, however, was henceforth dead, and the principle that the courts or the legislature could intervene in the employee-employer relationship to aid employees and effect certain public policies became unquestioned in American law.

Since the passage of the NLRA, Congress has passed numerous laws protecting employee witnesses or whistleblowers, including whistleblower provisions in the Fair Labor Standards Act,[41] the Occupational Safety and Health Act,[42] the Toxic Substances Control Act,[43] the Civil Service Reform Act,[44] the Clean Air Act,[45] and the Federal Mine Health and Safety Act,[46] to name a few.

The Supreme Court has broadly interpreted these whistleblower protection or witness protection statutes. For example, the Court has held that Section 8(a)(4) of the NLRA must be given a "broad" interpretation[47] in order to allow employees to be "completely free from coercion" when they provide information to the National Labor Relations Board.[48] This broad interpretation of the law was necessary to "prevent the Board's channels of information from being dried up by employer intimidation of prospective complainants and witnesses."[49]

Thirty years after *NLRB v. Jones and Laughlin Steel Co.*, the U.S. Supreme Court took the next major step in protecting employee whistleblower rights. The Court implied from the First and Fourteenth Amendments of the U.S. Constitution a wrongful discharge suit for state employees who engaged in protected free speech activities. The NLRA contained an explicit provision prohibiting the discharge of employees and providing for an administrative remedy. But neither the First or Fourteenth Amendments contain employee protection provisions. Whistleblowing, however, is a form of free speech. In the 1968 landmark case of *Pickering v. Board of Education*, [50] the Supreme Court held that for a public school teacher the "exercise of his right to speech on issues of public importance may not furnish the basis for his dismissal from public employment."[51] The Court derived a wrongful discharge cause of action from the constitutional rights embodied in the First Amendment. Thus the First Amendment created an exception to the at-will doctrine concerning the termination of state employees.

In *Pickering* the Supreme Court also acknowledged that the veracity of the speech did not determine whether the speech was protected: "*Erroneous* public statements upon issues then currently the subject of public attention, which are critical of his ultimate employer" are protected.[52] *Pickering* did not, however, protect all forms of speech. Specifically excluded from protection was speech which "interfered with the regular operation" of the schools, speech which would "impede" a teacher's performance of daily duties, speech which did not concern matters of public concern, and the issuance of "false statements knowingly or recklessly made."[53]

After *Pickering*, First Amendment limitations on a state's right to discharge at-will employees was expanded to prohibit discharge on the basis of other First Amendment activities, including political associations and beliefs.[54] The Court has also protected nonpublic speech directed solely at the state employees' supervisor.[55]

By the early 1970s the U.S. Supreme Court had developed an exception to the at-will doctrine covering state employees under the First and Fourteenth Amendments. The proper exercise of constitutional rights became a bar to such terminations, even if Congress did not pass any statutory protection prohibiting such discharge.[56] Where statutory provisions did exist, the Court upheld their constitutionality and required that they be broadly interpreted.

CONCLUSION

Modern whistleblower protection law is a synthesis of the historic powers of government to protect witnesses and parties to litigation, and a constitutional recognition of the power of government to regulate the private employee–employer relationship. If whistleblowers were not protected under law the ability of the general public or the government to learn of potential threats to the social welfare would be chilled. Employees could be economically threatened by their employer if they attempted to exercise their free speech rights, or their rights to initiate litigation and to testify. Although most of the laws which protect whistleblowers have only recently been enacted, the roots of whistleblower protection run deep in law. The need to protect people who disclose illegality of dangers to public safety from intimidation is a principle fundamental to democracy.

NOTES

1. *Nye v. U.S.*, 313 U.S. 33 (1941).

2. *Nye*, 61 S. Ct. at 816.

3. See *Shires v. Magnavox Co.*, 432 F. Supp. 231, 233 (E.D. Tenn. 1976).

4. See *Petermann v. International Brotherhood of Teamsters*, 344 P.2d 25 (Cal. App. 1959).

5. See Kohn and Kohn, "An Overview of Federal and State Whistleblower Protection," 4 *Antioch Law Journal* 99, 101–107 (Summer, 1986).

6. *Marbury V. Madison*, 5 U.S. (1 Cranch) 137, 163, 2 L.Ed. 60 (1803). In *EEOC v. Lorals 14 and 15*, 438 F. Supp. 876, 879 (S.D. N.Y. 1977) a U.S. federal district court granted an injunction against a defendant from "harassing, intimidating" and discriminating against employee for testifying in a Title VII suit. The court relied, in part, upon the historic power of government to protect witnesses:

Part of this duty of the government to provide the protection of law is that litigants and witnesses who appear before federal courts do so secure in the knowledge that they cannot be harassed, intimidated, punished or otherwise suffer harm because they availed themselves of the judicial system.

The insult that such retaliation against litigants or witnesses would produce goes beyond the injuries suffered by the individuals themselves: the integrity of the court's process and proceedings suffers the inevitable and intolerable destruction that accompanies any retaliation against the witnesses.

7. See 23 A.L.R. 183.

8. Stewart Rapalje, *A Treatise on Content*, §22, page 27 n. 1 (New York, 1884).

9. *Turk v. State*, 123 Ark. 341, 185 S.W. 472 (1916).

10. Ibid.

11. See *Wilson v. Irwin*, 144 Ky. 311, 138 S.W. 373 (1911); *McCarthy v. State*, 89 Tenn. 543, 15 S.W. 736 (1891); *Snow v. Hawkes*, 183 N.C. 365, 111 S.E. 621 (1922); *Sharland v. Sharland*, 1 Times L.R. (Eng., 1885); *Bromilow v. Phillips*, 40 Week Rep. (Eng., 1892); *Smith v. Lakeman*, 2 Jur. N.S. 1202, 26 L.J. Ch N.S. 305 (Eng. 1856); *Re Muloch*, 10 Jur. N.S. 1188, 33 L.J. Prob. N.S. 205, 13 Week Rep. 278 (Eng., 1864). See 23 A.L.R. 183.

12. *Turk v. State*, 185 S.W. at 473.

13. *Nye v. U.S.*, 313 U.S. 33 (1941).

14. 313 U.S. at 52.

15. 313 U.S. at 50.

16. 313 U.S. at 49.

17. Justice Douglas was referring to the Reconstruction era Civil Rights Act which criminalized attempts to "intimidate or impede" a witness or otherwise "obstruct or impede the due administration of justice." 18 U.S.C. 241, cited at 313 U.S. 46–47.

18. 81 Tenn. 507 (1884).

19. 81 Tenn. at 519–520 (1884).

20. 81 Tenn. at 519.

21. 81 Tenn. at 519.

22. *Payne*, 81 Tenn. at 544 (dissent of J. Freeman).

23. Act of Congress, June 1, 1898, 30 Stat. 424.

24. 30 Stat. 424, Section 10.

25. *Adair v. U.S.*, 208 U.S. 161 (1908).

26. 198 U.S. 45 (1905}.

27. *Adair v. U.S.*, 208 U.S. at 174–75.

28. 208 U.S. at 175.

29. See the dissent of Justice Holmes in *Lochner v. New York*, 198 U.S. 45, 75, in which he criticized the court for embodying "a particular economic theory" of laissez-faire capitalism into the Constitution.

30. *Adair*, 208 U.S. at 173.

31. *Adair v. U.S.*, 208 U.S. at 191 (dissent of J. Holmes).

32. The U.S. Supreme Court did uphold a number of state laws abridging the employee's right of contract, citing to the inherent state police power to protect employee health, *Holden v. Hardy*, 169 U.S. 366 (1898); *Bunting v. Oregon*, 243 U.S. 426 (1917).

33. Francis Piven, Richard Cloward, *Poor People's Movements* (New York: Pantheon, 1977); Howard Zinn, *A People's History of the United States* (New York: Harper, 1980); Jeremy Brecher, *Strike!* (Boston: South End Press, 1972).

34. Act of July 5, 1935, 49 Stat. 449.

35. 29 U.S.C. 141, et. seq.

36. Section 8(4) of the NLRA, 29 U.S.C. 158(a)(4).

37. *NLRB v. Jones & Laughlin Steel Co.*, 301 U.S. 1 57 S. Ct. 615 (1937).

38. Ibid, 57 S. Ct. at 624.

39. See *Adair v. U.S.* 208 U.S. 161 (1908); and *Coppage v. Kansas*, 35 S. Ct. 240 (1915).

40. *NLRB v. Jones & Laughlin Steel Corp.*, 57 S. Ct. at 641 (dissent of J. McReynolds).

41. 29 U.S.C. 206(d).

42. 29 U.S.C. 660(c).

43. 15 U.S.C. 2622.

44. 5 U.S.C. 2302.

45. 42 U.S.C. 7622.

46. 30 U.S.C. 815(c).

47. *NLRB v. Scrivener*, 405 U.S. 117, 92 S. Ct. 798, 801–2 (1972).

48 *Nash v. Florida Industrial Commission*, 389 U.S. 235, 88 S. Ct. 362, 365 (1967).

49. *NLRB v. Scrivener*, 92 S. Ct. 798, 801 (1972), quoting from *John Hancock Mut. Life Ins. Co. v. NLRB*, 191 F.2d 483, 485 (D.C. Cir. 1951).

50. 88 S. Ct. 1731 (1968).

51. 88 S. Ct. at 1738.

52. 88 S. Ct. at 1737.

53. 88 S. Ct. at 1737, 1738. Also see, *Connick v. Myers*, 461 U.S. 138 (1983) for a full discussion of the protection of speech made for private or public purposes. The *Connick* Court held: "When a public employee speaks not as a citizen upon matters of public concern, but instead or an employee upon matters only of personal interest, absent the most unusual circumstances, a federal court is not the appropriate forum in which to review the wisdom of personnel decision taken by a public agency allegedly in reaction to the employee's behavior." 461 U.S. 138, 147 (1983).

54. *Perry v. Sindermann*, 408 U.S. 593, 92 S. Ct. 2694 (1972); *Elrod v. Burns*, 427 U.S. 347, 96 S Ct. 2673 (1976); *Branti v. Finkel*, 445 U.S. 507, 100 S. Ct. 1287 (1980). The court did recognize that certain employees engaged in policy making or employees that have access to confidential information or work involving similar special circumstances could be discharged despite First Amendment limitations. See *Elrod*, 95 S. Ct. at 2686; *Branti* 100 S. Ct. at 1294.

55. See *Givhan v. Western Line Consol. School*, 439 U.S. 410, 99 S. Ct. 693 (1979).

56. In *Bush v. Lucas*, 103 S. Ct. 2404 (1983) the Supreme Court declined to allow federal civil service employees protection under a *Pickering* cause of action. The court held that federal employees must utilize the Civil Service Reform Act, which contained extensive provisions for protecting employee whistleblowers or employees who engage in protected activity. The Court looked at the unique "history and development of the civil service remedies and the comprehensive nature of the remedies." The court found that the federal Civil Service Reform Act provided exclusive remedy for federal civil servants covered under the act's protections. *Bush v. Lucas*, 103 S. Ct. at 2416.

3

FEDERAL PROTECTION FOR
EMPLOYEE WHISTLEBLOWERS

There is no comprehensive federal law that prohibits employers from retaliating against employees who disclose potential corporate or governmental violations of law. Instead, over the past fifty years there has been a steady growth of specific statutory protections for employee whistleblowers. These statutory remedies cover a significant cross section of the American workforce, but are riddled with loopholes.

Although the creation of federal rights for whistleblowers has enhanced the ability of employees to disclose employer violations of law, the patchwork nature of these remedies has hindered aggressive litigation and enforcement of whistleblower protection provisions. For example, only employees who engage in certain specific whistleblower conduct in certain specifically protected industries are covered under federal law. Each federal whistleblower statute has its own filing provisions, its own statute of limitations, and its own administrative or judicial remedies. Thus, each potential whistleblower case must be evaluated on the basis of who the employer is, what the disclosure concerns, and in which state the whistleblowing occurred. On the basis of these variables, an attorney must review various federal laws to determine if the employee is protected and exactly what procedures should be followed in filing a claim for redress.[1]

Each federal statute generally includes its own definition of what type of speech rights the statute protects, the statute of limitations for filing an action under the law, and its own administrative or judicial rules for adjudication of the claim. Although each statute is different, courts and administrative agencies regularly apply the case law and legal analysis developed under one statute in interpreting other statutes. This has occurred because the basic elements in a retaliatory discharge claim tend to be identical. For example, courts have used retaliation case law developed in retaliation cases for exercising First Amendment rights (the *Mt. Healthy* test) in other retaliation cases— such as wrongful discharge for exercising rights under the National Labor Relations Act.[2] Likewise, Congress has modeled some whistleblower protection statutes after others—for example, the Clean Air Act whistleblower protection statute was modeled after the 1969 Federal Mine Health and Safety Act, and the nuclear whistleblower statute was modeled after the Clean Air Act statute.[3] The interpretive interrelationship between these statutes is highly significant. Often, there is little or no case precedent under one law and the practitioners must utilize case law from other areas. The extensive body of case law dealing with retaliatory discharge under some statutes, such as the NLRA or Title VII, can be extremely useful for analyzing wrongful discharge cases under other less litigated statutes.

The following is an outline of federal statutes and constitutional protections for employee whistleblowers.

CONSTITUTIONAL PROTECTION

Under the First and Fourteenth Amendments to the U.S. Constitution, state and local government officials are prohibited from retaliating against whistleblowers. In 1968 the Supreme Court held that the First Amendment protects government employees who express public dissent.[4] The First Amendment protects employees who blow the whistle either publicly, or privately and directly to their supervisors.[5] Whether any specific exercise of free speech or disclosure of potential wrongdoing is protected under the First Amendment depends upon a case–by–case analysis under the rule pronounced in *Pickering v. Board of Education*: "absent proof of false statements knowingly or recklessly made . . . [the] exercise of his right to speak on issues of public importance may not furnish the basis for his dismissal from public employment."[6]

The rights of federal employees under the First Amendment were severely restricted by the Supreme Court in *Bush v. Lucas*.[7] Essentially, if an administrative remedy is available to a federal civil servant, the federal employee must utilize that administrative remedy and cannot bring an independent tort action under the First Amendment. If a federal employee is not covered, however, under a federal administrative scheme (i.e., the Federal Civil Service Reform Act), or if the administrative remedy does not cover the retaliation alleged by the employee, the federal whistleblower may be able to use the First Amendment as the basis of whistleblower retaliation cause of action.[8] Retaliatory discharge committed by certain public officials may be nonactionable due to the immunity granted some government officials and state governmental bodies.[9]

In order for a state or local public employee's speech to be protected it must pass a two-prong test. First, a court must determine whether the speech can be "fairly characterized as constituting speech on a matter of public concern," and not just a matter of "personal interest."[10] Second, the court must balance "the interest of the (employee) as a citizen, in commenting upon matters of public concern and the interests of the state, as an employer, in promoting the efficiency of the public service it performs through its employees."[11] Whistleblowers are covered under this constitutional approach: "An employee's First Amendment interest is entitled to more weight where he is acting as a whistleblower exposing government corruption."[12]

Even if the employee's speech was subject to constitutional protection, the employee still must state a claim sufficient to meet the Mt Healthy test.[13] Under Mt. Healthy an employee has the initial burden to demonstrate that the protected speech or conduct was a "motivating factor" in the adverse employment decision. Once this is demonstrated, the burden shifts to the employer to demonstrate, "by a preponderance of the evidence" that it "would have" taken the same action absent the employee's protected conduct. The Mt. Healthy test has been applied to analyzing the legality of employer actions under other wrongful discharge statutes.[14]

Discharge of employees in violation of their constitutional rights can provide the basis for a preliminary or permanent injunction enjoining a discharge.[15]

ENVIRONMENTAL LAWS

Employee protection provisions of the Toxic Substances Control Act (TSCA),[16] the Superfund,[17] the Water Pollution Control Act,[18] the Solid Waste Disposal Act,[19] the Clean Air Act,[20] the Atomic Energy and Energy Reorganization Acts,[21] and the Safe Drinking Water Act (SDWA),[22] contain whistleblower provisions which protect employees who disclose potential violations of these environmental laws. The seven laws are all substantially identical and provide for an administrative investigation and hearing within the U.S. Department of Labor. Relief includes reinstatement, back pay, compensatory damages, and attorneys' fees. All of the laws require that a complaint be filed with the U.S. Department of Labor within thirty days of the alleged discriminatory reprisal.[23] Both the TSCA and SDWA also contain provisions for the award of exemplary damages.[24]

Under the nuclear whistleblower protection law [42 U.S.C. 5851] the U.S. Courts of Appeal are presently split as to whether making a disclosure just to management (and not the U.S. Nuclear Regulatory Commission) is protected under the act.[25] The U.S. Court of Appeals for the Fifth Circuit narrowly construed the act and held that whistleblowers must have actual contact with the NRC. This holding was strongly criticized by the NRC and has been rejected by the U.S. Secretary of Labor and the U.S. Court of Appeals for the Tenth Circuit.[26] Except the Fifth Circuit, all other courts that have reviewed this issue have given the act an expansive interpretation and have protected purely internal whistleblowing.[27]

CONSPIRACIES TO INTIMIDATE WITNESSES AND OBSTRUCT JUSTICE IN FEDERAL COURT PROCEEDINGS [42 U.S.C. 1985 (2)]

A new and developing area for whistleblower protection is 42 U.S.C. 1985 (2). This clause, which was passed as part of the Reconstruction era, anti-Ku Klux Klan civil rights legislation, contains very broad provisions prohibiting conspiracies to intimidate parties or witnesses in proceedings before courts of the United States:

If two or more persons in any State or Territory conspire to deter, by force, intimidation, or threat, any party or witness in any court of the United States from attending such court, or from testifying for any matter pending therein, freely, fully, and truthfully, or to injure such party or witness in his person or property on account of his having so attended or testified. . . . the party so injured or deprived may have an action for the recovery of damages.[28]

Clause 2 of 42 U.S.C. 1985 applies to any conspiracy to interfere with the administration of justice in the United States courts—regardless of whether that conspiracy is class- or race-based. The requirement of "racial or class based" invidious discrimination, which the U.S Supreme Court held was necessary to have a cause of action under clauses of 42 U.S.C. 1985,[29] is not necessary for suits under clause 2.[30] The U.S. Supreme Court, in *Kush v. Rutledge* held:

Given the structure of §2 of the 1871 Act, it is clear that Congress did not intend to impose a requirement of class-based animus on persons seeking to prove a violation of their rights under the first clause of §1985 (2). The legislative history supports the conclusion we have drawn from the language of the statute. Protection of the processes of the federal courts was an essential component of Congress' solution to disorder and anarchy in the Southern States. Neither proponents nor opponents of the bill had any doubt that the Constitution gave Congress the power to prohibit intimidation of parties, witnesses, and jurors in federal courts.[31]

Additionally, unlike other Reconstruction-era civil rights laws (i.e., 42 U.S.C. 1983), Clause 2 of 1985 does not require any state action. Purely private conspiracies are actionable.[32]

The jurisprudence of 1985 (2) in its application to whistleblower protection is still new and relatively uncharted. The *Kush* decision, which opened up the application of 1985 (2) to a wide area of whistleblower-related actions, was only decided in April of 1983. The contours of this action remain undefined, but its potential for whistleblower protection is immense. Essentially, whistleblowers are often "witnesses" or parties to U.S. court actions. When a whistleblower makes a disclosure he or she is often participating in the first step of a federal suit—be it as a party in a False Claims Act or environmental citizen suit, or as a witness before a federal criminal or civil proceeding. Likewise, witnesses who provide information to a plaintiff in a federal wrongful discharge action are covered, as are any conspiracies by the employer to impede a federal whistleblower suit.

A 1985 (2) suit is not a wrongful discharge action—the tortious conduct is not the termination, per se, but the conspiracy to intimidate.[33] Certain forms of proof that are commonplace in a wrongful discharge suit, such as the *Mt. Healthy* "but for" test, may be inapplicable under 42 U.S.C. 1985 (2). The tortious conduct is the conspiracy to intimidate the witness—whether the witness is ever fired is only relevant to prove intimidation or injury. It is the conspiracy, not the discharge, which is the actionable conduct. Consequently, the *prima facie* case for a 1985 (2) action is very different from that of a traditional wrongful discharge case.

The U.S. Courts of Appeal have articulated the following *prima facie* case for a 1985 (2) action:

The essential allegations of a 1985 (2) claim of witness intimidation are (1) a conspiracy between two or more persons (2) to deter a witness by force, intimidation or threat from attending court or testifying freely in any pending manner, which (3) results in injury to the plaintiffs.[34]

Within this framework, a number of crucial threshold issues remain unresolved—such as whether a corporation is a single "person" under the act, or whether two members of the same corporation can conspire with each other.[35]

The most significant case interpreting 1985 (2) in the context of employee protection was *Irizarry v. Quiros*.[36] In *Irizarry* the U.S. Court of Appeals for the First Circuit held that the denial of reemployment (blacklisting) constituted both intimidation and an "injury" sufficient to state a claim under Clause 2. The court went on to hold that an action based upon an illegal conspiracy to blacklist was not preempted under labor law, and that plaintiffs were entitled to both statutory attorney fees under 42 U.S.C. §1988 and punitive damages.[37]

FALSE CLAIMS ACT

The newest federal whistleblower protection law was contained in the 1986 amendments to the False Claim Act (FCA).[38] The False Claims

Act establishes civil liability against persons or corporations who defraud the government.[39] The whistleblower protection provision is extremely liberal and protects "any employee" who is discharged or discriminated against on the basis of assisting in the preparation of litigation or in filing a False Claims Act suit. The act was passed to "halt companies and individuals from using the threat of economic retaliation to silence 'whistleblowers,' as well as assure those who may be considering exposing fraud that they are legally protected from retaliatory acts."[40] Whistleblowers are protected even if there was no underlying violation of the False Claims Act, as long as the allegations were filed in "good faith."[41]

The False Claims Act whistleblower clause has liberal damage provisions, including reinstatement, compensation for "special damage," two times the amount of back pay, and attorney's fees and costs.[42] There is a six-year statute of limitations,[43] and suits must be filed in the appropriate federal district court.[44]

In addition to the actual whistleblower protection clause, employees can take advantage of the liberal civil action provisions of the False Claims Act. Essentially, the law gives an individual citizen, who is an original informational source of any fraud against the U.S. government, standing to file a False Claims Act suit against individuals or corporations who have defrauded the federal government.[45] If the U.S. government joins in the suit, and fraud is proven, the citizen plaintiff receives between 15 and 25 percent of the proceeds of the action or settlement, and attorney's fees.[46] If the U.S. government fails to join in the suit, and the citizen plaintiff prevails in judgment or settlement, then the citizen plaintiff is entitled to "not less than 25 percent and not more than 30 percent" of the proceeds, plus attorney's fees.[47] Thus, an employee whistleblower who exposes fraud against the U.S. government (e.g. defense contract mischarging), can sue his or her employer in an attempt to halt the corrupt practices. If fraud is found to exist, the employee is entitled to a percentage of the civil liability or fraud found to have existed. The whistleblower employee would have standing to file a False Claims Act suit even if she or he was *not* discharged or discriminated against for making the disclosure. The whistleblower protection clause of the False Claims Act becomes operative only if the employee who files a FCA, or who assists or testifies in such a claim is subject to retaliation.

SURFACE TRANSPORTATION ASSISTANCE ACT

The Surface Transportation Assistance Act[48] protects employee whistleblowers (generally truck drivers) who file a complaint, testify in or cause to be instituted proceedings to enforce a commercial motor vehicle safety rule, regulation, or standard.[49] In certain circumstances, an employee has the right to refuse to operate a vehicle if, after contacting the employer, the employee has "reasonable apprehension" that operating the vehicle would cause "serious injury to himself or the public."[50] Additionally, an employee also can refuse to operate a vehicle if such operation would constitute a "violation of any federal rules, regulations, standards or orders applicable to commercial motor vehicle safety or health.[51]

A complaint must be filed with the Secretary of Labor within 180 days of the alleged discriminatory act.[52] Within sixty days of filing the complaint the Secretary of Labor must have the allegation investigated. If the results of the investigation indicate that there is "reasonable cause" to find that the "complaint has merit," then the secretary shall issue a preliminary order in support of the employee—this includes immediate temporary reinstatement pending the outcome of a full evidentiary hearing.[53] Either the employee or the employer can appeal, within thirty days, the preliminary investigative finding. If the preliminary finding is appealed, the parties are entitled to a full evidentiary hearing, which must be "expeditiously conducted."[54]

If a final order of the secretary is issued in support of the employee, the employee is entitled to reinstatement, back pay, compensatory damages, costs, and attorney's fees.[55] Appeals of the secretary's order must be filed in the U.S. Court of Appeals, for the circuit in which the violation occurred, within sixty days of the issuance of the secretary's order.[56]

The temporary reinstatement order of the Secretary of Labor was unsuccessfully subjected to a constitutional challenge in the U.S. Supreme Court case of *Brock v. Roadway Express, Inc.*[57] In *Roadway Express*, the Court found that Congress, in passing this law, "recognized that employees in the transportation industry are often best able to detect safety violations" but often do not do so "because they may be threatened with discharge."[58] Additionally, the Supreme Court found that Congress "recognized that the employee's protection against having to choose between operating an unsafe vehicle and losing his job would lack practical effectiveness if the employee could not be reinstated pending complete review. The longer a discharged employee remains unemployed, the more devastating are the consequences to his personal financial condition and prospects for re-employment."[59]

OCCUPATIONAL SAFETY AND HEALTH ACT

The Occupational Safety and Health Act (OSHA) protects employees from any form of retaliation for raising complaints concerning workplace health and safety.[60] This has been interpreted to include a right to refuse hazardous work under certain specified and limited circumstances.[61]

Employees who believe that they have been discriminated or retaliated against for exercising safety and health rights under OSHA must file a complaint with the local OSHA office within thirty days of the time they learn of the alleged discrimination. The Secretary of Labor (SOL) must investigate the allegation. If the SOL determines that there was a violation under OSHA, the secretary must sue on behalf of the employee to obtain appropriate relief, including reinstatement and back pay.[62]

OSHA was enacted to "assure as far as possible every working man and woman in the nation safe and healthful working conditions."[63] The whistleblower protection provisions were designed to "encourage employee reporting of OSHA violations."[64] Employees have been protected for raising OSHA-related safety complaints to the U.S. Department of Labor, and also for reporting such violations to their unions,[65] to management,[66] and to the newspapers.[67]

Under OSHA, an employee does not have a federal statutory right to initiate his or her own suit for retaliatory discharge.[68] The U.S. Courts of Appeal that have reviewed the issue have uniformly held that OSHA does not authorize an implied private cause of action for wrongful discharge.[69] Consequently, if the U.S. Department of Labor does not initiate an action on behalf of a wrongfully discharged employee, that employee apparently does not have another legal remedy under federal OSHA. The employee may, however, still have an action under state law.

FEDERAL MINE HEALTH AND SAFETY ACT

The Federal Mine Health and Safety Act (FMHSA) provides for an administrative remedy for any miner, miner's representative, or applicant for employment in a mine, who files or makes a complaint regarding a potential violation of the FMHSA.[70] Complaints both to management and to governmental authorities are statutorily protected. A complaint must be filed with the U.S. Department of Labor within sixty days of the alleged retaliatory action.[71]

The FMHSA broadly covers almost all mining activities, including coal or "*other* miners."[72] Its purpose was to provide broad safety protection to miners: "the first priority and concern of all in the coal and other mining industries must be the health and safety of its most precious resource—the miner."[73] The FMHSA was first passed in 1969, and was significantly strengthened in 1977.[74] Under both the 1969 and 1977 laws, courts have continuously stressed for "liberal construction" on whistleblower protection provisions.[75]

Once a complaint is filed, the Department of Labor's Mine Safety and Health Administration and the Federal Mine Safety and Health Review Commission must expeditiously process the complaint. If a determination is made that the complaint was "not frivolously brought," the commission must order the "immediate reinstatement" of the miner "pending" the full adjudication of the complaint.[76] A similar temporary reinstatement provision was recently found constitutional under the Surface Transportation Act.[77] If, after an investigation, the Secretary of Labor finds discrimination, the secretary must file a complaint with the commission, and the commission will hold a full evidentiary hearing.[78] If the secretary rules against the employee, the employee may file a complaint with the commission on his or her own behalf. Once again, the commission must afford the employee a full evidentiary hearing.[79] Appeals from a decision of the commission must be filed within thirty days of receipt of an adverse decision, to either the U.S. Court of Appeals for the circuit in which the violation arose, or to the District of Columbia Circuit.[80] Successful employees are entitled to reinstatement, back pay, costs, and attorney's fees.[81]

NATIONAL LABOR RELATIONS ACT

The National Labor Relations Act (NLRA) protects from retaliation employees who testify or file charges alleging a violation of the NLRA. A complaint should be filed with the regional director of the National Labor Relations Board (NLRB) for the region in which the violation allegedly occurred.[82] The statute of limitations for filing an unfair labor practice charge is six months.[83] Claims filed under this clause of the NLRA are prosecuted by the NLRB, the General Counsel, and Regional Directors of the NLRB as an unfair labor practice.[84]

Extensive case law has been developed under this clause of the NLRA, and under the other antiretaliation provisions of the NLRA.[85] Courts regularly apply principles developed in NLRA retaliation cases to other antiretaliation laws. For example, NLRA case law principles have been applied to whistleblower cases under the Atomic Energy Act[86] and the Federal Mine Health and Safety Act.[87]

SECTION 301 OF THE LABOR–MANAGEMENT RELATIONS ACT AND DUTY OF FAIR REPRESENTATION CLAIMS

Employees who are covered under a collective bargaining agreement (CBA), are protected from retaliatory discharge if such a firing is a violation of the union-management contract. If an employee is terminated in violation of the CBA, the employee must exhaust the contractual grievance procedures, such as arbitration, prior to filing a breach of contract claim under Section 301 of the Labor Management Relations Act, 29 U.S.C. 185.[88] The statute of limitations for a Section 301 suit is six months.[89] If the labor union fails to properly utilize the grievance and arbitration machinery on behalf of an employee, then both the union and the employee must be sued under Section 301 of the judicially created "Duty of Fair Representation" (DFR) doctrine. The U.S. Supreme Court established the DFR doctrine due to the special nature of a collective bargaining agreement.

Specifically, the NLRA statutorily empowers labor unions to represent all covered employees and sign a CBA that covers the entire workforce. Given their power, unions were held to have a "statutory duty" to "fairly" represent "all employees" in its collective bargaining process and in its "enforcement of the resulting collective bargaining agreement."[90] A union breaches its duty of fair representation if it handles or ignores a meritorious grievance in a "perfunctory manner,"[91] or when the union's conduct towards a member of a collective bargaining unit is "arbitrary, discriminatory or in bad faith."[92] The DFR was envisioned by the Supreme Court as a "bulwark" for the protection of "individuals stripped of traditional forms of redress" by the provisions of federal labor law. DFR claims are filed in federal district or state court.

DFR claims are important for whistleblowers who are unpopular with their local unions. Often, union leadership may be hostile to a whistleblower and fail to properly arbitrate their grievance. Additionally, union members who are engaged in efforts to reform local unions or expose the wrongdoing of union officials can utilize a DFR remedy in the appropriate situation.[93]

Dissident union members subject to retaliatory actions by their union may also have valid claims under the free speech clauses of the Labor Management and Disclosure Act.[94] Such suits are filed in federal district court directly against the union.[95]

IMPLIED FEDERAL CAUSES OF ACTION

Even if a statute has no express provision providing a civil or administrative remedy for the protection of whistleblowers, such a protection can be found through the doctrine of implied private cause of action. In *Cort v. Ash*, Supreme Court Justice Brennan outlined the four-step analysis for implying private right of action from a statute:

1. Does the statute create a federal right in favor of the plaintiff?
2. Is there any indication of legislative intent, explicit or implicit, either to create such a remedy or deny one?
3. Is it consistent with the underlying purposes of the legislative scheme to imply such a remedy for the plaintiff?
4. Is the cause of action one traditionally relegated to state law, in an area basically the concern of the States, so that it would be inappropriate to infer a cause of action based solely on federal law?[96]

If a whistleblower can point to a federal statute which grants his or her class of employees consistent with the *Cort v. Ash* analysis, the whistleblower may be able to state an implied federal cause of action. Such implied causes of action have been upheld under the Railway Labor Act for the retaliatory discharge of employees for union organizing,[97] and for testifying or furnishing information pursuant to an action under the Federal Employers Liability Act.[98] Private implied causes of action have been rejected under the Consumer Credit Protection Act[99] and the Federal Aviation Act.[100] There are no cases directly interpreting the statutory prohibition against terminating employees who report violations of the Institutionalized Persons Act.[101] But the statutory language and legislative history strongly imply such a right.[102] In most cases, termination prohibited by this law would probably be in violation of the First Amendment or 42 U.S.C. §1983.

SURFACE MINING CONTROL AND RECLAMATION ACT

This act protects employee whistleblowers who raise an environmental allegation, or allege a violation of the Surface Mining Control and Reclamation Act.[103] An employee must file a complaint within thirty days to the Department of Interior.[104] The law provides for reinstatement, back pay and attorney's fees.[105] Administrative regulations contain a mechanism for temporary relief from discrimination.[106] In *Leber v. Pennsylvania Dept. of Environmental Resources*, the U.S. Court of Appeals for the Third Circuit held that states were not prohibited from discriminating against their employees under this act.[107]

JOB TRAINING AND PARTNERSHIP ACT

The Job Training and Partnership Act (JTPA) prohibits retaliation against employees who allege that a recipient of a JTPA grant violated the JTPA, or federal, or state law, or has filed a complaint under JTPA.[108] The Department of Labor regulations implementing this act require that the granted employee initially utilize the internal grievance procedure.[109] After exhausting the local grievance procedure,[110] the employee may file a complaint directly with the Department of Labor.[111] Complaints can also be filed pursuant to 29 C.F.R. 629.51.

EXERCISE OF CIVIL RIGHTS AND FREE SPEECH

The Civil Rights Act of 1871,[112] prohibits any person from violating, under "color of law," the civil rights of any other person.[113] Whistleblowing is essentially the exercise of a First Amendment free speech right. Consequently, where there is state action. a whistleblower victimized by retaliation or any other form of discrimination has a potential Civil Rights

Section 1983 action.[114] Even if there is *no* state action, whistleblower retaliation which concerns a private conspiracy to retaliate against an employee may have a valid cause of action.[115] Under the state common law public policy exception, even in the absence of state action, the exercise of free speech rights might also be protected.[116]

MARITIME EMPLOYEES

The U.S. Court of Appeals for the Fifth Circuit recognized that a seaman could file a maritime tort against his or her employer for retaliating against an employee "seeking legal redress" under the Jones Act, 46 U.S.C. 688.[117] The court essentially adopted a public policy exception to the termination "at-will" doctrine, although the Fifth Circuit declined to permit punitive damages under this maritime tort.[118]

EMPLOYEE RETIREMENT INCOME SECURITY ACT (ERISA)

It is against federal law to retaliate against any person for participating in an ERISA retirement or benefit plan.[119] This includes retaliation against persons who give information or testify concerning ERISA, or the Welfare and Pension Plans Disclosure Act.[120] A whistleblower complaint under ERISA should be filed in federal district court, and a copy of the complaint should be served on the Secretary of Labor and the Secretary of Treasury.[121] Some courts have required ERISA plaintiffs to exhaust their administrative remedies prior to filing a suit in federal court.[122]

FAIR LABOR STANDARDS ACT

The Fair Labor Standards Act (FLSA) contains whistleblower provisions protecting all employees covered under the FLSA from retaliation for complaining, testifying, or filing charges regarding a violation of the FLSA.[123] This includes the FLSA's provision concerning child labor, minimum wage, and sex discrimination under the Equal Pay Act.[124] A complaint must be filed within two years of when the employee learns about the alleged retaliatory action,[125] and may be filed with the U.S. Department of Labor or in federal or state court with competent jurisdiction.[126] Remedies include reinstatement, back pay, liquidated damages, appropriate equitable relief, and a reasonable attorney's fee.[127] The U.S. Department of Labor has special regulations concerning child labor protection under the FLSA.[128]

FEDERAL EMPLOYEES (CIVIL SERVICE)

Federal law prohibits retaliation against federal whistleblowers covered under the Civil Service Reform Act.[129] If a federal employee is not covered under the Civil Service Reform Act, or the form of retaliation is not specifically covered under the act, the federal employee may be able to file a tort claim under the First Amendment of the U.S. Constitution.[130] Federal employees are also protected under some other federal antiretaliation statutes, and can file claims directly under those laws.[131]

The most common remedy for federal civil servant whistleblowers is the Civil Service Reform Act, which prohibits a federal agency from taking an adverse "personnel action" against a civil servant in retaliation for a variety of whistleblowing activities.[132] Under the Civil Service Reform Act, an employee alleging illegal retaliation must file a complaint with either the Merit Systems Protection Board and/or the Office of Special Counsel, depending upon the form of alleged retaliation.[133]

LONGSHOREMAN'S AND HARBOR WORKER'S COMPENSATION ACT

The Longshoreman's and Harbor Worker's Compensation Act (LHWCA) protects from retaliation employees who either claim protection or compensation under the act, or who testify in a proceeding under the act. Employers who violate the act are subject to a civil fine,[134] and the employee is entitled to reinstatement and back pay.[135] A complaint under this section should be filed with the U.S. Department of Labor.[136]

The LHWCA is a maritime worker's compensation law, which covers employees engaged in maritime employment (including longshoremen, harbor workers, and shipbuilders)[137] when an injury occurs on navigable waters of the United States, or upon adjoining piers, wharfs, or other adjoining areas customarily used for loading, building, or unloading a vessel.[138] The act also covers employees in the District of Columbia.[139] Claimants seeking relief under the act have a "light standard of proof in making their claims." This standard is less than the burden of proof "borne by plaintiffs in civil cases."[140]

MIGRANT AND SEASONAL AGRICULTURAL WORKERS PROTECTION ACT

The Migrant and Seasonal Agricultural Workers Protection Act has a provision which protects migrant workers who file a complaint, institute proceedings, testify, or exercise rights under the act.[141] Any employee who alleges discrimination in violation of this act must file a complaint with the Secretary of Labor within 180 days after the employee first learns of the alleged violation.[142]

Once the employee files the complaint, the Secretary of Labor must conduct an investigation into the allegations. If the secretary determines that a violation of the law occurred, then the secretary must file a suit in federal district court on behalf of the employee.[143]

Employees also have a right to initiate a private cause of action against any person who intentionally violates any provision of the Migrant and Seasonal Agricultural Worker Protection Act. Such suits must be filed in federal district court, and may be maintained "without regard to exhaustion of any alternative administrative remedies" provided under the act.[144]

UNSAFE CONTAINERS

The Safe Containers for International Cargo Act[145] contains a whistleblower protection provision.[146] Any employee who reports a violation of the act, or who reports the existence of an unsafe container that will be used in international transport, is protected from retaliation. A complaint must be filed with the U.S. Secretary of Labor within sixty days after the alleged violation occurs.[147]

The statute does not provide for a private cause of action. Instead, if the Secretary of Labor, after a thirty-day investigation, determines that a violation of the act occurred, the secretary must file a complaint for "appropriate relief" in federal court.[148] The law contains no provision for compensatory damages or attorney's fees.

DISCRIMINATION BASED ON RETALIATION CAUSED BY DISCLOSURES OF EMPLOYEE'S RACE, COLOR, SEX, AGE, RELIGION OR NATIONAL ORIGIN

Title VII of the Civil Rights Act of 1964[149] contains broad language protecting employees who object to discriminatory practices, or who file a complaint against such discrimination.[150] The law protects all employees—white and black, men and women—who oppose or disclose discriminatory practices. For example, a white employee who discloses that black employees are being subjected to discrimination is protected under Title VII,[151] as are employees who "witness" discrimination and blow the whistle on such practices.[152]

An employee alleging discrimination under Title VII must file a timely complaint with the Equal Employment Opportunity Commission (EEOC).[153] In order to contest a discharge under Title VII in federal court, an employee must file a complaint with the court within ninety days of receiving a "right to sue" letter from the EEOC.[154]

Remedies under Title VII include reinstatement, back pay, and attorney's fees and costs.[155] Liquidated damages, compensatory damages, and punitive damages are generally not allowed.[156]

The Age Discrimination in Employment Act contains a whistleblower protection clause nearly identical to that found in Title VII.[157] Also, the Equal Pay of the Fair Labor Standards Act[158] protects employees who disclose that an employer pays different wages to employees of the opposite sex for equal work.[159] Remedies under the Equal Pay Act are similar to Title VII, but the employee is also entitled to liquidated damages earned to the amount of back pay.[160]

A victim of racial discrimination in employment can also sue under the Civil Rights Act of 1870, 42 U.S.C. 1981. Section 1981 prohibits racial discrimination in both the public and private sectors, and allows the wrongfully discharged employee to sue in federal court.[161] Under this law employees are entitled not only to full back pay, but also, in the appropriate circumstances, compensatory and punitive damages.[162]

CRIMINAL AND OTHER SANCTIONS

Under certain state and federal laws it is criminal to harass or intimidate whistleblowers. Although these laws are rarely enforced, they do provide an outlet for a criminal investigation, indictment, or conviction of persons who violate these laws.[163]

The most significant federal law which potentially protects whistleblowers was enacted as part of the Reconstruction era civil rights statutes—18 U.S.C. 241. Section 241 criminalizes conspiracies to "oppress, threaten, or intimidate" citizens in their "free exercise or enjoyment of any right or privilege secured for (them) by the Constitution or laws of the United States." Any person who violates Section 241 is subject to imprisonment for ten years and a ten-thousand-dollar fine.[164] The U.S. Supreme Court, in *U.S. v. Price*, interpreted Section 241 extremely broadly: "The language of §241 is plain and unlimited. . . . [I]ts language embraces *all* the rights and privileges secured for citizens by *all* of the Constitution and *all* of the laws of the United States."[165] Under Section 241, conspiracies to intimidated witnesses[166] or government informants are illegal.[167] Even if no conspiracy exists, intimidation of a witness or a party in a proceeding before a U.S. court is a criminal act.[168]

Although it is unrealistic to expect the U.S. Department of Justice to criminally prosecute anything but the most outrageous criminal harassment of a whistleblower, preindictment government investigations into such allegations can be a useful source of information or assistance in the civil prosecution of a whistleblower case.[169]

Other criminal statutes can also be used by whistleblowers. For example, the False Claims Act includes provisions for criminal sanctions, and laws exist making it a criminal offense to "knowingly and willfully" provide information to the U.S. government.[170] The Racketeer Influenced and Corrupt Organizations Act (RICO) contains provisions for both civil and criminal penalties.[171] Whistleblowers who are direct victims of RICO violations may also have a civil cause of action for treble damages and attorneys' fees against the violating parties.[172]

NOTES

1. For a detailed criticism of the patchwork nature of the federal laws see Eugene Fidell, "Federal Protection of Private Sector Health and Safety Whistleblowers: A Report for the Administrative Conference of the United

States," Washington, D.C., March 1987. Litigators also should be alert to the fact that federal and state whistleblower protections often overlap. There is a growing body of case law discussing the relationship between federal statutory and state common law whistleblower actions. See *Silkwood v. Kerr-McGee Corp.*, 464 U.S. 238 (1984); *Farmer v. Carpenters*, 430 U.S. 290 (1977); *Olguin v. Inspiration Consolidated Copper Company*, 740 F.2d 1468 (9th Cir. 1984); *Garibaldi v. Lucky Food Stores, Inc.*, 726 F.2d 1367 (9th Cir. 1984); *Walsh v. Consolidated Freightways, Inc.*, 278 Or. 347, 563 P.2d 1205 (1977); *Hentzel v. Singer Co.*, 138 Cal. App. 3d 290 (1982); *Stokes v. Bechtel North American Power Corp.*, 614 F. Supp. 732 (N.D. Cal. 1985); *Wheeler v. Caterpillar Tractor Co.*, 108 Ill.2d 502, 485 N.E.2d 372 (1985), cert. denied, U.S. (1986); *Lingle v. Norge Division of Magic Chef*, ____ S. Ct. ____ (June 6, 1988).

2. *NLRB v. Transportation Management Corp.*, 462 U.S. 393 (1983); *Mackowiak v. University Nuclear Systems, Inc.*, 735 F.2d 1159, 1163–64 (9th Cir., 1984).

3. See *Kansas Gas & Electric v. Brock*, 780 F.2d 1505, 1511–12 (10th Cir. 1985).

4. *Pickering v. Board of Education*, 391 U.S. 563 (1968).

5. *Givhan v. Western Line Consolidated School District*, 439 U.S. 410 (1979).

6. *Pickering v. Board of Education*, 391 U.S. 563, 574 (1968).

7. 462 U.S. 367 (1983).

8. *Bush v. Lucas*, 103 S. Ct. 2404, 2418 (1983) (concurring opinion of J. Marshall); *Bartel v. Federal Aviation Administration*, 725 F.2d 1403, 1415 (D.C. Cir. 1984).

9. See *Nixon v. Fitzgerald*, 457 U.S. 731 (1982); *Harlow v. Fitzgerald*, 457 U.S. 800 (1982); U.S. Constitution, 11th Amendment; *Edelman v. Jordan*, 415 U.S. 651 (1974); *Moor v. County of Alameda*, 411 U.S. 693, 717–721 (1973).

10. *Connick v. Myers*, 461 U.S. 138, 147 (1983); *Rankin v. McPherson*, ____ U.S. ____ 107 S. Ct. 2891 (1987) (slip op. at 6). In *Connick* the court articulated the prong as follows:

We hold that when a public employee speaks not as a citizen upon matters of public concern, but instead as an employee upon matter of personal interest, absent the most unusual circumstances, a federal court is not the appropriate forum in which to review the wisdom of a personnel decision taken by a public agency allegedly in reaction to the employee's behavior. Cf. *Bishop v. Wood, supra*, at 349–350. Our responsibility is to ensure that citizens are not deprived of fundamental rights by virtue of working for the government; this does not require a grant of immunity for employee grievances not afforded by the First Amendment to those who do not work for the State.

Whether an employee's speech addresses a matter of public concern must be determined by the content, form, and context of a given statement, as revealed by the whole record.

Connick, 461 U.S. at 147–48. The First Amendment also prohibits some discharges based solely on political beliefs. *Branti v. Finkel*, 445 U.S. 507 (1980).

11. *Pickering*, 391 U.S. at 568; *Rankin* ____ U.S. at ____ (slip op. at 9); *Cox v. Dardanelle Public School Dist.*, 790 F.2d 668, 672 (8th Cir. 1986). *Cox* outlines the *prima facie* case for a First Amendment action.

12. *Brockell v. Norton*, 688 F.2d 588, 593 (8th Cir. 1982); *Brockell v. Norton*, (2nd Appeal), 732 F.2d 664, 668 (8th Cir. 1984).

13. *Mt. Healthy City School District Bd. of Ed. v. Doyle*, 429 U.S. 279, 287 (1977).

14. See *N.L.R.B. v. Transportation Management Corp.*, 462 U.S. 393 (1983); *Mackowiak v. University Nuclear Systems*, 735 F.2d 1159, 1163–64 (9th Cir. 1984).

15. See *American Postal Workers Union v. U.S. Postal Service*, 595 F. Supp. 403 (D. Conn. 1984); *Fujiwara v. Clark*, 703 F.2d 357 (9th Cir. 1983).

16. 15 U.S.C. 2622.

17. 42 U.S.C. 9610.

18. 33 U.S.C. 1367.

19. 42 U.S.C. 6971.

20. 42 U.S.C. 7622.

21. 42 U.S.C. 5851.

22. 42 U.S.C. 300j–9.

23. See 29 C.F.R. part 24, 29 C.F.R. Part 18, and Stephen M. Kohn, *Protecting Environmental and Nuclear Whistleblowers: A Litigation Manual*, Nuclear Information and Resource Service, Washington, D.C. (1985). The statutory and administrative weakness of the laws have recently been highlighted by the Administrative Conference of the United States, Recommendation 87–21, 1 C.F.R. §305.87–2 (June 11, 1987).

24. SDWA, 42 U.S.C. 300j–9(i)(2)(B)(ii); TSCA, 15 U.S.C. 2622(b)(2)(B).

25. See generally Stephen M. Kohn and Thomas Carpenter, "Nuclear Whistleblower Protection and the Scope of Protected Activity under Section 210 of the Energy Reorganization Act," 4 *Antioch Law Journal* 73 (Summer 1986).

26. See Kohn and Carpenter, Ibid., and *Kansas Gas & Electric Co. v. Brock*, 780 F.2d 1505 (10th Cir. 1985).

27. See *Mackowiak v. University Nuclear Systems*, 735 F.21d 1159 (9th Cir. 1984); *Consolidated Edison v. Donovan*, 673 F.2d 61 (2nd Cir. 1982); *Wheeler v. Caterpillar Tractor Co.*, 108 Ill.2d 502, 485 N.E.2d 372 (1985). Also see *DeFord v. Secretary of Labor*, 700 F.2d 281 (6th Cir. 1983) which held that the act should be broadly construed.

28. 42 U.S.C. 1985(2).

29. See *Griffin v. Breckenridge*, 403 U.S. 88, 102 (1971) which held that actionable conspiracies under 42 U.S.C. 1985(3) must be motivated by "racial, or perhaps otherwise class-based, invidiously discriminatory animus."

30. *Kush v. Rutledge*, 460 U.S. 719 (1983).

31. 460 U.S. 719, 726–27.

32. Ibid.

33. *Irizarry v. Quiros*, 722 F.2d 869, 872 (1st Cir. 1983). In *Irizarry*, the court refused to hold that 42 U.S.C. 1985(2) was preempted by other labor laws, such as the Labor Management Relations Act, because 1985(2) was designed to punish conspiracies.

34. *Chahal v. Paine Webber*, 725 F.2d 20, 23 (2nd Cir. 1984); *Malley–Duff & Associates v. Crown Life Insurance Co.*, 792 F.2d 341, 235 (3rd Cir. 1986).

35. Compare *Novotny v. Great American Federal S. & L. Association*, 584 F.2d 1235, 1256–59 (en banc) (3rd Cir. 1978), reversed on other grounds, 442 U.S. 366 (19____), holding that employees of a single corporation can conspire with each under 1985(3), against *Dombrowski v. Dowling*, 459 F.2d 190, 196 (7th Cir. 1972) which requests the intracorporate conspiracy analysis. Also see Note, intracorporate conspiracies under 42 U.S.C. 1985(c), 92 *Harvard Law Review* 470 (1978).

36. 722 F.2d 869 (1st Cir. 1983).

37. Ibid at 872.

38. 31 U.S.C. 3730(h).

39. 31 U.S.C. 2729. See also Wall and Joseph, "The False Claims Reform Act," *Wisconsin Bar Bulletin* (Ocrober 1987).

40. 1986 U.S. Code Cong. and Adm. News, p. 5266, 5299.

41. Ibid.

42. 31 U.S.C. 3730(b).

43. 31 U.S.C. 3731(b).

44. 31 U.S.C. 3730(b).

45. 31 U.S.C. 3730(b).

46. 31 U.S.C. 3730 (d)(1).

47. 31 U.S.C. 3730 (d)(2).

48. 49 U.S.C. 2305 (Appendix 13).

49. 49 U.S.C. 2305(a).

50. 49 U.S.C. 2304(b).

51. 49 U.S.C. 2305(b).

52. 49 U.S.C. 2304 (c)(1).

53. 49 U.S.C. 2305 (c)(2)(A).

54. 49 U.S.C. 2305 (c)(2)(A).

55. 49 U.S.C. 2305 (c)(2)(B).

56. 49 U.S.C. 2305 (d)(1).

57. 107 S.Ct. 1740 (April 22, 1987).

58. 107 S.Ct. 1745.

59. 107 S.Ct. 1745–46.

60. 29 U.S.C. 660(c).

61. See *Whirlpool Corp. v. Marshall*, 445 U.S. 1(1980). A right to refuse hazardous work was also recognized in certain specific situations under NLRA, *NLRB v. Washington Aluminum Co.*, 370 U.S. 9 (1962); Section 502 of the LMRA, *Gateway Coal Co. v. United Mine Workers*, 414 U.S. 368(1974); the Fed. Mine Health and Safety Act, *Miller v. Fed. Mine Safety Commission*, 687 F.2d 194 (7th Cir. 1982); Section 210 of the Energy Reorganization Act, *Pennsyl. v. Catalytic, Inc.*, 83-Energy Reorganization Act-2, Opinion of Secretary of Labor (Jan. 13, 1984).

62. 29 C.F.R. Part 1977.

63. 29 U.S.C. 651(b).

64. *Donovan v. Square D Co.*, 709 F.2d 335, 338 (5th Cir. 1983).

65. *Donovan v. Diplomat Envelope Corp.*, 587 F.Supp. 1417, 1424–25 (E.D.N.Y. 1984).

66. *Marshall v. Springville Poultry Farm, Inc.*, 445 F.Supp 2 (M.D. Pa. 1977).

67. *Donovan v. R.D. Anderson*, 552 F.Supp 249 (D. Kan. 1982).

68. Some courts have used the federal OSHA law as a source of authority for a state public policy tort. See *Kilpatrick v. Delaware Courts soc.*, 632 F.Supp. 542, 546 (E.D. Pa. 1986).

69. *Taylor v. Brighton Corp.*, 616 F.2d 256 (6th Cir. 1980); *George v. Aztec Rental Center, Inc.*, 763 F.2d 184, 186 (5th Cir. 1985).

70. 30 U.S.C. 815(c) (1977).

71. See generally, James A. Broderick and Daniel Minahan, "Employment Discrimination Under the Federal Mine Safety and Health Act, 84 *West Virginia Law Review* 1023 (1982).

72. 30 U.S.C. 802(g).

73. 30 U.S.C. 801(a).

74. In the 1969 law, the whistleblower provision was codified as 30 U.S.C. 820(b). After the 1977 amendments, the employee protection provision was codified at 30 U.S.C. 815(c).

75. *Phillips v. Interior Bd. of Mine Op. App.*, 500 F.2d 772, 782 (D.C. Cir. 1974).

76. 30 U.S.C. 815 (c)(2).

77. *Brock v. Roadway Express, Inc.*, ____ U.S. ____ 107 S.Ct. 1740 (1987).

78. 30 U.S.C. 815 (c)(2).

79. 30 U.S.C. 815 (c)(3).

80. 30 U.S.C. 815 (c)(3); 30 U.S.C. 816.

81. 30 U.S.C. 815 (c)(3).

82. 29 C.F.R. 102.10; see 29 U.S.C. 158 (a)(4).

83. 29 U.S.C. 160(b); *Ernst v. Indian Bell Tel. Co., Inc.*, 717 F.2d 1036, 1038 (7th Cir. 1983), cert. den. 104 S.Ct. 707 (1984).

84. See generally, 29 C.F.R. 101.2–101.16; 102.9–102.59.

85. See generally, cases under 42 U.S.C. 158(a).

86. See *Mackowiak v. University Nuclear Systems*, 735 F.2d 1159 (9th Cir. 1984).

87. See *Phillips v. Int. Bd. of Mine Op. App.*, 500 F.2d 772 (D.C. Cir. 1974).

88. See *Vaca v. Sipes*, 386 U.S. 171, 183–185 (1967).

89. *Del Costello v. International Brotherhood of Teamsters*, 462 U.S. 151 (1983).

90. *Vaca v. Sipes*, 386 U.S. 171, 177 (1967). Also see *Ford Motor Co. v. Huffman*, 345 U.S. 330 (1953); *Humphrey v. Moore*, 375 U.S. 335 (1964); *Steele v. Louisville & N.R. Co.*, 323 U.S. 192 (1944).

91. *Hines v. Anchor Motor Freight, Inc.*, 424 U.S. 554, 568–569 (1976).

92. *Vaca v. Sipes*, 386 U.S. 171, 190 (1967).

93. See *Taschner v. Hill*, 589 F.Supp. 127 (E.D. Penn. 1984).

94. 29 U.S.C. 411 *et seq.*

95. 29 U.S.C. 412; *Taschner v. Hill*, 589 F.Supp. 127, 131 (E.D. Penn. 1984).

96. 422 U.S. 66, 78 (1974).

97. See *Stepanischen v. Merchants Dispatch Transportation Corp.*, 722 F.2d 922 (1st Cir. 1983); *Brown v. World Airways, Inc.*, 539 F.Supp. 179 (S.D.N.Y. 1982).

98. *Gonzalez v. Southern Pacific Transportation Co.*, 773 F.2d 637 (5th Cir. 1985).

99. 15 U.S.C. 1674(a); see *LeVick v. Skaggs Companies, Inc.*, 701 F.2d 777 (9th Cir. 1983).

100. 49 U.S.C. 1301 *et seq.*; *Buethe v. Britt Airlines*, 581 F.Supp. 200 (S.D. Ind. 1984).

101. 42 U.S.C. 1997d.

102. See 1980 *U.S. Code Congress and Administrative News* at 816.

103. 30 U.S.C. 1293; 43 C.F.R. Part 4; C.F.R. Part 865.

104. Idem.

105. 30 U.S.C. 1293(b).

106. 43 C.F.R. 4.1203.

107. 780 F.2d 372 (3rd Cir. 1986).

108. 29 U.S.C. 1574(g).

109. 20 C.F.R. 636.3.

110. 20 C.F.R. 636.5.

111. 20 C.F.R. 636.6.

112. 42 U.S.C. 1983.

113. 42 U.S.C. 1983 reads in part, "Every person who, under color of any statute . . . subjects or causes to be subjected, any citizen . . . to the deprivation of any rights, privileges or immunities secured by the constitution under laws, shall be liable to the party injured in an action at law, suit in equity, or other proper proceeding for redress."

114. *Pickering v. Board of Education,* 391 U.S. 563 (1968).

115. See 42 U.S.C. 1985; *Griffin v. Breckenridge,* 403 U.S. 88 (1971). But also see, *Carpenter's Local 610 v. Scott,* 463 U.S. 825 (1983); *Buschi v. Kirven,* 775 F.2d 1240 (4th Cir. 1985); *Taylor v. Brighton Corp.,* 616 F.2d 256 (6th Cir. 1980).

116. See *Novosel v. Nationwide Ins. Co.,* 721 F.2d 894 (3rd Cir. 1983); *Jones v. Memorial Hospital System* 677 S.W. 2d 221 (Tex. App. 1984).

117. *Smith v. Atlas Off-Shore Boat Service,* 653 F.2d 1057, 1062 (5th Cir. 1981).

118. *Smith,* 653 F.2d at 1064. Also see *Robinson v. Rebstock Drilling Co., Inc.,* 749 F.2d 1182 (5th Cir. 1985); *Buchanan v. Bott Brothers' Construction Company, Inc.,* 741 F.2d 750 (5th Cir. 1984).

119. 29 U.S.C. 1140.

120. Idem.

121. 29 U.S.C. 1132; see also, 29 C.F.R. Part 2560.

122. *Kross v. Western Electric Company,* 701 F.2d 1238 (7th Cir. 1983); but see, *Zipf v. American Telephone and Telegraph,* 799 F.2d 889 (3rd Cir. 1986).

123. 29 U.S.C. 215.

124. 29 U.S.C. 206(d).

125. 29 U.S.C. 255.

126. 29 U.S.C. 216.

127. 29 U.S.C. 215–216.

128. 29 C.F.R. Part 579.

129. 5 U.S.C. 2302. Also see, special provisions covering employees in the foreign service, 22 U.S.C. 4133.

130. *Bush v. Lucas,* 462 U.S. 367 (1983).

131. See the Civil Rights Act of 1964, 42 U.S.C. 2000e 16; the Age Discrimination in Employment Act, 29 U.S.C. 631; the Fair Labor Standards Act, 29 U.S.C. 206(d); the Rehabilitation Act of 1973; 29 U.S.C. 791; the Clean Air Act Congressional History, 1977 U.S. Code Cong. and Ad. News 1405; *Conley v. McCellan Air Force Base,* 84-WPC-1; the Water Pollution Control Act—slip op. of Department of Labor Administrative Law Judge, September 12, 1984.

132. The Civil Service Reform Act, 5 U.S.C. 2302(b)(8), defines protected activity as:

(A) a disclosure of information by an employee or applicant which the employee or applicant reasonably believes evidences—

    (i) a violation of any law, rule or regulation,

    (ii) mismanagement, a gross waste of funds, an abuse of authority, or a substantial and specific danger to public health or safety if such disclosure is not specifically prohibited by law and if such information is not specifically required by Executive order to be kept secret in the interest of national defense or the conduct of foreign affairs; or

(B) a disclosure to the Special Counsel of the Merit Systems Protection Board, or to the Inspector General of an agency or another employee designated by the head of the agency to receive such disclosures, or information which the employee or applicant reasonably believes evidences—

    (i) a violation of any law, rule or regulation, or

    (ii) mismanagement, a gross waste of funds, an abuse of authority, or a substantial and specific danger to public health or safety.

133. 29 C.F.R. Part 1200; see Vaughn, "Statutory Protection of Whistleblowers in the Federal Executive Branch," 3 *University of Illinois Law Review* 615 (1982); Devine, "Abuse of Authority: The Office of the Special Counsel and Whistleblower Protection," 4 *Antioch Law Journal* 5 (1986).

134. 33 U.S.C. 948(a).

135. Idem.

136. See 20 C.F.R. Ch. VI, Section 702.271 (1985 Edition).

137. 33 U.S.C. 902(3).

138. 33 U.S.C. 903(a).

139. *Geddes v. Benefits Review Board U.S. Dept of Labor*, 735 F.2d 1412, 1414, N. 5 (D.C. Cir. 1984); D.C. Code Ann. §36–501 (1968).

140. Ibid, at 1416.

141. 29 U.S.C. 1855.

142. 29 C.F.R. 500.9(b).

143. 29 U.S.C. 1855(b).

144. 29 U.S.C. 1854.

145. 46 U.S.C. 1501 *et. seq.*

146. 46 U.S.C. 1506.

147. 46 U.S.C. 1506(d).

148. 46 U.S.C. 1506(c) and (d).

149. 42 U.S.C. 2000e, *et. seq.*

150. 42 U.S.C. 2000e–4(a). This provision states:

It shall be an unlawful employment practice for an employer to discriminate against any of his employees or applicants for employment, for an employment agency, or joint labor–management committee controlling apprenticeship or other training or retraining, including on–the–job training programs, to discriminate against any individual, or for a labor organization to discriminate against any member thereof or applicant for membership, because he has opposed any practice made an unlawful employment practice by this title, or because he has made a charge, testified, assisted, or participated in any manner in an investigation, proceeding, or hearing under this title.

See *Pettway v. American Cast Iron Pipe Co.*, 411 F.2d 998 (5th Cir. 1969).

151. See *Abel v. Bonfant*, 625 F. Supp. 263 (S.D. N.Y. 1985); *Parker v. Baltimore and O.R. Co.*, 652 F.2d 1012 (D.C. Cir. 1981). Also, under 42 U.S.C. §1981 white employees who are punished for trying to vindicate the rights of racial minorities are protected. See *Abel v. Bonfant*, 625 F. Supp. at 267; *DeMatteis v. Eastman Kodak Co.*, 511 F.2d 306, reh'g on other grounds, 520 F.2d 409 (2nd Cir. 1975).

152. See *E.E.O.C. v. St. Anne's Hospital*, 664 F.2d 128, 132 (7th Cir. 1982).

153. If the state in which the discrimination occurred has no appropriate state or local agency authorized to grant relief, a Title VII charge must be filed with the EEOC within 180 days of the discriminatory act, 42 U.S.C. §2000e–5(c). If a state has an appropriate agency which can grant relief, the employee must

file with the state or local agency before filing with the EEOC, but also must file a complaint with the EEOC within three hundred days of the initial discriminatory act, or within thirty days of a notice from the state, that the state either will take no action on behalf of the employee or has denied the complaint—whichever is earlier. 42 U.S.C. 2000e–5(e). Sixty days after an employee initiates an action with a state or local agency he or she has standing to file directly to the EEOC, even if the state has not completed it own investigation. Ibid.

154. See *Lynn v. Western Gillette, Inc.*, 564 F.2d 1282 (9th Cir. 1977). For a detailed description of the procedure under Title VII, and the general substantive and procedural law under all the federal civil rights laws, see Honorable Charles R. Richy, *Manual on Employment Discrimination and Civil Rights Actions in the Federal Courts* (N.Y., N.Y.: Kluwer Law Book Publishers, Inc., 1985).

155. 42 U.S.C. 2000e–5(g); 42 U.S.C.; 42 U.S.C. 2000e–5(k).

156. See *Walker v. Ford Motor Co.*, 684 F.2d 1355, 1363–64 (11th Cir. 1982).

157. 29 U.S.C. 623(d).

158. 29 U.S.C. 206(d).

159. See *Crockwell v. Blackmon-Mooring Steamatic*, 627 F. Supp. 800, 804 (W.D. Tenn. 1985).

160. *Crockwell*, 627 F. Supp. at 805.

161. Also see 42 U.S.C. 1983 which prohibits all violations of federal civil rights under color of state law.

162. See *Johnson v. Railway Express Agency*, 421 U.S. 454, 460 (1975).

163. The state of California passed a law which makes it a criminal misdemeanor to terminate a whistleblower. California Labor Code §1102.5.

164. 18 U.S.C. 241.

165. 383 U.S. 787, 800 (1965).

166. See *U.S. v. Smith*, 623 F.2d 627, 629 (9th Cir. 1980); *U.S. v. Thevis*, 665 F.2d 616 (5th Cir. 1982); *Foss v. U.S., 266 F. 881 (9th Cir. 1920)*; *U.S. v. Bufalino*, 518 F. Supp. 1190 (S.D. N.Y. 1981).

167. See *U.S. v. Smith*, 623 F.2d 627, 629 (9th Cir. 1980); *Motes v. U.S.*, 178 U.S. 458 (1900); *Nicholson v. U.S.*, 79 F.2d 387 (8th Cir. 1935).

168. 18 U.S.C. 1503.

169. See *U.S. v. Ehrilichman*, 546 F.2d 910 (D.C. Cir. 1976); cert. den. 97 S.Ct. 1155 (1977).

170. 18 U.S.C. 1001.

171. 18 U.S.C. 1961 *et. seq.*

172. *Nodine v. Textron, Inc.*, 819 F.2d 347 (1st Cir. 1987); *Morast v. Lance*, 807 F.2d 926 (11th Cir. 1987).

4

STATE PROTECTION FOR EMPLOYEE WHISTLEBLOWERS

The most important development in whistleblower protection has been the development of a state cause of action for retaliatory discharge. A majority of states have recognized a *public policy exception* to the common law termination at-will doctrine. This public policy exception has revolutionized the rights of whistleblowers. Instead of offering protection to employees covered under special laws or employees who work for the federal or state governments, the public policy exception cause of action usually protects *all* private sector employees in the states that have adopted the exception. Additionally, most states classify a retaliatory discharge cause of action as a tort, and consequently employees who file claims under this cause of action are entitled to jury trials and, if successful, punitive damage awards.

Under traditional state common law, in the absence of an employment contract, an employee at-will could be terminated for any reason, or for no reason.[1] Over the past twenty years, however, a majority of states have carved out a public policy exception to the termination at-will doctrine.[2] If the termination of an at-will employee was activated by an intent that contravenes some important public policy, state courts have recognized a public policy exception to the common law doctrine, and have awarded damages either in contract or tort. This national trend was summarized by the Supreme Court of California:

[i]n a series of cases arising out of a variety of actual settings in which a discharge clearly violated an express statutory objective or undermined a firmly established principle of public policy, courts have recognized that employers' traditional broad authority to discharge an at-will employee may be limited by statute or by considerations of public policy.[3]

The definition of what type of activity is protected under a public policy exception is still evolving. Some states, such as Indiana, have limited the exception to cases "where the employee is discharged solely for exercising a right conferred on him by a statute, constitution, or other positive law."[4] Other states apply a broader interpretation of public policy. For example, New Jersey adopted a "clear mandate" standard for defining what type of activity is protected under the public policy exception:

[w]e hold that an employee has a cause of action for wrongful discharge when the discharge is contrary to a clear mandate of public policy. The sources of public policy include legislation; administrative rules, regulations, or decisions; and judicial decisions. In certain instances, a professional code of ethics may contain an expression of public policy. However, not all such sources express a clear mandate of public policy.[5]

When litigating in state court, employees are not required to limit their cause of action to just the public policy exception.[6] Employees often include other causes of action in their complaints, such as intentional interference with contracts,[7] breach of contract based on the terms of the employment contract or employee manual,[8] an implied covenant of good faith and fair dealing,[9] intentional infliction of emotional distress,[10] fraud,[11] negligence,[12] invasion of privacy,[13] defamation,[14] and an implied contract.[15] A number of states have passed statutes protecting employee whistleblowers in the public sector,[16] or protecting private and public sector whistleblowers.[17]

If there is a state or federal statutory remedy covering a whistleblower claim, some courts have required the employee to invoke the statutory remedy instead of the public policy common law remedy.[18]

Following is a breakdown of the public policy exception cause of action in the fifty states.

ALABAMA

After years of rejecting a public policy exception to the termination at-will doctrine, the Alabama Supreme Court has apparently adopted this cause of action.[19] In *Harrell v. Reynolds Metals Co.*, the court held: "An employee at will cannot be wrongfully terminated unless such termination is for a reason which contravenes public policy."[20] The court also indicated that a cause of action for "outrageous conduct" (i.e., intentional infliction of emotional distress) may also be available to an employee discharged for reasons which contravene public policy.

ALASKA

The Supreme Court of Alaska has upheld causes of action for both the public policy exception, and the breach of the implied covenant of good faith and fair dealing. Both causes of action lie in contract.[21]

The tort of intentional interference with another's contract has also been recognized. The following elements must be shown: (1) that a contract existed (or can be implied); (2) that defendant knew of the contract and intended to induce a breach; (3) that the contract was breached; (4) that defendant's wrongful conduct engendered the breach; (5) that the breach caused plaintiff's damages; and (6) that the defendant's conduct was not privileged or justified.[22]

In *Bald v. R.C.A. Alascom*, plaintiff alleged that she was wrongfully discriminated against by both her employer and the union in violation of state antidiscrimination legislation.[23] The Supreme Court of Alaska held that a state cause of action was maintainable and that the National Labor Relations Act did not preempt or deprive state courts from hearing the case.[24]

ARKANSAS

No Arkansas case has held that a cause of action for wrongful discharge exists as an exception to the at-will doctrine. In *M.B.M. Co. v. Counce*,[25] however, the Supreme Court indicated a willingness to recognize an exception to the at-will rule if plaintiff had been discharged for exercising a statutory right, for performing a duty required by law, or for reasons in violation of some other well-established public policy.[26] A termination repugnant to the general good or forbidden by the legislature would violate public policy.[27] A United States Court of Appeals has interpreted Arkansas state law to permit both a tort and contract claim for a discriminatory discharge.[28] Title VII of the U.S. Civil Rights Act was held not to preempt a state law contract claim.[29]

An employee who has been wrongfully discharged may also bring an action in tort for intentional infliction of emotional distress.[30] To be actionable, such a termination must be so extreme and outrageous as to go beyond all possible bounds of decency, and to be atrocious and utterly intolerable in a civilized society.[31]

ARIZONA

In 1985 the Arizona Supreme Court adopted the public policy exception to the at-will doctrine in the case of *Wagenseller v. Scottsdale Memorial Hospital*.[32] The court held that an at-will employer may fire an employee for good cause or for no cause, but not for "bad cause"—i.e., that which violates public policy.[33] In *Wagenseller*, the employee was fired for refusing to participate in activities allegedly in violation of the state's indecent exposure statute.[34] The court expressly stated that the public policy exception would not be limited to cases involving a violation of a criminal statute,[35] and could be articulated by constitutional, statutory, or decisional law.[36]

A tort for wrongful discharge exists upon a showing by the plaintiff that the termination was due to his or her refusal to perform some act contrary to public policy, or the performance of some act which the employee had a right to do as a matter of public policy.[37] Moreover, a cause of action in contract is also maintainable under an implied-in-fact contract.[38] A personnel manual can become part of an employment contract and modify the employment relationship so as to require an employer to show good cause when firing an employee.[39]

CALIFORNIA

California was the first state to adopt the public policy exception to the at-will doctrine in the landmark case of *Petermann v. International Brotherhood of Teamsters*, where an employee was discharged for refusing to commit perjury.[40] California courts have since upheld the holding in *Petermann* despite the fact that California Labor Code §2922 provides, in relevant part, that "An employment, having no specified term, may be terminated at-will of either party on notice to the other."[41]

A cause of action for wrongful discharge is recognized in contract,[42] and in tort.[43] Additionally, California has acknowledged a cause of action resulting from a wrongful discharge for breach of implied-at-law covenant of good faith and fair dealing,[44] for intentional negligent infliction of emotional distress,[45] for defamation and invasion of privacy,[46] for fraud,[47] and for interference with contractual relations.[48]

In addition, the California Labor Code §1102.5 imposes criminal liability on employers who:

(a) . . . adopt, or enforce any rule, regulation, or policy preventing an employee for disclosing information to a government or law enforcement agency, where the employee has reasonable cause to believe that the information discloses a violation of state or federal statute, or violation or noncompliance with a state or federal regulation.

(b) . . . retaliate against an employee for disclosing information to a government or law enforcement agency, where the employee has reasonable cause to believe that the information discloses a violation of state or federal statute, or violation or noncompliance with a state or federal regulation.[49]

An employee who has been discharged for engaging in any such protected activity can, in addition to filing a civil action, file criminal misdemeanor charges and subject his or her employer to a fine, imprisonment or both.[50]

Generally, California state courts have not required employees to exhaust administrative remedies prior to filing a wrongful discharge suit.[51] Statutory remedies are generally considered cumulative.[52] For example, California courts upheld an action for wrongful discharge despite the fact that OSHA also provided a remedy.[53] The administrative remedies created by OSHA were held to be independent of those available under a wrongful discharge action and plaintiff was not required to first exhaust his administrative remedies.[54] Recent decisions by the United States federal courts in California indicate that the federal judicial system has taken a more narrow approach to the preemption and exhaustion issues in California than has the state judicial system.[55]

COLORADO

Colorado has not specifically adopted a public policy exception to the at-will doctrine. A United States district court sitting in diversity, however, held that Colorado would uphold such an action for wrongful discharge if confronted with the appropriate circumstances.[56] A salesman's tort claim for wrongful discharge, issued for refusing to violate federal antitrust laws, was upheld.[57]

In *Corbin v. Sinclair Marketing*,[58] a Colorado state court stated that a public policy exception to the at-will doctrine was not available when the statute at issue provided employees with a wrongful discharge remedy.[59] The court did not address what would occur in the absence of such a statute or remedy, but indicated that a public policy exception, in the appropriate circumstances, could be upheld.[60]

Moreover, in *Lampe v. Presbyterian Medical Center*,[61] a state court noted that the at-will doctrine would not apply if a plaintiff claimed that he or she was discharged for exercising a "specifically enacted right [or] duty," such as the right to file for workmen's compensation or the duty to serve on a jury.[62] Colorado has specifically enacted legislation to protect employees from discharge or other coercion for receiving a summons, responding thereto, serving as a juror, or attending court for prospective jury service.[63]

CONNECTICUT

The Supreme Court of Connecticut has recognized an exception to the at-will doctrine where a termination involves "impropriety ... derived from some important violation of public policy."[64] A wrongful discharge claim can be framed in either tort or contract.[65]

In *Magnan v. Anaconda Industries, Inc.*,[66] the Connecticut Supreme Court adopted the implied covenant of good faith and fair dealing as another theory that limits an employer's right to discharge an employee at will.[67] The court held, however, that a breach of such an implied covenant cannot be predicated simply upon the absence of good cause.[68] An employee must prove that the employer was motivated by bad faith or malice, or that the employer's actions constituted fraud, deceit or misrepresentation.[69] This cause of action can be defended if the employer "honestly believed" the discharge was for good cause.[70]

Intentional infliction of emotional distress has also been recognized by Connecticut in employment context.[71] It must be shown: (1) that defendant intended to inflict emotional distress or knew, or should have known, that it was likely to result from his or her conduct; (2) that the conduct was extreme and outrageous; (3) that defendant caused plaintiff's distress; and (4) that the emotional distress sustained by plaintiff was severe.[72] The court in *Murray v. Bridgeport Hospital*[73] acknowledged that a claim for tortious interference with a contract could be maintained in an employment context.[74]

In addition to state common law remedies, the Connecticut legislature has passed a whistleblower protection statute.[75] The statute protects employees in the private sector from retaliation for disclosing an employer's illegal activities.[76] An employee who is discharged or otherwise penalized by his or her employer in violation of this statute may bring a civil action after exhausting all available administrative remedies.[77]

The remedies provided by the whistleblower statute include reinstatement of previous job, payment of back wages, reestablishment of employee benefits, costs of litigation, and reasonable attorney's fees.[78] The statue further provides that the rights and remedies created by the statute shall not be construed to diminish or impair the rights of a person under any collective bargaining agreement.[79]

DELAWARE

Delaware has not yet adopted a public policy exception to the termination at-will doctrine.[80] An employee handbook was held not to alter the employment status of an at-will employee.[81] The booklet in question, however, was issued by the employer after the commencement of the employee's employment.[82]

Delaware has enacted legislation to protect *public* employees from being discharged, threatened, or otherwise discriminated against for reporting suspected violations of law.[83] A federal district court, sitting in diversity, held that Delaware would adopt a public policy exception cause of action for wrongful discharge.[84]

DISTRICT OF COLUMBIA

A cause of action for wrongful discharge is not recognized in the District of Columbia. In *Ivy v. Army Times Publishing Co.*, the court insisted upon strict adherence to the doctrine that employment for an indefinite term was terminable at will.[85] The courts have upheld this doctrine when an employee was discharged for giving truthful testimony against an employer,[86] as well as when a female bartender was fired for her association with a black person.[87]

FLORIDA

The Florida Supreme Court has adopted a narrow public policy exception claim when a statute "confers by implication" such an action.[88]

GEORGIA

Georgia is unique in that it is the only state that adheres to an ironclad interpretation of a statute which codified the at-will doctrine.[89] Georgia courts strictly abide by the statutory language of the code, which does not encompass an exception.[90] The courts have confined themselves to the statute even when an employee is terminated in an attempt to cover up illegal activities.[91]

HAWAII

In 1982, the Hawaii Supreme Court in *Parnar v. American Hotels, Inc.*,[92] recognized the right of an at-will employee to bring an action for retaliatory discharge against her employer. The plaintiff bears the burden of proving that the discharge violated a clear mandate of public policy.[93] In determining whether a clear mandate of public policy is violated, the *Parnar* court stated that courts should inquire whether the employer's conduct contravenes the letter or purpose of a constitutional, statutory, or regulatory provision or scheme.[94] The employer's motivation for discharging an employee is a material issue subject to jury determination.[95] The public policy exception lies in tort, and an employee can be awarded punitive damages where appropriate.[96]

The Supreme Court refused to impose upon an employer a duty to terminate only in good faith. Whether a wrongful discharge can give rise to a cause of action for intentional infliction of emotional distress has not been addressed.[97]

An employee's complaint for unlawful discharge from employment, having its source in state statute, is not preempted by collective bargaining agreement or federal labor laws.[98] Additionally, Hawaii has codified a right of action for an unlawful suspension or discharge from employment.[99]

IDAHO

The employment at-will rule in Idaho is not an absolute bar to a claim for wrongful discharge.[100] In *Jackson v. Minidoka*,[101] the court held that an employee may claim damages for wrongful discharge when the motivation for the firing contravenes public policy.[102] Being terminated for refusing to give false testimony, reporting an injury in order to file for workmen's compensation, refusing to date one's supervisor, and serving on jury duty against the wishes of an employer were all cited as examples of violations of public policy by the Supreme Court of Idaho.[103]

ILLINOIS

Illinois joined the growing number of states recognizing the tort of retaliatory discharge with the decision of *Kelsay v. Motorola , Inc.*[104] The Illinois Supreme Court held, "All that is required is that the employer discharge the employee in retaliation for the employee's activities, and that the discharge be in contravention of a clearly mandated public policy."[105] In *Palmateer v. International Harvester Co.*, the court stated that no public policy was more fundamental than the one favoring the effective protection of the lives and property of citizens.[106] Where, however, no clear mandate of public policy is violated or where only private interests are involved, an employer may discharge an at-will employee without liability.[107]

The state Supreme Court in 1985 held that the protection of the lives and property of citizens from the hazards of radioactive material was as important and fundamental a public policy as protecting them from crimes of violence.[108] The state common law remedy was not preempted by the federal nuclear whistleblower protection law, Section 210 of the Energy Reorganization Act.[109]

Moreover, a wrongfully discharged employee whose employment is covered by a collective bargaining agreement providing for grievance procedures was not required to exhaust those procedures prior to bringing an action for the tort of retaliatory discharge.[110] The U.S. Supreme Court, however, has taken *certiorari* on the issue of whether arbitration provisions in collective bargaining agreements preempt state law retaliatory discharge claims.[111] A wrongfully discharged employee may be able to sue for intentional infliction of emotional distress.[112] Under Illinois law, a plaintiff seeking recovery for intentional infliction of emotional distress must allege facts showing: (1) that the conduct by defendant was extreme and outrageous; (2) that the plaintiff suffered emotional distress; (3) that the defendant's conduct was intentional, or so reckless that the defendant knew severe emotional distress was substantially certain to result; and (4) that defendant's conduct was the actual and proximate cause of plaintiff's emotional distress.[113]

INDIANA

The state Supreme Court in *Frampton v. Central Indiana Gas Co.*, established that a public policy exception to the traditional at-will rule exists whenever an employee is discharged for exercising a statutorily conferred right.[114] In *Frampton* the employee was permitted to sue her employer for retaliatory discharge resulting from filing a worker's compensation claim.[115] The *Frampton* rule is not limited just to workers' compensation claims.[116] To fall within the public policy exception recognized in Frampton, *supra*, a plaintiff must demonstrate that he or she was discharged in retaliation for either having exercised a statutorily conferred personal right, or having fulfilled a statutorily imposed duty.[117]

Indiana has required an employer to show good cause for terminating an at-will employee when adequate independent consideration is exchanged.[118] An employee's release of personal injury claims against an employer, assignment of a valuable lease to the employer, abandoning his or her competing business, and surrendering his or her own permanent exployment are all examples of adequate consideration and require an employer to show good cause for termination.[119] Moving a household and surrendering employment alone, however, are insufficient to require a showing of good cause.[120] Punitive damages are awarded upon a clear and convincing evidence of malice, fraud, gross negligence or oppressive conduct.[121]

Indiana has statutorily outlined employment protection provisions for state employees in the State Employees' Bill of Rights.[122] In relevant part, the law provides that no state employee may be dismissed, have benefits withheld, be transferred, or be demoted[123] for reporting in writing the existence of a state, federal or regulatory violation,[124] or the misuse of public resources.[125]

IOWA

Although Iowa continues to adhere to the "general rule" that an at-will employee may be terminated at any time, for any reason,[126] the state Supreme Court has hinted that "under the proper circumstances we would recognize a common law claim for a discharge violating public policy."[127] The court has reasoned that if it did uphold the exception, the public policy would have to be very "clear" and based upon statutory policies.[128] Also, if an independent statutory remedy exists covering that discharge, the employee must utilize that remedy, and not the common law.[129]

KANSAS

Kansas courts adopted a limited public policy exception to the at-will doctrine in *Murphy v. City of Topeka-Shawnee Cty.*[130] Retaliatory discharge under Kansas law is a tort.[131] The plaintiff in *Murphy* was discharged for filing a worker's compensation claim. Such activity was found to subvert the purpose of the Worker's Compensation Act designed to promote the welfare of the people in the state, and consequently violated public policy.[132] Punitive damages may be awarded to deter like wrongs from being committed in the future.[133]

The holding in *Murphy* has been narrowly drawn. The Supreme Court of Kansas interpreted it to apply to interests protected by state law.[134] Terminating an employee because of his outspoken advocacy for consumers and investors, allegedly encouraged by the Kansas Securities Act, was held by the Court of Appeals not to seriously contravene a very clear public policy and therefore was inactionable.[135]

The Federal District Court of Kansas, sitting with pendent jurisdiction, found that the elimination of racial discrimination is a significant public policy objective in Kansas,[136] allowing the employee to maintain a state cause of action for retaliatory discharge on the basis of race.[137] The state action was held to be independent of the federal remedies available under Title VII.[138]

KENTUCKY

An exception to the employment at-will doctrine has been adopted by the Kentucky Supreme Court.[139] A cause of action for retaliatory discharge can lie if the termination was motivated by an employer's desire to punish an employee for seeking benefits to which he or she is entitled by law.[140] The following factors set out the exceptions to the at-will doctrine:

1. The discharge must be contrary to a fundamental and well defined public policy as evidenced by existing law.
2. That policy must be evidenced by a constitutional or statutory provision.
3. The decision of whether the public policy asserted meets these criteria is a question of law for the court to decide, not a question of fact.[141]

Where a statute both declares the act unlawful and specifies the civil remedy available, the aggrieved party is limited to the remedy provided by statute.[142]

So far two situations have been found to exist in Kentucky where grounds for discharging an employee are so contrary to public policy that they are actionable absent explicit legislative statements prohibiting the discharge. The first situation exists when an employee is discharged for refusing to violate a law during the course of employment.[143] The second situation exists when an employee is discharged as a result of his or her exercise of a right conferred by a well-established legislative enactment.[144]

LOUISIANA

Louisiana statutory law allows employers to discharge at-will employees without cause,[145] and the state courts have not yet adopted a broad public policy exception.[146] Federal courts hearing cases under diversity jurisdiction have refused to recognize a public policy exception under Louisiana law.[147] Wrongful discharge claims, however, have been upheld under the worker's compensation law,[148] and under common law intentional tort theories.[149]

MAINE

The Supreme Judicial Court of Maine carved out an exception to the at-will doctrine in *Larrabee v. Penobscot Frozen Foods, Inc.*,[150] An at-will employment contract is terminable for good cause.[151] No consideration other than services to be performed or promised is necessary from either employer or employee to fall under the good cause public policy exception.[152] Likewise, an employee who accepts a job based on oral representations and other reasonable inferences that employment would continue until his or her retirement, has a cause of action for breach of employment contract if terminated before retirement.[153]

A cause of action for breach of an express or implied contract has been recognized when an employee relies on personnel policies, handbooks, manuals and performance review procedures.[154] Punitive damages are available only upon a showing of a willful, independent tort arising from the employer's actions which constitute a breach.[155]

MARYLAND

Maryland courts recognize a cause of action for the tort of abusive discharge when the motivation for the termination contravenes public policy.[156] Plaintiff may rely on both state and federal law as the source of the public policy that would be undermined by refusing an exception to the at-will doctrine.[157] Punitive damages are awardable for abusive discharge.[158]

MASSACHUSETTS

The public policy exception to the at-will doctrine has been recognized under contract law in Massachusetts.[159] An at-will employee who brings a wrongful discharge action on breach of contract theory is not entitled to recover punitive damages nor future lost wages and benefits.[160]

A covenant of good faith and fair dealing was applied to an at-will employment relationship in *Fortune v. National Cash Register Co.*.[161]

Where the discharge is for a reason contrary to public policy the courts will find a breach of contract based on the good faith and fair dealing doctrine.[162]

In a wrongful discharge claim based on age discrimination before a federal district court in Massachusetts, the court held the action was preempted by a state antidiscrimination statute which provides employees with a statutory remedy.[163] In so holding, however, the court recognized a contrary decision in *McKinney v. National Dairy Council*[164] holding that a discharge motivated by age discrimination was actionable under the implied covenant of good faith and fair dealing.[165]

MICHIGAN

The Michigan courts recognize an exception to the at-will rule and maintain that an employee cannot be discharged in violation of a clearly articulated, well accepted public policy.[166] To state a cause of action for wrongful discharge, plaintiff must establish that: (1) (s)he was engaged in protected activity;[167] (2) (s)he was discharged; and (3) his or her discharge was due to performing the protected activity.[168] In *Sventko v. Kroger Co.*,[169] the court upheld a retaliatory discharge claim because the termination violated an employee's exercise of a right conferred by statute.[170] In addition, refusing to violate a law in the course of employment is protected conduct under the public policy exception.[171]

The state supreme court cited approvingly a United States district court case which held that a discharge for refusing to fix prices in violation of the Sherman Act violated state public policy.[172] But, a federal Discrimination Employment Act[173] was used to preempt a common law wrongful discharge action.[174] A federal district court reasoned that statutory remedies were provided to protect employees from discharge on the basis of sex or age, and that it was therefore unnecessary to expand the public policy exception to include sex and age discrimination.[175]

Michigan enacted a Whistleblowers' Protection Act in 1981.[176] The act is a statutory recognition that the protection of employees who report violations of laws, regulations, and rules is a part of Michigan public policy.[177] Another Michigan statute provides similar protection against retaliatory discharges to employees who file complaints with the Michigan Civil Rights Commission.[178]

MINNESOTA

An action in tort for wrongful discharge in Minnesota has been upheld under the public policy exception to the at-will doctrine rule.[179] The Minnesota courts held that terminating an employee for refusing to violate federal law was against state public policy.[180]

MISSISSIPPI

A public policy exception to the at-will doctrine has not been recognized by the Supreme Court of Mississippi.[181] The court refused to create a cause of action for retaliatory discharge, asserting that creation of a remedy was appropriate for legislative amendment and not judicial adoption.[182] In *Shaw v. Burchfield*,[183] however, the court indicated that a cause of action for tortious interference with a contract may be recognized in an at-will employment situation. Mississippi does have some statutes which govern the employment practices of public employees.[184]

MISSOURI

In 1985 the court of appeals analyzed the public policy exception and concluded that employers "are not free to require employees, on pain of losing their jobs, to commit unlawful acts or acts in violation of a clear mandate of public policy expressed in the constitution, statutes, and regulations promulgated pursuant to statute."[185]

Prior to this decision Missouri held an employer liable for wrongful discharge on at least two occasions. In *Smith v. Arthur Baue Funeral Home*,[186] an employee was fired for asserting his right to be covered by a collective bargaining agreement. The court allowed the wrongful discharge claim, reasoning that the Missouri Constitution created a modified at-will doctrine by declaring a right which was violated by the employer.[187] In *Hansome v. Northwestern Cooperage Co.*,[188] the court upheld a cause of action for wrongful discharge where plaintiff was discharged for exercising his right granted under Missouri's Worker's Compensation statute.[189]

Where a collective bargaining agreement provides a grievance procedure for the settlement of disputes between employers and employees, the aggrieved party must exhaust the remedies provided by the agreement before resorting to the courts for redress.[190]

The Missouri Court of Appeals in *Beasley v. Affiliated Hosp. Products*[191] expressly allowed an employee to sue for wrongful termination, and negligent and intentional infliction of emotional distress.[192] The court held that terminating an employee for refusal to violate a law was in clear violation of public policy as announced by both the Missouri and United States legislatures.[193]

MONTANA

The Supreme Court of Montana has adopted the public policy cause of action.[194] Terminating an employee for refusing to perjure himself or herself, for asserting his or her right to obtain Workers' Compensation

Everett Library
Queens College
1900 Selwyn Avenue
Charlotte, N. C.   28274

benefits, and for refusing sexual relations were listed by the court as examples of conduct in clear violation of public policy.[195]

Montana recognized the implied covenant of good faith and fair dealing doctrine.[196] The implied covenant protects employees who, in good faith, accept and maintain employment, reasonably believing their job is secure so long as their duties are performed satisfactorily.[197] An action for emotional, mental, and financial distress arising from a wrongful termination has also been recognized.[198]

NEBRASKA

The common law at-will doctrine remains intact in Nebraska.[199] On at least two occasions the Supreme Court of Nebraska has considered whether to adopt the public policy exception. In both cases the court explicitly declined the invitation to clarify the state's common law on this issue, and held that the facts of each case did not warrant creating a public policy exception, even if the state was to recognize the exception.[200]

NEVADA

Nevada first recognized the public policy exception in 1984.[201] Conduct is against public policy when a state enacts legislation forbidding certain behavior.[202] The failure of the legislature to enact a statute expressly forbidding retaliatory discharge does not preclude the courts from providing a remedy for behavior in violation of public policy.

As with any intentional tort, punitive damages are awardable for the tort of retaliatory discharge where plaintiff can demonstrate malicious, oppressive, or fraudulent conduct on the part of defendant.[203]

Sex or age discrimination was held to fall within the public policy exception to the at-will doctrine by a federal district court interpreting Nevada law.[204] The tort of breach of covenant of fair dealing, and damages for humiliation, embarassment, anxiety, harm to reputation and health were also upheld in the employee context by the district court.[205]

NEW HAMPSHIRE

New Hampshire has adopted a broad public policy exception to the at-will doctrine.[206] The state supreme court in *Monge v. Beebe Rubber Co.* held that "a termination by the employer of a contract of employment at will which is motivated by bad faith or malice or based on retaliation is not in the best interest of the economic system or the public good and constitutes a breach of the employment contract.[207]

The holding in *Monge* has been applied only to situations where an employee is discharged because he performed an act that public policy would encourage, or refused to do that which public policy would condemn.[208] To state a claim for wrongful discharge from employment, plaintiff must show that defendant was motivated by bad faith, malice, or retaliation, and demonstrate that the discharge violated public policy.[209] In most cases, whether public policy exists is a question for the jury and can be based on statutory or nonstatutory principles.[210]

Other causes of action may also be recognized in the employment context. The tort of intentional infliction of emotional distress and the tort of defamation, for example, were upheld by a federal district court interpreting New Hampshire law.[211]

NEW JERSEY

New Jersey recognizes a cause of action for wrongful discharge in both contract and tort.[212] An action in contract may be predicated on the breach of an implied provision that an employer will not discharge an employee for refusing to perform an act that violated a clear mandate of public policy,[213] whereas a tort action may be based on the employer's duty not to discharge an employee for such reasons.[214] Punitive damages may be awarded in a tort action but not in a contract action.[215] The sources of public policy include legislation (administrative rules, regulations or decisions), and judicial opinions.[216]

In 1986 the New Jersey state legislature passed the Conscientious Employee Protection Act,[217] one of the country's strongest state statutes protecting whistleblowers. The law covers both public and private sector employees who disclose allegations of wrongdoing to a "public body" after they attempted to resolve the matter, if possible, with their supervisor.[218] The law has a one-year statute of limitations, provides for a civil remedy in state court, punitive damages, attorney's fees, and reinstatement with full back pay. The law explicitly did not act to waive other common law or statutory remedies which exist in New Jersey, but if an employee utilizes the law she or he waives the right to pursue other remedies. If utilized, the Conscientious Employee Protection Act is an exclusive remedy.[219] Other New Jersey statutes also prohibit employees from wrongful discharge.[220]

NEW YORK

Although New York state courts have rejected establishing a public policy exception,[221] the state passed a statute in 1984 to protect employees from retaliatory discharge for whistleblowing. The statute prohibits an employer from taking any retaliatory personnel action[222] against an employee, if such employee does any of the following:

(a) discloses, or threatens to disclose to a supervisor or to a public body an activity, policy or practice of the employer that is in violation of law, rule or regulation which violation creates and presents a substantial and specific danger to the public health or safety;

(b) provides information to, or testifies before, any public body conducting an investigation, hearing or inquiry into any such violation of a law, rule or regulation by such employer; or

(c) objects to, or refuses to participate in any such activity, policy or practice in violation of a law, rule or regulation.[223]

To be protected under the state for disclosure to a public body, however, the employee must first bring the disclosure to the attention of a supervisor,[224] and afford the employer a reasonable opportunity to correct its alleged misconduct.[225] The statute of limitations for an action under this statute is one year after the alleged retaliatory personnel action was taken.[226]

Independent contractors are not protected by the statutory provisions.[227] Furthermore, the fact that the personnel action was predicated upon grounds other than the employee's exercise of any activity protected in the statute will constitute a defense to the action.[228] The statute does not in any way diminish the rights of employees under any other law, statute, contract or collective bargaining agreement, but institution of an action under the statute will be deemed a waiver of the rights and remedies available under any other contract, collective bargaining agreement, law, rule or regulation or under the common law.[229]

New York has also statutorily prohibited an employer from discharging or in any way discriminating against an employee for asserting or attempting to assert a worker's compensation claim from such employer.[230]

NEW MEXICO

New Mexico adopted a judicial exception to the at-will doctrine in *Vigil v. Arzola.*[231] A cause of action in tort was allowed upon plaintiff's identification of a specific expression of public policy, and proof by clear and convincing evidence of a sufficient nexus between the public policy and the discharge.[232] Damages include lost wages and punitive damages.[233]

The legislature has further limited the at-will doctrine by prohibiting employers from penalizing employees for their participation in jury service;[234] for their particular political opinions or beliefs;[235] or for asserting rights provided in the state workmen's compensation statute.[236]

NORTH CAROLINA

A claim for wrongful discharge was first recognized by the North Carolina Supreme Court in *Sides v. Duke Hospital*, where an anesthetist was fired for testifying truthfully in a civil action.[237] The court held that no employer in North Carolina has the right to discharge an employee because he refused to testify untruthfully.[238] Actions for intentional infliction of emotional distress, breach of contract, and malicious interference with an employment contract are also recognized.[239]

Punitive damages may be recovered only for tortious conduct.[240] To recover punitive damages, the employee must prove that the employer acted willfully, with malice, or with reckless disregard for the employee's rights.[241]

Actions by employees who have been demoted or discharged in retaliation for instituting a worker's compensation proceeding in good faith, or for testifying in regard to it, are expressly authorized by the General Assembly.[242]

NORTH DAKOTA

North Dakota continues to adhere to the traditional at-will rule.[243] The North Dakota Supreme Court did, however, express a willingness to hold that employment manuals or handbooks could, in the proper circumstances, create an implied employment contract.[244]

OHIO

The Supreme Court of Ohio has not recognized the public policy exception.[245] In *Phung v. Waste Managements, Inc.*, the court held that public policy does not require an exception to the employment at-will doctrine, even when an employee is discharged for demanding that his employer cease violating legal and societal obligations in its disposal of toxic waste.[246] One judge strongly dissented, asserting that the majority overlooked the fact that Phung, employed at a nuclear waste disposal site, was under an obligation imposed by Ohio's General Assembly to assist in enforcing Ohio's environmental laws, violation of which constitutes a criminal offense.[247]

OKLAHOMA

Absent a contractual abridgment, Oklahoma still adheres to the termination at-will doctrine.[248] A personnel manual can constitute an employment contract.[249] Oklahoma has some statutory exceptions to the at-will doctrine.[250]

OREGON

The state of Oregon has recognized the public policy exception to the at-will doctrine.[251] Public policy actions have fallen into three categories: (1) where plaintiff is discharged for fulfilling a societal obligation;[252] (2) where plaintiff is discharged for pursuing private statutory rights;[253] and (3) where an adequate statutory remedy exists, an additional common law remedy of wrongful discharge may not be upheld.[254]

Under the Workers' Compensation Act, an employee aggrieved by an unlawful employment practice can either file a claim with the Bureau of Labor or the state.[255] The damages awardable include, but are not limited to, injunctive relief, reinstatement, back pay,[256] and punitive damages.[257]

PENNSYLVANIA

The Pennsylvania Supreme Court acknowledges a cause of action for wrongful discharge of an at-will employee where some recognized facet of public policy is threatened.[258] Public policy can be derived directly from Pennsylvania's Constitution,[259] federal law,[260] or state law.[261]

To state a cause of action, an employee must first establish that some public policy[262]was threatened or violated by the discharge.[263] The employee must further prove that she or he was terminated for refusing to perform an illegal act or engaging in an act protected by public policy.[264] However, even if an important public policy is involved, the discharge will be deemed lawful if the employer shows a separate, plausible, and legitimate reason for firing the employee.[265]

Several statutory remedies to protect employees from retaliatory discharges have also been recognized by Pennsylvania.[266]

RHODE ISLAND

Rhode Island continues to adhere to the traditional common law termination at-will rule.[267] Federal courts, interpreting Rhode Island law, have refused to allow public policy exception actions for wrongful discharge.[268]

SOUTH CAROLINA

The state Supreme Court of South Carolina adopted the public policy exception to the at-will doctrine in *Ludwick v. Minute of Carolina, Inc.*[269] A retaliatory discharge of an at-will employee for refusing to violate the law was held to constitute violation of a clear mandate of public policy.[270] The court in *Ludwick* made no attempt to narrowly define cases involving the public policy exception of refusal to violate the law, and stated that:

An at will prerogative without limits could be suffered only in an anarchy, and there not for long—it certainly cannot be suffered in a society such as ours without weakening the bond of counter balancing rights and obligations that holds such societies together. Thus, while there may be a right to terminate a contract at will for no reason, or for an arbitrary or irrational reason, *there can be no right to terminate such a contract for an unlawful reason or purpose that contravenes public policy.*[271]

The court qualified the exception by ruling that plaintiff has the burden of establishing that the retaliatory discharge contravenes a clear violation of a mandate of public policy.[272]

SOUTH DAKOTA

South Dakota continues to follow the traditional termination at-will doctrine.[273]

TENNESSEE

In a case concerning the termination of an employee for utilizing her rights under a worker's compensation act, the Supreme Court of Tennessee upheld a public policy wrongful discharge tort, stating:

A cause of action for retaliatory discharge, although not explicit, created by the statute, is necessary to enforce the duty of the employer, to secure the rights of the employee and to carry out the intention of the legislature. A statute need not expressly state what is necessarily implied in order to render it effectual.[274]

The court also found that punitive damages were recoverable under a retaliatory discharge tort.[275]

TEXAS

Texas has judicially created a public policy exception to the at-will doctrine.[276] The exception was adopted to prohibit employers from discharging their employees for refusing to perform an illegal act.[277] The Texas legislature has enacted other exceptions to the at-will doctrine.[278]

UTAH

Utah has not formally adopted a judicially created public policy exception to the at-will doctrine.[279] State officers and employees are, however, statutorily protected against retaliation for reporting governmental violations of law.[280]

VERMONT

In 1986 Vermont adopted the public policy exception to the termination at-will doctrine. The Vermont Supreme Court broadly defined public policy, rejecting the proposition that courts are limited to statutory directives in defining exactly what are protected disclosures or what is protected conduct.[281] Quoting from an old Ohio Supreme Court definition of "public policy" the Vermont court stated: "In substance (public policy) may be said to be the community common sense and common conscience.[282]

VIRGINIA

Virginia's Supreme Court has recognized a public policy exception to the at-will rule by allowing a cause of action in tort for improper discharge.[283] A cause of action for wrongful discharge may also exist where the employer expressly and/or impliedly promised that the employee would only be fired for just cause.[284]

WASHINGTON

The state of Washington joined the growing majority of jurisdictions and recognized a cause of action in tort for wrongful discharge.[285] The employee has the burden of proving the dismissal violates a clear mandate of public policy. A clear mandate of public policy is violated if an employer's conduct contravenes the purpose of a constitutional, statutory, or regulatory provision or scheme.[286] Once the employee has demonstrated that his or her discharge may have been motivated by reasons that contravene a clear mandate of public policy, the burden shifts to employer to prove that the dismissal was for reasons other than those alleged by the employee.[287]

The Washington courts have also held that an at-will employment relationship can be modified by provisions found in an employee policy manual.[288] Some limitations on an employer's right to discharge are also based upon state statutes.[289]

WEST VIRGINIA

West Virginia adopted the public policy exception to the at-will doctrine in *Harless v. First National Bank in Fairmont*.[290] The court in *Harless* held that where an employer's motivation for the discharge contravenes some substantial public policy principle, the employer may be liable in tort for retaliatory discharge.[291] The public policy contravened was established by the state's legislature protecting credit consumers.[292] The state Supreme Court, however, has since held that the public policy exception need not be based on a statute.[293]

A tort for intentional infliction of emotional distress arising from a retaliatory discharge was also recognized in *Harless*.[294] The action was allowed even though there was no impact and no physical injury caused by defendant's wrong. The plaintiff need only show that an emotional or mental disturbance resulted from defendant's intentional or wanton wrongful act.[295]

WISCONSIN

Wisconsin has instituted a contract-based exception to the at-will doctrine.[296] The law in Wisconsin now implies a provision that the employer will not discharge an employee for refusing to perform an act that violates a clear mandate of public policy. The employee must show that the dismissal violated such a public policy. It then becomes the employer's burden to go forward with evidence to show that the firing resulted from just cause and not from refusal to commit an illegal act.[297]

An employee fired for refusing a command to violate public policy does not have to prove that the employer had evil intent in discharging him or her.[298] An employee may, however, be required to exhaust administrative remedies before bringing a state action.[299]

WYOMING

Wyoming continues to adhere to the traditional at-will doctrine.[300] Under the appropriate set of circumstances, however, an employee handbook has been found to constitute a contract and consequently provides an exception to the at-will doctrine.[301]

NOTES

1. See 12 ALR 4th 544, *Discharge of At-Will Employees.*

2. The first state to carve out this exception was California in the landmark case *Peterman v. International Brotherhood of Teamsters*, 174 Cal. App. 2d 184, 344P.2d 25 (1959). See also one of the first law review articles that powerfully endorsed a new state tort for retaliatory discharge, Blades "Employment at Will v. Individual Freedom: On Limiting the Abusive Exercise of Employer Power," 67 *Columbia Law Review* 1404 (1957).

3. *Tameny v. Atlantic Richfield Co.*, 27 Cal. 3d 167, 610 P.2d 1330, 1332–1333, 164 Cal. Rptr. 83 (1980).

4. *Pepsi-Cola General Bottlers, Inc. v. Woods*, 440 N.E.2d 696, 697 (Ind. Ct. App. 1982). See also *Carrillo v. Illinois Bell Tel. Co.*, 538 F. Supp. 793, 799 (N.D. Ill. 1982) (applying Illinois law).

5. *Pierce v. Ortho Pharmaceutical Corp.*, 84 N.J. 58, 417 A.2d 505, 512 (1980).

6. Larsen, Lex. *Unjust Dismissal* (N.Y.: Matthew Bender, 1988), Section 3–1 through 4–10.

7. See *Bowman v. State Bank of Keysville*, 311 S.E.2d 797 (Va. 1985); *Stewart v. Ost*, 491 N.E.2d 1306 (Ill. 1986); *Empiregas, Inc. v. Hardy*, 487 So.2d 244 (Ala. 1985).

8. *Pine River State Bank v. Mettille,* 333 N.W.2d 622 (Minn. 1983); *Arie v. Intertherm,* 648 S.W.2d 142 (Mo. App. 1983); *Morris v. Lutheran Medical Center,* 215 Neb. 677, 340 N.W.2d 388 (1983); *Hammond v. N.D. State Personnel Bd.,* 345 N.W.2d 359 (N.D. 1984); *Landgon v. Saga Corp.,* 569 P.2d 524 (Okla. App. 1976); *Jackson v. Minidoka Irrigation,* 98 Idaho 330, 563 P.2d 54 (1977); *Magnan v. Anaconda Industries, Inc.,* 37 Conn. Supp. 38, 479 A.2d 781 (1984); *Terrio v. Millinocket Community Hospital,* 379 A.2d 135 (Me. 1977); *Toussaint v. Blue Cross & Blue Shield,* 408 Mich. 579, 292 N.W.2d 880 (1980).

9. *Mitford v. de Lasala,* 666 P.2d 1000 (Alaska 1983); *Monge v. Beebe Rubber Co.,* 114 N.H. 130, 316 A.2d 549 (1974); *Fortune v. National Cash Register Co.,* 364 N.E.2d 1251 (Mass. 1977); *Cleary v. American Airlines, Inc.,* 111 Cal. App. 3d 443, 168 Cal. Rptr. 722 (1980).

10. *Agis v. Howard Johnson Co.,* 355 N.E.2d 315 (Mass. 1976); *Lucas v. Brown & Root, Inc.,* 736 F.2d 1202 (8th Cir. 1984); *Kelly v. Gen. Tel. Co.,* 136 Cal. App. 3d 278, 186 Cal. Rptr. 184 (1982).

11. *DuSesoi v. United Refining Co.,* 540 F. Supp. 1260 (W.D. Pa. 1982).

12. *Chamberlain v. Bissell, Inc.,* 547 F. Supp. 1067 (W.D. Mich. 1982); *Kelly v. Gen. Tel. Co.,* 136 Cal. App. 3d 278, 186 Cal. Rptr. 184 (1982).

13. *Payton v. City of Santa Clara,* 183 Cal. Rptr. 17, 132 Cal. App. 3d 152.

14. *Kelly v. Gen. Tel. Co.,* 136 Cal. App. 3d 152.

15. *Pugh v. See's Candies, Inc.,* 116 Cal. App. 3d 311, 171 Cal. Rptr. 917 (1981).

16. See Delaware (29 Section 5115); Hawaii (Sec. 621–10.5); Illinois (Ch. 127, Section 636119c.1.); Indiana (4–15–10–4); Maine (26 Section 832); Texas (A.Rt. 6252–16A); Washington (42.40.010); Wisconsin (230.80).

17. See: California (Section 1102.5); Connecticut (Section 31–51m); Maine (26 Section 831); Michigan (Section 15.361 *et seq.*); New York (Section 740).

18. *Mein v. Masonite Corp.,* 124 Ill. App. 3rd 617, 464 N.E.2d 1137 (1937); *Ohlsen v. DST Industries, Inc.,* 111 Mich. App. 580 (1982); *Strauss v. A.L. Randall Co.,* 144 Cal. App. 3rd 514 (1983); *Wolk v. Saks Fifth Ave.,* 728 F.2d 221 (3rd Cir. 1984). But also see *Holien v. Sears Roebuck Co.,* 298 Or. 76, 689 P.2d 1292 (1984); *McKinney v. National Dairy Council,* 491 F.Supp. 732 (D. Mass. 1980); *Wheeler v. Caterpillar Tractor Co.,* 108 Ill. 2d 502, 485 N.E.2d 372 (1985); *Garibaldi v. Lucky Food Stores, Inc.,* 726 F.2d 1367 (9th Cir. 1984); *Alexander v. Gardner-Denver Co.,* 415 U.S. 36 (1974); *Colorado Anti-Discrimination Commission v. Continental Air Lines, Inc.,* 372 U.S. 714 (1963). In *Greenwald v. City of North Miami Beach,* 587 F.2d 779, 781 (5th Cir. 1979), the court held that the federal administrative remedies for whistleblowers under the Safe Drinking Water Act were "entirely independent of any state or local remedies."

19. See *Meeks v. Opp. Cotton Mills, Inc.,* 495 So.2d (Ala. 1984); *Hinrichs v. Tranquilaire Hospital,* 352 So.2d 1130 (Ala. 1977).

20. *Harrell v. Reynold Metal Co.,* 495 So.2d 1381, 1387 (Ala. 1986).

21. *Knight v. American Guard and Alert, Inc.,* 714 P.2d 788, 791–92 (Alaska, 1986).

22. *Knight, supra,* at 793.

23. 569 P.2d 1328 (1977).

24. *Idem* at 1335 (long distance operator refused to pay union dues because of religious beliefs).

25. 596 S.W.2d 681 (Ark. 1980).

26. *Idem* at 683; the court in *Newton v. Brown & Root,* 658 S.W.2d 370, 371 (1983) also indicated that a public policy exception to the at-will doctrine would

be recognized. But, because plaintiff was found to have contributed to this termination for violating a safety rule he could not obey, due to his employer's failure to provide safe working conditions, he was denied relief. Also see *Scholtes v. Signal Delivery Service, Inc.*, 548 F.Supp. 487, 494 (W.D. Ark. 1982).

27. Idem.

28. *Lucas v. Brown & Root, Inc.*, 736 F.2d 1202 (8th Cir. 1984) (plaintiff was fired for refusing to sleep with her foreman).

29. Idem at 1206; Title VII does not "exempt or relieve any person from any liability, duty, penalty, or punishment provided by any present or future law of any state, other than any such law which purports to require or permit the doing of any act which would be an unlawful employment practice under this title." 42 U.S.C. §2000e-7.

30. *Lucas*, 736 F.2d at 1206; *M.B.M. Co. v. Counce*, 596 S.W. 2d 681.

31. Idem at 687.

32. 710 P.2d 1025 (Ariz. 1985); Also see *Vermillion v. AAA Pro Moving & Storage*, 704 P.2d 1360 (Ct. App. 1985).

33. Idem at 1033.

34. Idem at 1035 (employee refused to "moon" co-workers in company skit).

35. *Wagenseller*, 710 P.2d at 1035.

36. Idem at 1036.

37. *Wagenseller*, 710 P.2d at 1044.

38. Idem at 1036.

39. Idem at 1036–37; citing *Leikvold v. Valley View Community Hospital*, 688 P.2d 170 (Ariz. 1984).

40. 344 P.2d 25 (Cal. 1959).

41. California Labor Code §2922.

42. *Petermann*, 344 P.2d 25 (1959).

43. *Tameny v. Atlantic Richfield Co.*, 610 P.2d 1330 (1980).

44. *Cleary v. American Airlines*, 111 Cal. App. 3d 443, 455 (1980), the court held that the "longevity" of the employee's service, together with the expressed policy of the employer [of adopting specific procedures for adjudicating employee disputes], operates as a form of estoppel, precluding any discharge of such an employee by the employer without good cause; also see *Grueberg v. Aetna Ins. Co.*, 510 P.2d 1032 (Cal. 1973); *Comunale v. Traders General Ins.*, 328 P.2d 198 (Cal. 1958).

45. *Lagies v. Copley*, 168 Cal. App. 3d 958 (1980); *Renteria v. County of Orange*, 82 Cal. App. 3d 833 (1978); *Agarwal v. Johnson*, 603 P2d 58 (1959).

46. See: *Williams vs. Taylor*, 129 Cal. App. 3d 745 (1982); *Kelly v. General Telephone Co.*, 136 Cal. App. 3d 278 (1982); and *Deaile v. General Telephone Co.*, 40 Cal. App. 3d 841 (1974).

47. *Childress v. Church's Fried Chicken*, 148 Cal. App. 3d (1983); *Johns Manville Prods. Corp. v. Superior Court*, 612 P.2d 948 (Cal. 1980); *Crocker-Citizen's National Bank v. Control Metals Corp.*, 566 F.2d 631 (9th Cir. 1977).

48. *Seamen's Direct Buying Service v. Standard Oil Co.*, 36 Cal. 3d 752 (1984).

49. Cal. Labor Code §1102.5(a),(b).

50. Cal. Labor Code §1103.

51. *Flores v. Los Angeles Turf Club*, 361 P.2d 921 (Cal. 1961).

52. Idem; see also *S.P. Growers Association v. Rodriguez*, 552 P.2d 721 (Cal. 1976), holding that a state may impose additional sanctions to those provided by a federal act prohibiting discrimination against a worker and prescribing remedies for such discrimination.

53. 188 Cal. App. 3d 290 (1982).

54. See *Hentzel v. Singer Co.*, 138 Cal. App. 3d 290, 188 Cal. Reptr. 159 (1982).

55. See *Snow v. Bechtel Const.*, 647 F. Supp. 1514 (C.D. Cal. 1986).

56. *Winther v. DEC International, Inc.*, 625 F. Supp. 100 (D. Colo. 1985).

57. Idem at 104.

58. 684 P.2d 265 (Colo. App. 1984).

59. Nonetheless, the court recognized that handbooks or policy manuals containing specific procedures for termination may give rise to a contractual duty on the part of the employer to comply with such procedures. Ibid at 267.

60. *Corbin v. Sinclair Marketing, Inc.*, 684 P.2d at 267.

61. 590 P.2d 513 (Colo. App. 1979).

62. Idem at 515; but also see *Sussman v. University of Colo. Health*, 706 P.2d 443 (Colo. App. 1985), where state employee was denied a remedy for wrongful termination due to filing a workmen's compensation claim because, if founded in tort, was barred by the Government Immunity Act, and if founded in contract, was precluded for failure to exhaust administrative remedies available under the State Personnel System Act, section 24–50–101 *et seq.*, C.R.S. (1982 Repl. vol. 10).

63. C.R.S. §13–71–118.

64. *Sheets v. Teddy's Frosted Foods, Inc.*, 427 A.2d 385, 386–387 (1980) (employee was discharged in retaliation for his reporting deviations from food quality standards to his employer; see Mooney, "Wrongful Discharge: A 'New' Cause of Action?", 54 *Connecticut Bar Journal* 213 (1980).

65. *Magnan v. Anaconda Industries, Inc.*, 479 A.2d 781, 789 (1984).

66. 479 A.2d 781 (1984).

67. Idem at 785.

68. Idem at 788.

69. Idem at 789–790.

70. Idem at 790.

71. *Murray v. Bridgeport Hospital*, 480 A.2d 610 (1984).

72. Idem at 614; See *Morris v. Hartford Courant Co.*, 513 A.2d 66 (Conn. 1986) holding that employee could not sustain claim for unintentional emotional distress without asserting risk of illness or bodily harm.

73. 480 A.2d 610 (1984).

74. Idem at 613 (the court in *Murray*, however, denied the action because there was no allegation that defendants profited in any way by inducing the alleged breach.

75. Conn. General Statutes §31–51m (1982).

76. No employer shall discharge, discipline or otherwise penalize any employee because the employee, or a person acting on behalf of the employee, reports, verbally or in writing, a violation or a suspected violation of any state or federal law or regulation or any municipal ordinance or regulation to a public body, or because an employee is requested by a public body to participate in an investigation, hearing or inquiry held by that public body, or a court action. The provisions of this subsection shall not be applicable when the employee knows that such report is false. Ibid §31–51m(b).

77. Idem §31–51m(c). An action must be brought within ninety days of the date of the final administrative determination or within ninety days of such violation, whichever is later, in the superior court for the judicial district where the violation is alleged to have occurred, or where the employer has its principal office.

78. Idem.

79. Idem, §31–51(m)(d).

80. *Heideck v. Kent General Hospital, Inc.*, 466 A.2d 1095, 1096 (1982); *Haney v. Laub*, 312 A.2d 330, 332 (Del. 1973); *Drake v. Hercules Power Co.*, 55 A.2d 630 (Del. 1946).

81. *Heideck, supra*, 466 A.2d at 1097.

82. Idem.

83. 29 Del. Laws, §5115 (1983).

84. *Hansrote v. American Indus. Tec.*, 586 F.Supp. 113, 115 (W.D. Penn. 1984).

85. 428 A.2d 831 (D.C. App. 1981).

86. Idem.

87. *Weaver v. Gross*, 605 F.Supp. 210 (D.D.C. 1985).

88. *Smith v. Piezo Technology & Prof. Admin.*, 427 So.2d 182, 184 (Fla. 1983).

89. Georgia Code §66–101.

90. *Goodroe v. Georgia Power Company*, 251 S.E. 2d 51, 52 (Ga. Ct. App. 1978), plaintiff alleged that he was fired because he was about to uncover criminal activities within his place of employment; also see *Miles v. Bibb Co.*, 339 S.E.2d 316 (Ga. Ct. App. 1985); *Jacobs v. Georgia-Pacific Corp.*, 323 S.E.2d 238 (Ga. Ct. App. 1984); and *Gunn v. Hawaiian Airlines, Inc.*, 291 S.E.2d 779 (Ga. Ct. App. 1982); a state is not required to adopt such a rigorous statutory interpretation of its codified at-will doctrine. In California, for example, the courts have adopted an exception to the at-will doctrine irrespective of the fact that it was codified in California's Labor Code §2922.

91. *Taylor v. Foremost-McKesson, Inc.*, 656 F.2d 1029 (1981); *Goodroe v. Georgia Power Co.*, 251 S.E.2d 52 (Ga. Ct. App. 1978).

92. *Parnar v. American Hotels, Inc.*, 652 P.2d 625 (1982).

93. Idem at 628.

94. Idem at 631.

95. Idem at 631–632.

96. Idem at 629.

97. Idem at 629 and at 631 n.16.

98. *Puchert v. Agsalud*, 677 P.2d 449, 455 (1984).

99. Haw. Rev. Stat. §621–10.5.

100. 563 P.2d 54 (1977); also see *Knee v. School Dist. No. 132*, 676 P.2d 727 (Idaho Ct. App. 1984).

101. Idem at 57.

102. Idem.

103. Idem at 57–58.

104. 384 N.E.2d 353 (1978).

105. *Palmateer v. International Harvester Co.*, 421 N.E.2d 876, 881 (Ill. 1981).

106. 421 N.E.2d at 879. Plaintiff was discharged for informing a local law enforcement agency that a co-worker may have committed a criminal violation.

107. *Cosentino v. Price*, 483 N.E.2d 297 (Ill. App. 1985); see *Rachford v. Evergreen Intern. Airlines Inc.*, 596 F.Supp. 384 (Ill. 1984); where United States district court interpreting Illinois law held that employee could not rely on federal law to establish a public policy exception in support of his claim; also see *Pratt v. Caterpillar Tractor Co.*, 500 N.E.2d 1001 (Ill. App. 1986).

108. *Wheeler v. Caterpillar Tractor Co.*, 485 N.E.2d 372, 377 (1985).

109. Idem, at 376–377.

110. *Cosentino v. Price*, 483 N.E.2d 297 (Ill. App. 1985); Midgett v. Sackett-Chicago, Inc., 473 N.E.2d 1280 (Ill. 1984); *Kelsay v. Motorola, Inc.*, 384 N.E.2d 353; but also see *Stoecklein v. Illinois Tool Works, Inc.*, 589 F.Supp. 139 (1984); and *Ring v. R.J. Reynolds Indus. Inc.*, 597 F. Supp 1277 (1984).

111. *Lingle v. Norge Div. of Magic Chef, Inc.*, U.S. Supreme Court, No. 87–259 (October Term, 1987). On June 6, 1988 the Supreme Court found that such claims were not pre-empted.

112. *Payne v. AHFI/Netherlands, B.V.*, 522 F.Supp. 18 (N.D. Ill. 1980); also see *Criscione v. Sears, Roebuck & Co.*, 384 N.E.2d 91 (1st Dist. 1978); *Stoecklein v. Illinois Tool Works, Inc.*, 589 F. Supp. 1277 (1984).

113. *Stoecklein v. Illinois Tool Works, Inc.*, 589 F.Supp. 139, 145–146 (1984); *Carrillo v. Illinois Bell Tel. Co.*, 538 F.Supp. 793 (N.D. Ill. 1982).

114. 297 N.E.2d 425 (1973).

115. Also see *Stack v. Allstate Ins. Co.*, 606 F.Supp. 472, 475 (1985); *Mead Johnson and Co. v. Oppenheimer*, 458 N.E.2d 668 (Ind. App. 1984).

116. *McClanahan v. Remington Freight Lines, Inc.*, 498 N.E.2d 1336 (Ind. App. 1986), truck driver fired for refusing to drive load in violation of state weight restrictions had wrongful discharge cause of action.

117. See *Campbell v. Eli Lilly & Co.*, 413 N.E.2d 1054, 1061 (Ind. App. 1980), Aff'd., 421 N.E.2d 1099 (1981). Plaintiff in *Campbell* alleged he was dismissed for reporting to his superiors the dangerous and lethal effects of various company-manufactured drugs. A summary judgment was granted in favor of the employer because plaintiff failed to demonstrate a statutory source for the public policy asserted to have been violated. Also see *Tri-City Comprehensive Community Health Center, Inc. v. Franklin*, 498 N.E.2d (Ind. App. 1986); and *Hamblen v. Danners, Inc.*, 478 N.E.2d 926 (Ind. App. 1985) holding that public policy was not violated by dismissing employee who refused to take polygraph test because no statute existed regarding the use of polygraphs as a condition of employment.

118. *Stack v. Allstate Ins. Co.*, 606 F.Supp. 472, 475 (1985).

119. *Ohio Table Pad Co. of Indiana v. Hogan*, 424 N.E.2d 144, 146 (Ind. App. 1981).

120. Idem, also see *Streckfus v. Gardenside Terrace Co-op., Inc.*, 481 N.E.2d 423, 425 (Ind. App. 1985).

121. *Morgan Drive Away v. Brant*, 479 N.E.2d 1336 (Ind. App. 1985); *Travelers Indem. Co. v. Armstrong*, 442 N.E.2d 349, 363 (1982).

122. Ind. Code 4–15–10–2 (except where otherwise provided by state or federal law).

123. Ind. Code 4–15–10–3.

124. Ind. Code 4–15–10–4.

125. Ind. Code 4–15–10–7.

126. See *Abrisz v. Pulley Freight Lines, Inc.*, 270 N.W.2d 454, 455 (Iowa 1978).

127. *Northrop v. Farmland Industries, Inc.*, 372 N.W.2d 193, 196 (Iowa 1985).

128. Ibid.

129. Ibid at 196–97.

130. 630 P.2d 186 (Kan. App. 1981).

131. Ibid at 190.

132. Ibid at 192.

133. Ibid at 193.

134. *Anco Const. Co., Ltd. v. Freeman*, 693 P.2d 1183, 1186 (Kan. 1985), NLRB held to preempt state action for alleged discharge in retaliation for petitioning management for higher wages.

135. *Cain v. Kansas Corp. Com'n.*, 673 P.2d 451 (Kan. App. 1983).

136. *Wynn v. Boeing Military Airplane Co.*, 595 F.Supp 727 (D. Kan. 1984).

137. Ibid at 729.

138. Ibid.

139. *Firestone Textile Co. v. Meadows*, 666, S.W.2d 730 (Ky. 1984); *Pari-Mutuel Clerk's Union v. Ky. Jockey Club, Ky.*, 551 S.W.2d 801 (Ky. 1977).

140. *Firestone* 666, S.W.2d at 733.

141. *Grzyb v. Evans*, 700 S.W.2d 399 (Ky. 1985).

142. *Grzyb*, 700 S.W.2d at 401–2, sex discrimination and freedom of association claims did not fall within the public policy exception because they lacked a specific constitutional or statutory provision upon which plaintiff could base a claim.

143. *Grzyb*, at 402.

144. Ibid.

145. La. Civ. Code Ann. art. 2747.

146. *Gil v. Metal Service Corp.*, 412 So.2d 706, 708 (La. App. 4th Cir. 1982), writ denied, 414 So.2d 379.

147. *Gillory v. St. Landry Parish Policy Jury*, 802 F.2d 822, 826 (5th Cir. 1986).

148. *Moore v. McDermott, Inc.*, 504 So.2d 982 (La. App. 1st Cir. 1987).

149. *Breaux v. South Louisiana Elec. Co-op Assn.*, 471 So.2d 967 (La. App. 1st Cir. 1985). Also see Bureau of National Affairs, State Labor Laws 28: 203 (La. State environmental whistleblower law).

150. 486 A.2d 97 (Me. 1984).

151. Ibid at 99–100.

152. Ibid.

153. *Buchanan v. Martin Marietta Corp.*, 494 A.2d 677, 679 (1985).

154. *Greene v. Union Mutual Life Ins. Co.*, No. 84–0126–P, slip. op. (D. Me. Nov. 15, 1985).

155. Ibid.

156. *Adler v. American Standard Corp.*, 538 F.Supp 572 (D. Md. 1982).

157. Ibid at 578.

158. Ibid at 580.

159. *De Rose v. Putnam Management Co., Inc.*, 496 N.E.2d 428 (1986); *Crews v. Memorex Corp.*, 588 F.Supp. 27, n.3 at 29 (D. Mass. 1984).

160. *De Rose*, at 432 (employee was fired for failing to give testimony implicating another as employer expected).

161. 364 N.E.2d 1251 (Mass. 1977).

162. *Cort v. Bristol-Myers Co.*, 431 N.E.2d 908 (1982); *Gram v. Liberty Mutual Ins. Co.*, 429 N.E.2d 21 (1981).

163. *Crews*, 588 F.Supp. 27.

164. 491 F.Supp. 1108 (D. Mass. 1980).

165. *Crews*, 588 F.Supp. 27 n.5 at 30.

166. *Clifford v. Cactus Drilling Corp.*, 353 N.W.2d 469, 474 (Mich. 1984).

167. Idem.

168. *Authier v. Ginsberg*, 757 F.2d 796, 798 (1985), cert. den. 106 S.Ct 208 (1985).

169. *Sventko v. Kroger Co.*, 245 N.W.2d 151 (1976).

170. A claim was maintained against an employer for discharging employee for having filed a workmen's compensation claim: *Goins v. Ford Motor Co.*, 347 N.W.2d 184 (Mich. App. 1983).

171. *Trombetta v. Detroit, T&R Co.*, 265 N.W.2d 385 (1978).

172. *Suchodolski v. Mich. Consolidated Gas Co.*, 316 N.W.2d 710, 714 (Mich. 1982).

173. 29 U.S.C. §621 *et seq.*

174. *Schroeder v. Dayton-Hudson Corp.*, 448 F.Supp 910 (E.D. Mich. 1977).

175. *Schroeder*, at 918; also see *Pompey v. General Motors Corp.*, 189 N.W.2d 243 (1971), holding that a civil action for wrongful discharge on the basis of race discrimination is a statutory right restricted by the statute of limitations prescribed by the State Fair Employment Practices Act.

176. M.C.L. §15.361 *et seq.*

177. The act provides that:

An employer shall not discharge, threaten, or otherwise discriminate against an employee regarding the employee's compensation, terms, conditions, location, or privileges of employment because the employee, or a person acting on behalf of the employee, reports or is about to report, verbally, or in writing, a violation or a suspected violation of a law or regulation or rule promulgated pursuant to law of this state, a political subdivision of this state, or the United States to a public body, unless the employee knows that the report is false, or because an employee is requested by a public body to participate in an investigation, hearing, or inquiry held by that public body, or a court action. (M.C.L. §15.362.)

178. The statute provides that an employer shall not retaliate or discriminate against an employee that has made a charge, filed a complaint, assisted or participated in an investigation, proceeding or hearing under the Michigan Elliott-Larsen Civil Rights Act. M.C.L. §37.2701.

179. *Phipps v. Clark Oil & Refining Corp.*, 396 N.W.2d 588 (Minn. App. 1986).

180. Ibid. Employee was terminated for refusing to violate the federal Clean Air Act.

181. *Kelly v. Mississippi Valley Co.*, 397 So.2d 874 (1981).

182. *Kelly*, 397 So.2d at 877.

183. 481 So.2d 247 (1985).

184. *Conley v. Board of Trustees of Grenada County Hosp.*, 707 F.2d 175, 179 (5th Cir. 1983); for example, see Miss. Code Ann. §21-3-5 (allowing municipalities to discharge police employees without cause) and compare with Miss. Code Ann. §41-13-5, expressly stating that in order for joint municipal–county hospitals to discharge employees, inefficiency or another good cause must be shown.

185. *Boyle v. Vista Eyewear, Inc.*, 700 S.W.2d 859 (Mo. App. 1985), employee was discharged for refusing to violate a Food and Drug Administration regulation.

186. 370 S.W.2d 249, 254 (Mo. 1963).

187. Ibid.

188. 679 S.W.2d 273 (Mo. 1984).

189. Missouri's Workers' Compensation statute provides that: "No employer or agent shall discharge or in any way discriminate against any employee for

exercising any of his rights under this chapter. Any employee who has been discharged or discriminated against shall have a civil action for damages against his employer." R.S. Mo. §287.780 (1978).

190. *McKinnes*, 667 S.W.2d at 741, if the arbitration clause is not susceptible to any interpretation that covers the asserted dispute, however, the grievance procedures provided by the collective bargaining agreement need not be exhausted.

191. 713 S.W.2d 557 (Mo. App. 1986).

192. *Beasley*, 713 S.W.2d at 561. Plaintiff need only plead the defendant should have realized its conduct involved an unreasonable risk of causing plaintiff's emotional distress and that the distress is "medically diagnosible" and "medically significant."

193. Ibid. at 561. Had plaintiff complied with his employer's demands he would have been subject to criminal prosecution.

194. *Keneally v. Orgain*, 606 P.2d (Mont. 1980); *Nye v. Department of Livestock*, 639 P.2d 498 (Mont. 1982) (administrative rules as a source of a public policy supporting a wrongful discharge action).

195. *Keneally*, at 129.

196. *Degnan v. Executive Homes, Inc.*, 696 P.2d (Mont. 1985); *Dare v. Montana Petroleum Marketing.*, 687 P.2d 1015, 1020 (Mont. 1984).

197. Ibid. Reliance upon an employment handbook was held not to be essential to a cause of action for breach of the implied covenant of good faith.

198. *Dare*, 687 P.2d at 1020.

199. *Mueller v. Union Pacific R.R.*, 371 N.W.2d 732, 737–38 (Neb. 1985).

200. *Mau v. Omaha Nat. Bank*, 207 Neb. 308, 299 N.W.2d 147 (Neb. 1980); *Mueller v. Union Pacific R.R.*, 371 N.W.2d 732 (Neb. 1985).

201. *Hansen v. Harrah's*, 675 P.2d 394 (Nev. 1984), the court recognized the tort of unlawful discharge in retaliation for filing a workers' compensation claim.

202. *Savage v. Holiday Inn Corp. Inc.*, 603 F.Supp. 311, 313 (D.C. Nev. 1985); *Wolber v. Service Corp. Intern.*, 612 F.Supp. 235, 237 (D.C. Nev. 1985).

203. *Hansen v. Harrah's*, 675 P.2d 394, 397 (1984).

204. *Savage*, 603 F.Supp. 311 (D.C. Nev. 1985).

205. Ibid. at 315; also see *Wolber v. Service Corp. Intern.*, 612 F.Supp 235 (D.C. Nev. 1985).

206. *Monge v. Beebe Rubber Co.*, 316 A.2d 549 (1974).

207. *Monge*, 316 A.2d at 551.

208. *Howard v. Dorr Woolen Co.*, 414 A.2d 1273 (1980), discharge due to sickness or age does not fall into public policy exception.

209. *Cloutier v. Great Atlantic & Pacific Tea Company*, 436 A.2d 1140 (1981).

210. *Lilley v. New Hampshire Ball Bearings, Inc.*, 514 A.2d 818, 821 (1986), public policy supports truthfulness and is violated when an employee is discharged for failing to lie to company president on official's behalf; *Cloutier*, 436 A.2d at 1144–45, the question is taken from the jury only when the existence of public policy can be established or not established as a matter of law, *Lilley*, at 821.

211. *Chamberlin v. 101 Realty, Inc.*, 626 F.Supp. 865 (D.N.H. 1985).

212. *Pierce v. Ortho Pharmaceutical Corp.*, 417 A.2d 505, 512 (1980).

213. *Pierce*, supra, at 512; cf. *Vasquez v. Glassboro Services, Inc.*, 415 A.2d 1156 (1980).

214. Idem.

215. Idem.

216. Idem. The code of ethics may also provide an expression of public policy.

217. N.J. Statutes 34:19.

218. N.J. Statutes 34:19–4.

219. N.J. Statutes 34:19–8..

220. See the New Jersey Law Against Discrimination, which prohibits employees from discharge due to race and sex. N.J. Statute section 10:5–1, *et seq.*

221. *Sabetay v. Sterling Drug Inc.*, 497 N.Y.Supp. 2d 655 (1986); *Salanger v. U.S. Air*, 560 F.Supp. 202 (N.D. N.Y. 1983); *Murphy v. American Home Products Corp.*, 448 N.E.2d 86 (N.Y. Ct. App. 1983); there is indication that New York, while not explicitly adopting a public policy exception, will allow a *prima facie* tort in the employment context. See *McCullough v. Certain Feed Products Corp.*, 417 N.W.S.2d 353 (1979); *Chin v. American Tel. & Tel. Co.*, 410 N.Y.S.2d 737 (1978).

222. Ibid., §740(1)(e). Such action includes the discharge, suspension or demotion of an employee, or other adverse employment action taken against an employee in the terms or conditions of employment.

223. Ibid., §740(2).

224. Ibid., §740(f), a supervisor means any individual within an employer's organization who has the authority to direct and control the work performance of the affected employee; or who has managerial authority to take corrective action regarding the violation of the law, rule or regulation of which the employee complains.

225. Idem, §740(3).

226. Idem, §740(4)(a).

227. Idem, §740(4)(c).

228. Idem.

229. Ibid., §740(b).

230. Workers' Compensation Law §120; *Lo Dolce v. Regional Transit Serv., Inc.*, 429 N.Y.S.2d 505 (App. Div. 1980).

231. 699 P.2d 613 (Ct. App. 1983).

232. *Vigil*, 699 P.2d at 620.

233. Ibid., at 620–21.

234. N.M.S.A. §38–5–18.

235. N.M.S.A. §1–20–13

236. N.M.S.A. §52–1–9; but also see *Williams v. Amex Chemical Corp.*, 720 P.2d 1234 (1986), holding that a state claim for the tort of retaliatory discharge is preempted by the Workmen's Compensation Act which creates exclusive rights and remedies.

237. 328 S.E.2d 818 (N.C. Ct. App. 1985).

238. *Sides*, 328 S.E.2d at 826.

239. *Sides*, 328 S.E.2d at 827–28.

240. *Fitzgerald v. Wolf*, 252 S.E.2d 523 (N.C. 1979); *Smith v. Ford Motor Co.*, 221 S.E.2d 282 (N.C. 1976).

241. *Sides*, 328 S.E.2d at 830 (citing *Hardy v. Toler*, 218 S.E.2d 342 (1975).

242. Idem.

243. Section 34–03–01, N.D.C.C.; *Bailey v. Perkins Restaurant,* 938 N.W. 120, 122 (N.D. 1986).

244. Ibid.

245. *Phung v. Waste Managements, Inc.,* 491 N.E.2d 1114 (Ohio 1986).

246. Ibid.

247. Ibid at 1117.

248. *Scrivener-Stevens Co. v. Boliaris,* 385 P.2d 911 (Okla. 1963).

249. *Langdon v. Saga Corp.,* 569 P.2d 524 (Okla. App. 1976).

250. Employers are prohibited from firing employees for serving on juries (Okla. Sta. Ann. 38 §34). Employers are also prohibited from firing employees who file workers' compensation claims in good faith or participate in any workmen's compensation proceeding [Okla. Stat. Ann. 85 §5]. Punitive damages are allowed where employer intended to retaliate when firing employee [*Freeman v. Chicago, Rock Island and Pacific Co.,* 239 F.Supp. 661 (W.D. Okla. 1965); *Hicks v. Tulsa Dynaspan, Inc.,* 695 P.2d 17 (Okla. App. 1985); *Zaragosa v. Oneok, Inc.,* 700 P.2d 662 (1984), *cert. den.* (1985); *Peabody Galion v. Dollar,* 666 F.2d 1309, 1317 (10th Cir. 1981)].

251. *Nees v. Hocks,* 536 P.2d 512 (1975), employee was discharged for serving on jury duty.

252. See *Nees.*

253. See *Campbell v. Ford Industries, Inc.,* 546 P.2d 141 (1976), employee was fired for exercising his statutory right to inspect corporate records.

254. *Walsh v. Consolidated Freightways,* 563 P.2d 1205 (1977), employee barred from state action when adequate statutory remedy protections against unsafe working conditions; but also see *Holien v. Sears, Roebuck & Co.,* 689 P.2d 1292 (1984), holding statutory remedies are not exclusive with respect to a discharge based on sex discrimination.

255. *Williams v. Waterway Terminals Co.,* 693 P.2d 1290, 1292 (Or. 1985), employer refused to reinstate employee following recovery of a compensable injury.

256. *Williams,* 693 P.2d at 1292.

257. *Delaney v. Taco Time International, Inc.,* 681 P.2d 114 (Or. 1984).

258. *Geary v. U.S. Steel Corp.,* 319 A.2d 174, 180 (Pa. 1974)

259. *Hunter v. Port Authority of Allegheny County,* 419 A.2d 631 (1980); *Reuther v. Fowler & Williams, Inc.,* 386 A.2d 119, 120 (Pa. Super. 1978); Art I, Section 7 of the Pennsylvania Constitution provides that "the free communication of thought and opinions is one of the invaluable rights of man, and every citizen may freely speak, write and print on any subject, being responsible for the abuse of that liberty."

260. *McNulty v. Borden, Inc.,* 542 F.Supp. 655 (E.D. Pa. 1982), the Robinson-Patman Act, 15 U.S.C. §13 was alleged to have been violated, but absent finding that act was actually violated by factfinder, without putting forth another public policy consideration, there is no contravention of public policy.

261. *Hansrote v. Amer. Indus. Technologies,* 586 F.Supp. 113 (W.D. Pa. 1984), employee was fired for refusing to violate Pennsylvania law making the acceptance of a commission bribe a criminal offense; *Wolk v. Saks Fifth Ave. Inc.,* 728 F.2d 221 (3rd Cir. 1984), employee was fired in retaliation for the refusal to succumb to sexual advances in violation of Pennsylvania Human Relations Act.

262. *Cisco v. United Parcel Service*, 476 A.2d 1340 (Pa. Super. 1984); *Perks v. Firestone Tire and Rubber Co.*, 611 F.2d 1363 (3rd Cir. 1979), employee was fired for refusing to take polygraph test contrary to Pennsylvania statute forbidding employers to require test; *Novosel v. Nationwide Ins. Co.*, 721 F.2d 894, 899 (3rd Cir. 1983), holding that freedom of political expression involves no less a compelling social interest than the fulfillment of jury service or the filing of a workman's compensation claim.

263. Idem.

264. *McNulty v. Borden, Inc.*, 542 F.Supp. 655, 656 (E.D. Pa. 1982); *Perks v. Firestone Tire and Rubber Co.*, 611 F.2d 1363 (3rd Cir. 1979).

265. *Betts v. Stroehmann Bros.*, 512 A.2d 1280, 1281 (Pa. Super. 1986); *Cisco*, 476 A.2d 1340.

266. The Pennsylvania Human Relations Act, for example, provides in relevant part that:

It shall be an unlawful discriminatory practice, unless based upon a bona fide occupational qualification, or in the case of a fraternal corporation or association, unless based upon membership in such association or corporation, or except where based upon applicable security regulations established by the United States or the Commonwealth of Pennsylvania: (a) For any employer because of the race, color, religious creed, ancestry, age, sex, national origin or non-job related handicap or disability of any individual to refuse to hire or employ, or to bar or to discharge from employment such individual, or to otherwise discriminate against such individual with respect to compensation, hire, tenure, terms, conditions or privileges of employment, if the individual is the best able and most competent to perform the services required.

State and federal circuit courts have differed on whether an action under this act is exclusive of state action. *Wolk v. Saks Fifth Ave. Inc*, 728 F.2d 221, 223 (3rd Cir. 1984), holding act to be exclusive remedy; *contra, Ire v. Central Transportation Inc.*, 409 A.2d 2, 4 (1979). Also see *Braun v. Kelsey-Hayes Co.*, 635 F.Supp. 75, 80 (E.D. Pa. 1986); and *Kilpatrick v. Delaware County Soc.*, 632 F.Supp. at 548–49 on issue of whether federal statutory remedies preempt state action.

267. *Payne v. K-D Manufacturing Co.*, 520 A.2d 569, 573 (R.I. Supreme Court, 1987).

268. *Brainard v. Imperial Manufacturing Co.*, 571 F.Supp. 37, 40 (D.R.I. 1983).

269. *Ludwick v. Imperial Manufacturing Co.*, 337 S.E.2d (1985).

270. *Ludwick*, 337 S.E.2d at 216 (employee was fired for obeying a subpoena).

271. *Ludwick*, 337 S.E.2d at 215, quoting *Sides v. Duke Hospital*, 328 S.E.2d 818 (N.C. 1985).

272. *Ludwick*, 337 S.E.2d at 215; Prior to *Ludwick*, the court articulated its willingness to adopt a public policy exception in *Todd v. South Carolina Farm Bureau Mut. Ins. Co.*, 321 S.E. 2d 602 (Ct. App. 1984) which denied a wrongful discharge claim for firing plaintiff who refused to take a polygraph test because South Carolina had no statute barring polygraph tests as a condition or continuation of employment.

273. *Hopes v. Black Hills Power & Light Co.*, 386 N.W.2d 490 (S.D. 1986).

274. *Clanton v. Cain-Sloan Co.*, 677 S.W.2d 441, 445 (Tenn. 1984).

275. Ibid.

276. *Sabine Pilots Service v. Hauck*, 687 S.W.2d 733 (1985), employee was discharged for refusing to dump oily bilge water into a river in violation of the federal Water Pollution Control Act.

277. *Hauck*, at 735.

278. The exceptions include discharges for filing a workers' compensation claim [Tex. Prev. Civ. Stat. Ann. Part. 8307c]; discharges based on union membership or nonmembership [Tex. Rev. Civ. Stat. Ann. art. 5207a]; discharges because of active duty in state military services [Tex. Rev. Civ. Stat. Ann. Art. 5765 §7A]; and discharges because of jury service [Tex. Rev. Stat. Ann. Art. 5207b]. Employee suing under workmen's compensation statute for wrongful discharge need only prove that her proceeding under the Workmen's Compensation Act was a determining factor. *Azar Nut Co. v. Caille*, 72 S.W.2d 685 (Tex. App. 1986).

The at-will doctrine is further modified by the Texas Commission on Human Rights Act, prohibiting discharges based on race, color, handicap, religion, national origin, age or sex [Tex. Rev. Civ. Stat. Ann. art. 5221k §1.02]. Moreover, legislation exists which expressly protects government employees from retaliatory and discriminatory discharges. [See, Tex. Rev. Civ. Stat. Ann. art. 6252–16].

279. *Bihlmaier v. Carson*, 603 P.2d 790 (Utah 1979); *Rose v. Allied Development Co.*, 719 P.2d 83 (Utah, 1986).

280. Utah Code Ann. §74–46–21 (1985); Utah Code Ann. §67–21–1, *et seq*; *Rose v. Allied Development Co.*, 719 P.2d 83, 85 (Utah 1986) (referring to the Civil Rights Act of 1964, 42 U.S.C. §2000e–2(a)(1)). Additionally, the doctrine is limited by state law extending the prohibited reasons for discharge to include age and handicaps. Utah Code Ann. §34–35–6 (1953); *Rose*, 719 P.2d at 85.

281. *Payne v. Rozendall*, 520 A.2d 586, 588 (Vt. 1986).

282. Ibid at 588.

283. *Bowman v. State Bank of Keysville*, 331 S.E.2d 797, 801 (1985).

284. *Frazier v. Colonial Williamsburg Foundation*, 574 F.Supp. 318, 320 (E.D. Va. 1983).

285. *Thompson v. St. Regis Paper Co.*, 685 P.2d 1081 (Wash. 1984).

286. *Thompson*, at 1088; the Foreign Corrupt Practices Act, 91 Stat. 1494, and the Securities Exchange Act, 15 U.S.C. §78a *et seq*. formed the basis of the public policy which was violated.

287. *Thompson*, at 1089.

288. Ibid. at 1087–88.

289. Discharges are prohibited if based on race, color, religion, sex, national origin, or any sensory, mental, or physical handicap. [R.C.W. 49.60.030, 49.60.180]. Like provisions protecting employees are found in the Industrial Safety and Health Act [R.C.W. 49.46.100] and the Minimum Wage Act [R.C.W. 49.44.090].

290. 246 S.E.2d 270 (W. Vir. 1978).

291. *Harless*, 264 S.E.2d at 275.

292. *Harless*, 264 S.E.2d at 276, referring to the West Virginia Consumer Credit and Protection Act, W.Va. Code 46–A–101.

293. *Cordle v. General Hugh Mercer Corp.*, 325 S.E.2d 111 (1984) held that the public policy exception is contravened when employer discharges an at-will employee for refusing a polygraph test, advocating the protection of individual privacy.

294. *Harless*, at 276.

295. *Harless*, at 276 (quoting *Monteleone v. Co-Operative Transit Co.*, 36 S.E.2d 475, 478 (1945)).

296. *Brockmeyer v. Dun & Bradstreet*, 335 N.W.2d 834, 838 (1983).

297. *Brockmeyer*, at 841.

298. *Bushko v. Miller Brewing Co.*, 396 N.W.2d 167 (1986).

299. See *Koehn v. Pabst Brewing Co.*, 763 F.2d 865 (7th Cir. 1985).

300. *Siebken v. Town of Wheatland*, 700 P.2d 1236 (Wyo. 1985). But also see *Mobil Coal Producing, Inc. v. Parks*, 704 P.2d 702, 708–09 (concurring opinion of Justice Rose) (Wyo. 1985).

301. *Mobil Coal Producing, Inc. v. Parks*, 704 P.2d 702 (Wyo. 1985).

5

OVERVIEW OF A
WHISTLEBLOWER CLAIM

Whistleblower protection law is rapidly developing. Attorneys planning to litigate such a claim must be aware of the dynamic nature of this area of law. There are no well-established boiler plate procedures for trial preparation. Each case tends to be very fact specific, and the applicable law changes from jurisdiction to jurisdiction. Despite these limitations, the following overview covers most of the issues and procedures which an attorney should consider when filing a whistleblower action.

DETERMINATION OF WHAT LAWS COVER
THE ALLEGED RETALIATION

The first step in reviewing a whistleblower claim is to determine what statutes or common law actions may provide a remedy. A case may be covered under more than one whistleblower protection provision. For example, if an employee working in the private sector blew the whistle in Louisiana on the dumping of toxic waste into the Mississippi River, that employee would be protected under two federal laws and one state law: the Toxic Substance Control Act,[1] the Water Pollution Control Act,[2] and a Louisiana state environmental whistleblower act provide remedy.[3] If the same violation was alleged in California, the federal laws would still apply, and the whistleblower might also have a tort cause of action under the state common law for punitive damages.[4] If the employee blew the whistle on the identical issue, but worked for the federal government in Washington, D.C., she or he would be covered under the Federal Civil Service Reform Act, and perhaps also the federal Toxic Substance Control Act and Water Pollution Control Act remedies, but would not have any state cause of action.[5]

As can be seen, depending upon whom one works for and in which state one is employed, the nature and scope of whistleblower protection is varied. Practitioners must review the state common law and statutory law, and federal statutory and constitutional law to determine which laws may provide a remedy for the employee.

In addition to explicit whistleblower protection laws, employees may also be protected under traditional tort or contract remedies for damages resulting from retaliation for whistleblowing, including such actions as intentional infliction of emotional distress,[6] defamation,[7] or breach of contract.[8] A remedy also may lie in a labor union contract or through union grievance procedures.[9]

REVIEW APPROPRIATE STATUTES OF LIMITATION

One major weakness in many statutory whistleblower protection laws is the short statute of limitations. For example, the employee protection provisions of the Atomic Energy Act,[10] the Clean Air Act,[11] the Safe Drinking Water Act,[12] the Water Pollution Act,[13] the Comprehensive Environmental Response, Compensation and Liability Act,[14] the Toxic Substance Control Act,[15] the Surface Mining Control and Reclamation Act,[16] and the Occupational Safety and Health Act,[17] all have only a *thirty-day* statute of limitations. Statute of limitations under other laws also can be very short—such as sixty days to six months.[18]

Failure to comply with a statute of limitations is one of the favorite defenses in whistleblower cases, and the statute is generally held to start running at the time an employer learns that he or she will be retaliated against—not on the last day of employment.[19] Although an employee may fail to comply with the statute of limitations, equitable or legal principles may be utilized to toll the running of the statute. The U.S. Supreme Court has held that statutes of limitation in employment cases are not jurisdictional bars to maintaining a cause of action, but instead, the time limits are subject to equitable modification.[20]

The doctrine of equitable tolling is narrow, and plaintiffs must be extremely careful to draft their complaints or affidavits in such a fashion as to qualify for relief under this doctrine. As the U.S. Court of Appeals for the Third Circuit stated in *School District of Allentown v. Marshall*: "The restrictions on equitable tolling must be scrupulously observed."[21] The court summarized the general grounds that a complainant must allege in order to obtain equitable relief from the statute of limitations:

1. the defendant has actively misled the plaintiff respecting the cause of action;
2. the plaintiff has in some extraordinary way been prevented from asserting his or her rights; or
3. the plaintiff has raised the precise statutory claim in issue but has mistakenly done so in the wrong forum.[22]

The exact definition of "actively misled" or fraudulent concealment of an employee's right to file a complaint is analyzed on a case-by-case basis.[23] But, an employee's subjective ignorance of the time provisions is not sufficient to invoke equitable modification of the statute of limitations.[24]

If there is a statutory or regulatory duty to post notice of an employee's right to file a discrimination suit under the whistleblower laws, the failure to post such a notice may toll the statute of limitations.[25] Equitable tolling may be available if the employee shows that she or he was lulled into inaction by the assurances of the employer,[26] faced substantial "threats of reprisal" or other acts of "intimidation,"[27] had no reason to know that he or she was the victim of discrimination until after the statutory period expired,[28] and where the employee can show the presence of a continuing violation.[29]

CHOICE OF REMEDIES

A plaintiff in a wrongful discharge case may have a choice of forums to pursue his or her claim. The decision on how to pursue the claim will determine what statute of limitations is applicable, the types of damages that are recoverable, and what forum the claim will be adjudicated in. For example, nuclear whistleblowers are explicitly protected under Section 210 of the Energy Reorganization Act.[30] Section 210 has a thirty-day statute of limitations, and provides for a full adversary administrative hearing before the U.S. Department of Labor.[31] Under Section 210 there is no jury trial, the rules of evidence are relaxed, and the proceedings are required to be expedited (a final determination is required to be issued within ninety days of the complaint). No punitive damages are provided for under the statute.

The Illinois Supreme Court ruled that an employee covered under Section 210 states a claim under the Illinois public policy exception tort. Thus, in Illinois, an employee could ignore the Section 210 claim, file in state court, get around the thirty-day statute of limitations, have a jury hear the case, and receive punitive damages.[32] In a recent California case, an employee attempted to utilize the state courts for such a tort, but a federal district court held that Section 210 preempted state action (in the area of atomic regulation) and dismissed the claim.[33] Preemption and preclusion have also been found when employees failed to utilize administrative remedies under OSHA,[34] the NLRA,[35] the Toxic Substances Control Act (TSCA),[36] and state human rights laws.[37]

Some employees have filed for both administrative and common law remedies. Once again, although this approach has been successful, it raises other issues beside preemption, such as *res judicata* and collateral *estoppel*. Where the law clearly provides only one legal remedy, the choice of forum is easy, but once a multitude of forums are opened for the employee, extreme care should be utilized in determining the pros and cons of each potential strategy.

The major questions that should be considered in choosing an appropriate remedy are:

1. Is the common law action preempted or precluded by a preexisting statutory remedy?
2. What effect would filing an administrative complaint have on a potential state common law action?
3. What procedure will the adjudicating body utilize and where is the practitioner experienced in litigation?
4. Does the case contain facts or issues which are not suitable for an administrative body, or a jury evaluating the facts and awarding damages?
5. Is the client willing to underwrite the costs of a long, grueling suit, or are less expensive administrative procedures more economical and practical?
6. What amount of time will a final determination reasonably take in forum?
7. Which forum is most appropriate for airing the public policy concerns raised by the whistleblowing activity?
8. What are the risks of simultaneously filing in multiple forums?
9. Are there potential unused forums or laws through which to pursue or ground a whistleblower claim?

In utilizing the available legal remedies and in trailblazing new approaches to the issue of whistleblower protection, attorneys for employees should be aggressive but selective; clients should be carefully informed of the potential drawbacks of each litigation strategy.

THE BASIC *PRIMA FACIE* CASE

Litigation strategy in whistleblower cases centers around proving the required *prima facie* case, and rebutting the most prominent management defense that the employee's discharge was for a legitimate business purpose, not improper retaliation. The specific elements of the *prima facie* case can change, dependent upon the state tort theory or federal statute which premises the suit. The following elements, however, are the basic components of most whistleblower protection claims:

1. that the plaintiff is an employee or person covered under the specific statutory or common law relied upon for the action;
2. that the defendant is an employer or person covered under the specific statutory or common law relied upon for the action;
3. that the plaintiff engaged in protected whistleblower activity;
4. that the defendant knew or had knowledge that the plaintiff engaged in such activity;
5. that retaliation against the employee was motivated, at least in part, by the employee engaging in protected activity;

6. that plaintiff was discharged or otherwise discriminated against with respect to his or her compensation, terms, conditions or privileges of employment; or suffered some other wrong actionable under state tort or contract theory;
7. that plaintiff acted in good faith when he or she engaged in protected activity;
8. that the defendant cannot demonstrate, by a preponderance of the evidence, that he or she would have reached the same decision as to plaintiff's employment in the absence of protected conduct.[38]

The eighth element listed in the *prima facie* case is technically a defense. Employers, however, almost always put forth an alleged legitimate business justification for the adverse action. Practically speaking, if an employee cannot meet this defense, at least under federal whistleblower protection law, he or she will lose (even if discriminatory motive can be demonstrated).[39]

PROOF OF DISCRIMINATORY MOTIVE

The heart of an employment discrimination case is proving that the discrimination arose because the employee engaged in protected activity.[40] Discriminatory motive can be demonstrated through direct or circumstantial evidence. In rare cases, the employer's conduct is so outrageous as to be "inherently discriminatory" unto itself. The more common case involves subtle discrimination, and requires the employee to carefully demonstrate a variety of circumstances which then give rise to a reasonable inference of discriminatory motive.

An employee is not required to produce direct testimony or evidence of retaliatory motive. In *Ellis Fischel State Cancer Hospital v. Marshall*,[41] the court held: "The presence or absence of retaliatory motive is a legal conclusion and is provable by circumstantial evidence even if there is testimony to the contrary by witnesses who perceived lack of such improper motive."[42]

The following general categories of facts or circumstances are used to establish a reasonable inference of discriminatory motive:

1. employer's hostile attitude toward matter underlying employee's protected conduct;
2. employer's knowledge of protected conduct;
3. nature of protected conduct;
4. special conditions of employment following protected conduct and leading up to discharge;
5. disparate treatment of discharged employee prior to protected conduct;
6. previous expressions of satisfaction with work record;
7. disparate treatment of similarly situated employees;
8. termination procedure;
9. timing of discharge; and
10. threats or retaliation against other employees for similar conduct.[43]

Other factors which have been used successfully to establish circumstantial evidence of discriminatory motive are:

1. high work performance ratings prior to engaging in protected activity, and
   low ratings or "problems" thereafter;[44]
2. manner in which the employee was informed of his or her transfer or termination;[45]
3. inadequate investigation of the charge against the employee;[46]
4. discipline, transfer, or termination shortly after employee engaged in protected activity;[47]
5. the magnitude of the alleged offense;[48]
6. absence of previous complaints against employee;[49]
7. differences in the way complainant and other employees were treated;[50]
8. determination that the employee was not guilty of violating work rule charged
   under;[51] and
9. charges of "disloyalty" against an employee for engaging in protected
   activity.[52]

The above list of factors is not exhaustive. Every case has unique circumstances and the courts do not apply a rigid test to determine
retaliatory motive. Many cases follow established patterns, but the circumstances that may potentially give rise to an inference of retaliatory
intent are as diverse as the labor force.[53]

DISCOVERY

One of the most important aspects of a plaintiff's whistleblower case
is discovery. Employees must utilize discovery, in the form of deposi-
tions and requests for documents, admission, and interrogatory
answers, in order to document their case and rebut the alleged
legitimate business justification the employer will inevitably postulate
to meet its burden under *Mt. Healthy.*

In a whistleblower case, discovery can also be used to probe into the
validity of the original allegations. Simply put, facts concerning the
underlying disclosure or misconduct are often extremely relevant for
the wrongful discharge case. This prosecutorial use of discovery can be
critical for an employee to obtain justice. The underlying misconduct,
if documented and fully uncovered, can have a devastating impact on a
corporate wrongdoer. Whistleblower allegations have led to the exposure of multi-billion-dollar cost overruns, fraud, and have resulted in
the closing of nearly completed nuclear power plants.[54]

In testimony before the United States Administrative Conference
regarding whistleblower protection statutes, attorneys who represent
many major industries in whistleblower cases recognized that the "potential collateral consequences" which may result from a whistleblower case can "dwarf" the actual consequences of losing the wrongful

discharge claim.[55] Discovery is essential to properly probe those "collateral consequences" of the employee's disclosure—as they can relate directly to employer motive, and employer credibility. Corporate embarrassment over the public airing of the original allegation may also facilitate settlement.

Courts have generally recognized the necessity for allowing extensive discovery in employment discrimination cases. In *McDonnell Douglas Corp. v. Green*, the Supreme Court made specific reference to the importance of pretrial discovery in enabling a worker to prove disparate treatment and the pretextual grounds for termination.[56] Refusal to adhere to the "liberal spirit" of discovery is an abuse of discretion, and is grounds for reversing the trial court's decision.[57] The courts have refused to allow "procedural technicalities" to impede liberal discovery,[58] and have "consistently allowed extensive discovery in employment discrimination cases."[59] The necessity for broad discovery is plain:

Generally, plaintiffs should be permitted a very broad scope of discovery in Title VII cases. Since direct evidence of discrimination is rarely obtainable, plaintiffs must rely on circumstantial evidence and statistical data, and evidence of an employer's overall employment practices may be essential to plantiff's prima facie case.[60]

In order to obtain discovery, the information requested must be relevant or must lead to information which is relevant.[61] A realistic possibility that the information sought may be relevant to the subject matter constitutes relevancy. The fact that the information sought may not be introduced at trial does not affect its relevancy for discovery purposes.[62]

As with relevancy, the scope of potential discovery is broad. For example, in an individual disparate treatment case an employee is entitled to evidence of general patterns of discrimination.[63] This includes company-wide information, information concerning employees in other departments, and personnel files on employees located at stores around the country.[64]

Likewise, information compiled for federal investigators or pursuant to law,[65] affirmative action plans,[66] statistical information,[67] organization charts and company reports,[68] information regarding prior corporation discriminatory actions or complaints,[69] and an individual's own personnel records are all discoverable.[70] Federal regulatory agencies can also be subpoenaed for information which may be relevant to the case.

Judges have the discretion to limit or quash discovery, or issue protective orders. When a trial judge oversteps his or her discretion, however, the decision may be reversed.[71] Failure to adhere to the liberal spirit of the rules of discovery, without sound reasons for limiting discovery, is grounds for the court of appeals to reverse.[72]

Typical discovery in a whistleblower claim includes document and interrogatory requests on the following topics:

1. the employee's personnel file and work history;
2. all management investigations, inquiries, evaluations or documents related to the original whistleblower allegation or concern;
3. all management documents which evaluate the employee and relate to his or her discipline, job performance, or termination;
4. copies of all personnel manuals and work rules;
5. evidence of disparate treatment, or evidence that the plantiff was treated differently or more harshly than other employees who may have committed similar or worse disciplinary infractions;
6. evidence or information regarding federal or state investigations, or legal actions which relate to underlying whistleblower disclosures;
7. all evidence or information regarding the termination decision, including who participated in it, exactly why it was made, all steps which led to the decision, the alleged reason for the discipline, the exact acts for which the discipline was administered, and who had knowledge of the incident which led to the discipline;
8. evidence and information on each element of the *prima facie* case;
9. the facts, evidence, and witness that the defendant will rely upon to prove its case that the discharge was not retaliatory.

In addition to civil discovery, an employee may also use the federal [5 U.S.C. 552] or state Freedom of Information Acts to obtain information from government agencies. Often, various government agencies have investigated the whistleblower claims, or regulated the area of the employer's business which was the subject of the whistleblower.

FORMULATION OF A THEORY OF THE CASE

The basic theory to every whistleblower case is premised upon proving the *prima facie* case: that the "employer discharged the employee in retaliation for the employee's activities," and that the discharge was in "contravention of a clearly mandated public policy."[73]

In demonstrating that the termination or discipline was retaliatory, an employee usually utilizes four major theories: that the adverse personnel action was pretextual, disparate, inherently discriminatory, or was taken in direct response against the employee's refusal to perform illegal or hazardous work. These four approaches are not mutually exclusive, and can be argued together in the alternative.

Pretext Theory

A pretext case is based upon proving that the alleged reason given for the discharge did not in fact exist, or was not in fact relied upon. In *Wright Line* the National Labor Relations Board defined pretext:

Examination of the evidence may reveal, however, that the asserted justification is a sham in that the purported rule or circumstance advanced by the employer did not exist, or was not, in fact, relied upon. When this occurs, the reason advanced by the employer may be termed pretextual. Since no legitimate business justification for the discipline exists there is, by strict definition, no dual motive.[74]

Demonstrating pretext can be extremely difficult, and the ultimate burden of proof always remains upon the employee to prove pretext.[75]

Dual Motive

The most common theory utilized to demonstrate retaliation, and overcome the defendant's alleged legitimate business reason for the termination or discipline, is the dual motive theory. Dual motive cases differ from pretext cases in that *both* valid and invalid reasons for a discharge exist. The dual motive test can be summarized as follows: The employee must initially establish, by a preponderance of the evidence, a *prima facie* case showing that illegal motives (among other factors) "played some part" in the disciplinary action or discharge.[76] Once the employee meets this burden, the burden of proof shifts onto the employer to persuade the court or jury that it would have discharged or disciplined the employee even if the protected activity had not occurred.

The dual motive test was spelled out by the U.S. Supreme Court in *Mt Healthy*.[77] In *Mt. Healthy*, a retaliation case based upon First and Fourteenth Amendment protection, the court held:

Initially, in this case, the burden was properly placed upon respondent [the employee] to show that his conduct was constitutionally protected, and that this conduct was a substantial factor—or to put it in other words, that it was a motivating factor in the Board's decision not to rehire him. Respondent having carried that burden, however, the District Court should have gone on to determine whether the Board had shown by a preponderance of the evidence that it would have reached the same decision as to respondent's reemployment even in the absence of the protected conduct.[78]

The shifting burden of proof can be extremely important. If the court cannot determine whether the employer disciplined the worker out of legitimate or illegitimate motives, the employee should prevail. The employer usually bears the risk that "the influence of legal and illegal motives cannot be separated."[79]

If management attempts to meet this burden and demonstrate a "legitimate," nondiscriminatory reason for terminating or disciplining the employee, the primary rebuttal evidence an employee can put forward is proof of "disparate treatment."[80] Disparate treatment simply means that an employee who engages in protected activity was treated differently, or disciplined more harshly, than an employee who did not engage in protected activity.[81] For example, in an NLRA context, where a union organizer and another employee were both caught drinking on the job and the company fired only the union organizer, the court found disparate treatment.[82]

Refusal to Perform Work

Often a discharge is sparked by an explicit refusal by an employee to perform a given task. Although refusal to follow orders is traditionally a valid business reason for a discharge, two limited grounds may exist for an employee to refuse to perform a job assignment. The first is a refusal to perform work that is illegal,[83] the second is a refusal to perform unsafe or immediately hazardous work.[84]

Refusal to work cases are often straightforward, since the act triggering the actual termination is usually not in dispute. The employee, however, has a high burden of proving that the requested act was illegal or unhealthy. In an OSHA case, the U.S. Supreme Court articulated the following for use in evaluating a wrongful discharge case on the basis of refusing hazardous work:

[C]ircumstances may sometimes exist in which the employee justifiably believes that the express statutory arrangement does not sufficiently protect him from death or serious injury. Such circumstances will probably not often occur, but such a situation may arise when (1) the employee is ordered by his employer to work under conditions that the employee reasonably believes pose an imminent risk of death or serious bodily injury, and (2) the employee has reason to believe that there is not sufficient time or opportunity either to seek effective redress from his employer or to apprise OSHA of the danger.[85]

This standard has been followed in right to refuse hazardous work cases under other statutes.[86]

Inherently Discriminatory Conduct

A fairly unexplored area of whistleblower protection is based upon the labor law theory that certain employer conduct inherently discriminates against whistleblowers, and constitutes a discriminatory act regardless of intent. Whistleblowers have raised such allegations against mass drug testing and polygraph testing.

In cases under the National Labor Relations Act, the Supreme Court has held that where conduct is "inherently discriminatory," the employer must be held to "consequences which forseeably and inescapably flow" from the conduct, even if there is no evidence of illegal or discriminatory intent.[87] In such cases, "good faith" is not a defense.[88]

In *Radio Officers v. NLRB*, the Supreme Court outlined this rule:

[T]hat specific proof of intent is unnecessary where employer conduct inherently encourages or discourages union membership is but an application of the common-law rule that a man is held to intend the foreseeable consequences of his conduct. Thus an employer's protestation that he did not intend to encourage or discourage must be unavailing where a natural consequence of his action was such encouragement or discouragement. Concluding that encouragement or discouragement will result, it is presumed that he intended such consequence. In such circumstances intent to encourage is sufficiently established.[89] [citations omitted]

ROLE OF THE INITIAL DISCLOSURE

Attorneys are trained in utilization of the law. But most employees do not become whistleblowers in order to get engaged in litigation—they blow the whistle to expose or stop problems which may raise major issues of social policy or public safety. Advocates for the whistleblower must be sensitive to the subjective importance the initial allegations may have for the employer, and the objective importance the allegations may raise for society.

For the most part, the validity of the underlying claim is never the focus of a wrongful discharge suit. Most laws protect the whistleblower even if the original disclosure is unproven—it is the act of raising the concerns which is important, not whether the concerns are valid.[90]

Although the validity of the underlying allegation is, for the most part, not a necessary element of proof, attorneys should still aggressively attempt to document the validity of the claim. First, if the underlying allegation was correct, it will help demonstrate that the original allegation was made in good faith and was not frivolous. Second, if the underlying allegation is correct, the credibility of the employee will be enhanced, and that of the employer will be diminished. Third, the validity of the underlying claim would provide circumstantial evidence of discriminatory motive, i.e., the employer's intent to cover up the problem. Fourth, as the employee gets closer to fully documenting and proving an illegal problem, the willingness of the employer to settle the case—on terms both favorable to the employee and the public—are enhanced.

Aggressively attempting to document and prove the validity of the underlying claim serves both the public interest and the legal interest of the client, and implicates the reason why the employee risked his or her job and livelihood.

CONCURRENT ENFORCEMENT ACTIONS

Employees are not limited to pursuing their whistleblower case only as a legal action for wrongful discharge. Employees, citizen organizations, and attorneys can also initiate concurrent enforcement actions aimed at remedying the underlying wrongful conduct. For example, if a whistleblower was terminated from a nuclear power plant for blowing the whistle to the Nuclear Regulatory Commission (NRC) about faulty welds, the employee can file a complaint with the NRC regarding the validity of the welds.[91] Thus, while the attorney and client are pursuing a wrongful discharge case, the NRC is required to investigate the quality of the welds. If the employee works closely with the regulatory authority or investigative body, the regulatory body may vindicate the underlying claim.

Conversely, employees should be leery of putting too much credence in an official, state, local, police, or federal inquiry into the underlying conduct. In the federal sector, the U.S. Office of the Special Counsel, which has responsibility for reviewing the validity of federal whistleblower complaints, has obtained a notorious reputation for participating in cover-ups of alleged problems. The Office of the Special Counsel has come under extreme criticism. The very congressional sponsors who wrote the legislation calling for its creation as a body to protect whistleblowers have introduced legislation calling for its abolition or its major reform.[92] Likewise, in the famous whistleblower case involving retaliation and wrongful death against Ms. Karen Silkwood, the original NRC investigation vindicated the outrageous actions of the Kerr-McGee Corporation.[93]

Even incomplete or inefficient governmental investigations, however, can be very useful for the employee. Employees can obtain access to the closed government investigation files through use of the Federal Freedom of Information Act or state FOIAs, and subpoena government records which may relate to their case.[94]

Additionally, members of the news media often have an interest in investigating and covering a whistleblower case. A media investigation can turn up many leads unavailable to the whistleblower, give the whistleblower added credibility, pressure the governmental regulatory agencies to conduct a thorough investigation, and prompt or facilitate politicians to give assistance to the whistleblower or statutorily address the issue raised by the allegations. Congressional and legislative action is often prompted by whistleblower disclosures.

Limiting a whistleblower case just to a traditional legal forum may, under the circumstance of each case, not be the best approach. Attorneys and other representatives for the whistleblower should familiarize themselves and review, on a case-by-case basis, exactly what state, federal, or private agencies may have jurisdiction over the allegations or may be interested in assisting the whistleblower. Agencies commonly used for this purpose are the NRC (nuclear power issues), the EPA (environmental), the Inspector General's Office of the various U.S. departmental agencies, the Office of the Special Counsel, the U.S. Attorney, the FBI and Department of Justice, public interest organizations involved in the area in which the whistleblower is concerned, the news media, and the U.S. Congress (both local Congress members, and the Washington D.C. committee staff who are involved in oversight work concerning the area relating to the disclosures).

NOTES

1. 15 U.S.C. 2622.
2. 33 U.S.C. 1367.
3. Bureau of National Affairs (BNA), State Labor Laws 28:203.
4. *Tameny v. Atlantic Richfield Co.*, 164 Cal. Rptr. 839, 610 P.2d 1330 (1980).
5. 5 U.S.C. 2302.
6. *Agis v. Howard Johnson, Co.*, 355 N.E.2d 315 (Mass. 1976); *Lucas v. Brown & Root, Inc.*, 736 F.2d 1202 (8th Cir. 1984).
7. *Kelly v. Gen. Tel. Co.*, 136 Cal. App. 3d 311, 186 Cal. Rptr. 917 (1981).
8. *Pine River State Bank v. Mettille*, 333 N.W.2d 622 (Minn. 1983); *Arie v. Intentherm*, 648 S.W.2d 142 (Mo. App. 1983); *Morris v. Lutheran Medical Center*, 215 Neb. 677, 340 N.W.2d 388 (1983); *Hammond v. N.D. State Personnel Bd.*, 345 N.W.2d 359 (N.D. 1984); *Langdon v. Saga Corp.*, 569 P.2d 524 (Okla. App. 1976); *Jackson v. Minidoka Irrigation*, 98 Idaho 330, 563 P.2d 54 (1977); *Magnan v. Anaconda Industries, Inc.*, 37 Conn. Supp. 38 (1984); *Terrio v. Millenocket Community Hospital*, 379 A.2d 135 (Me. 1977); *Toussaint v. Blue Cross & Blue Shield*, 408 Mich. 579, 292 N.W.2d 880 (1980).
9. *Stokes v. Bechtel North American Power Corp.*, 614 F. Supp. 732 (D.C. Cent. D. Cal. 1986).
10. 42 U.S.C. 5851.
11. 42 U.S.C. 7622.
12. 42 U.S.C. 300j–9.
13. 33 U.S.C. 1367.
14. 42 U.S.C. 9610.
15. 15 U.S.C. 2622.
16. 30 U.S.C. 1293.
17. 29 U.S.C. 660(c).
18. See the Federal Mine Health and Safety Act, 30 U.S.C. 815(c) (60 days); the National Labor Relations Act, 29 U.S.C. 158 (6 months); the Surface Transportation Act, 49 U.S.C. 2305 (180 days); and the Safe Containers Act, 46 U.S.C. 1506 (60 days).
19. *Delaware State College v. Ricks*, 449 U.S. 250 (1982).
20. *Zipes v. Transworld Airlines, Inc.*, 455 U.S. 3803, 385 (1982).
21. 657 F.2d 16, 19 (3rd Cir. 1981).
22. 657 F.2d 16, 18 (3rd Cir. 1981); *Dartey v. Zack Co.*, 82–ERA– 2, slip op. of the SOL at 5–6 (April 25, 1983). The Supreme Court has recognized that failure to comply with short employment discrimination filing periods is not a jurisdictional bar to maintaining a cause of action, but instead, the time limits are subject to equitable modification. *Zipes v. Transworld Airlines, Inc*, 455 U.S. 385, 393 (1982).
23. See *Richards v. Mileski*, 662 F.2d 65, 70 (D.C. Cir. 1981); *Meyer v. Riegal Products Corp.*, 720 F.2d 303, 307–308 (3rd Cir. 1983).

24. *Kocian v. Getty Refining & Marketing Co.*, 707 F.2d 748, 753 (3rd Cir. 1983); *Earnhardt v. Comm. of Puerto Rico*, 691 F.2d 69, 71 (1st Cir. 1982); *Geromette v. General Motors Corp.*, 609 F.2d 1200 (6th Cir. 1979); *Smith v. American President Lines, Ltd.*, 571 F.2d 102, 109 (2nd Cir. 1978); *Martinez v. Orr*, 738 F.2d 1107, 1110 (10th Cir. 1984).

25. *Bonham v. Dresser Industries, Inc.*, 569 F.2d 187, 193 (3rd Cir. 1977) cert. denied, 439 U.S. 821 (1978); *Charlier v. S.C. Johnson & Son, Inc.*, 556 F.2d 761 (5th Cir. 1977); *Dartt v. Shell Oil Co.*, 539 F.2d 1256, 1262 (10th Cir. 1976).

26. *Carlile v. South Routt School Dist. RE 3-J*, 652 F.2d 981, 985 (10th Cir. 1981).

27. *Fleischhaker v. Adams*, 481 F.Supp. 285, 292 (D.D.C 1979).

28. *Oaxaca v. Roscoe*, 641 F.2d 386 (5th Cir. 1981); *Reeb v. Economic Opportunity Atlanta, Inc.*, 516 F.2d 924 (5th Cir. 1975); *Stoller v. Marsh*, 682 F.2d 971, 974 (D.C. Cir. 1982); *Bickham v. Miller*, 584 F.2d 736 (5th cir. 1978); *Cooper v. Bell*, 628 F.2d 1208 (9th Cir. 1980).

29. *McKenzie v. Sawyer*, 684 F.2d 62, 72 (D.C. Cir. 1982); *Olson v. Rembrandt Printing Co.*, 511 F.2d 1228, 1234 (8th Cir. 1975). See also, *Terry v. Bridgeport Brass Co.*, 519 F.2d 806 (7th Cir. 1975); *Hiscott v. General Elec. Co.*, 521 F.2d 632, 635 (6th Cir. 1975); *Prophet v. Armco Steel Co.*, 575 F.2d 579 (5th Cir. 1978).

30. 42 U.S.C. 5851.

31. 29 C.F.R. Part 24 and 18.

32. *Wheeler v. Caterpillar Tractor Co.*, 108 Ill. 2d 502, 485 N.E.2d 372 (1988) cert. denied, 106 S.Ct. 1641 (1986).

33. *Snow v. Bechtel*, 647 F.Supp. 1514 (C.D. Cal. 1986). But also see, *Stokes v. Bechtel*, 614 F. Supp. 732 C.D.C. (Cal. 1985) and *Silkwood v. Kerr-McGee Corp.*, 464 U.S. 238, 104 S. Ct. at 625–26 (1984).

34. *Ohlsen v. DST Industries, Inc.*, 314 N.W.2d 699, 704 (Mich. App. 1982).

35. *Allis-Chalmers Corp. v. Lueck*, 105 S. Ct. 1904, 1912 (1985). But also see, *Alexander v. Gardner-Denver Co.*, 415 U.S. 36 (1974); *Garibaldi v. Lucky Food Stores, Inc.*, 726 F.2d 1367 (9th Cir. 1984).

36. *Braun v. Kelsey-Hayes*, 635 F. Supp. 75, 79–80 (E.D. Pa. 1986).

37. *Stoecklein v. Illinois Tool Works, Inc.*, 589 F. Supp. 139, 145 (N.D. Ill. 1984).

38. *Mt. Healthy City School District v. Doyle*, 97 S. Ct. 568, 576 (1977); *NLRB v. Transportation Management Corp.*, 103 S. Ct. 2469 (1983); *Mackowiak v. University Nuclear Systems, Inc.*, 735 F.2d 1159 (9th Cir. 1984); (Energy Reorganization Act) Stephen Kohn, "Protecting Environmental and Nuclear Whistleblowers: A Litigation Manual" (Washington, D.C.: N.I.R.S., 1985); "Shepard's Causes of Action," 1 COA 273; American Jurisprudence, *Proof of Facts* (2nd), "Proof of Retaliatory Discharge; *Munsey v. Morton*, 507 F.2d 1202 (D.C. Cir. 1974); (Federal Mine Health and Safety Act) *Cox v. Dardanelle Public School District*, 790 F.2d 668 (8th Cir. 1986); (First Amendment) *Sims MME Paulette Dry Cleaners*, 580 F. Supp. 593 (S.D.N.Y. 1984) (Title VII).

39. *Mt. Healthy City School District v. Doyle*, 97 S. Ct. 568, 576 (1977).

40. *DeFord v. Secretary of Labor*, 700 F.2d 281, 286 (6th Cir. 1983); *Mackowiak v. University Nuclear Systems, Inc.*, 735 F.2d 1159, 1162 (9th Cir. 1984). Cf. *NLRB v. Mount Desert Island Hosp.*, 695 F.2d 634, 638 (1st Cir. 1984), employer's action construed broadly to prevent intimidation of others in exercise of their rights; *John Hancock Mutual Life Ins. Co. v. NLRB*, 191 F.2d 483, 485 (D.C. Cir. 1951), broad construction necessary to prevent intimidation of prospective complainants and witnesses.

41. 629 F.2d 563, 566 (8th Cir. 1980), cert. denied, 450 U.S. 1040 (1981).

42. See also, *Mackowiak v. University Nuclear Systems, Inc.*, 735 F.2d 1159, 1162 (9th cir. 1984); *Zoll v. Eastern Allamkee Community School Dist.*, 588 F.2d 246, 250 (8th cir. 1978); *Rutherford v. American Bank of Commerce*, 565 F.2d 1162, 1164 (10th Cir. 1977).

43. American Jurisprudence, *Proof of Facts* (2nd), "Proof of Retaliatory Termination," Sec. 7–1.

44. *Ellis Fischel State Cancer Hospital v. Marshall*, 629 F.2d 563 (8th Cir. 1980); *Brown & Root–Northrop*, 174 N.L.R.B. 1048, 1050–51 (1969).

45. *DeFord v. Secretary of Labor*, 700 F.2d 281 (6th Cir. 1983).

46. *Consolidated Edison Co. of N.Y. v. Donovan*, 673 F.2d 61 (2nd Cir. 1982).

47. See also *McCarthy v. Cortland County Community Action Program*, 487 F. Supp. 333, 340 (N.D. N.Y. 1980); *Melchi v. Burns Int'l Security Serv., Inc.*, 597 F. Supp. 575, 584 (E.D. Mich. 1984); *Jim Causley Pontiac v. NLRB*, 620 F.2d 122, 125 (6th Cir. 1980); *Womack*, 619 F.2d at 1296; *G & S Metal Products Co.*, 199 N.L.R.B. 705, 708 (1972), enforced 489 F.2d 441 (6th Cir. 1973).

48. *NLRB v. Wright Line, A Div. of Wright Line*, 662 F.2d 899, 907–908 (1st Cir. 1981), cert. denied, 455 U.S. 989 (1982).

49. *Kendall Co.*, 188 N.L.R.B. 805, 809 (1971).

50. *Viracon, Inc. v. NLRB*, 736 F.2d 1188, 1192 (7th Cir. 1984); *M & S Steel Co.*, 148 N.L.R.B. 789, 795 (1964), enforced, 353 F.2d 80 (5th Cir.).

51. *G & S Metal Products Co.*, 199 N.L.R.B. 705, 708 (1972), enforced, 489 F.2d 441 (6th Cir. 1972).

52. *NLRB v. Mount Desert Island Hosp.*, 695 F.2d 634, 640–641 (1st Cir. 1982).

53. See John P. Ludington, *Employer Discrimination Against Employee for Filing Charges or Giving Testimony Under NLRA*, 35 ALR Fed. 8–24.

54. See Stephen M. Kohn and Thomas Carpenter, "Nuclear Whistleblower Protection and the Scope of Protected Activity Under Section 210 of the Energy Reorganization Act, 4 *Antioch Law Journal*, 73, 74–77, 94–96 (summer 1986).

55. N. Reynolds, R. Walker, P. Dykems, "Comments on Preliminary Recommendations of the Administrative Conference of the United States Regarding Private Sector Health and Safety Whistleblower Statutes" (Washington, D.C., April 10, 1987).

56. 411 U.S. 792, 804–805 (1973).

57. *Duke v. University of Texas at El Paso*, 729 F.2d 994, 997 (5th Cir. 1984).

58. *Duke*, 729 F.2d at 997.

59. *Morrison v. City and County of Denver*, 80 F.R.D. 289, 292 (D. Colo. 1978).

60. *Morrison*, 80 F.R.D. at 292.

61. *LaChemise LaCoste v. The Alligator Co.*, 60 F.R.D. 164, 170–171 (D. Del. 1973).

62. *Fonseca v. Regan*, 98 F.R.D. 694, 700 (E.D. N.Y. 1983); *Zahorik v. Cornell Univ.*, 98 F.R.D. 27, 29 (N.D. N.Y. 1983); *Roesberg v. Johns-Manville Corp.*, 85 F.R.D. 292, 295–297 (E.D. Pa. 1980); *United States v. International Business Machines Corp.*, 66 F.R.D. 215, 218 (S.D. N.Y. 1974); *McDonnell Douglas Corp. v. Green*, 411 U.S. 792 (1973); *Wirtz v. Capitol Air Serv., Inc.*, 42 F.R.D. 641, 642 (D. Kan. 1967); *Milner v. National School of Health Technology*, 73 F.R.D. 628, 632 (E.D. Pa. 1977).

63. *Zahorik v. Cornell Univ.*, 98 F.R.D. 27, 31 (N.D. N.Y. 1983); *Lieberman v. Gant*, 630 F.2d 60, 68 (2nd Cir. 1980); *Milner v. National School of Health*

Technology, 73 F.R.D. 628, 632 (E.D. Pa. 1977). Racial discrimination pattern: NOW, Inc. etc. v. Minnesota Mining & Mfg. Co., 73 F.R.D. 467, 472 (D. Minn. 1977); Johnson v. W.H. Stewart Co., 75 F.R.D. 541, 543 (W.D. Okla. 1976). Civil rights discrimination pattern: Dunn v. Midwestern Indemnity, 88 F.R.D. 191, 196 (S.D. Ohio 1980).

64. Held v. National R.R. Passenger Corp., 101 F.R.D. 420, 425 (D. D.C. 1984); Georgia Power Co. v. Equal Employment Opportunities Comm'n, 412 F.2d 462, 468 (5th Cir. 1969); NOW, Inc. etc. v. Minnesota Mining & Mfg. Co., 73 F.R.D. 467, 472 (D. Minn. 1977); Haykel v. GFL Furniture Leasing Co., 76 F.R.D. 386, 390 (N.D. Ga. 1976); Duke v. University of Texas at El Paso, 729 F.2d 994 (5th Cir. 1984).

65. Witten v. A.H. Smith & Co., 100 F.R.D. 446, 454 (D. Md. 1984); Resnick v. American Dental Ass'n, 90 F.R.D. 530, 541 (N.D. Ill. 1981); Georgia Power Co. v. EEOC, 412 F.2d 462 at 468 (5th Cir. 1969).

66. Witten v. A.H. Smith & Co., supra; Zahorik v. Cornell Univ., 98 F.R.D. 27, 32 (N.D. N.Y. 1983); Johnson v. W.H. Stewart Co., 75 F.R.D. 541, 543 (W.D. Okla. 1976).

67. Sweat v. Miller Brewing Co., 708 F.2d 655, 657 (11th Cir. 1983); NOW, Inc. etc. v. Minnesota Mining and Mfg. Co., 73 F.R.D. 467, 472 (D. Minn. 1977); Alabama v. United States, 304 F.2d 583, 586 (5th Cir. 1962).

68. Held v. National R.R. Passenger Corp., 101 F.R.D. 420, 425 (D. D.C. 1984); Zahorik, supra at 33; Holliman v. Redman Dev. Corp., 61 F.R.D. 488, 490 (D. S.C. 1973).

69. Resnick, supra; two years prior to earliest date EEOC claim filed, Zahoric, supra; four and one-half years prior to plaintiff's discharge and two years after, Milner v. National School of Health Technology, 73 F.R.D. 628, 632 (E.D. Pa. 1977).

70. Milner, supra.

71. Wallin v. Fuller & Nationwide Mutual Ins. Co., 476 F.2d 1204 (5th Cir. 1973).

72. See Duke v. University of Texas at El Paso, 729 F.2d 494 (5th Cir. 1984).

73. Cosentino v. Price, 483 N.E.2d 297, 300 (Ill. App. 1 Dist. 1985), citing from Palmateer v. Int. Harvester Co., 85 Ill.2d 124, 134, 421 N.E.2d 876 (1981).

74. Wright Line, 251 N.L.R.B. 1083 (1980), aff'd, 662 F.2d 899 (1st Cir. 1981), cert. denied, 455 U.S. 989 (1982). Also see DeFord, 700 F.2d 281 (6th Cir. 1983).

75. NLRB v. Transportation Management Corp., 103 S. Ct. 2469, 2473 N.5 (1983); Texas Dept. of Community Affairs v. Burdine, 101 S. Ct. 1089 (1981); McDonnell Douglas Corp. V. Green, 93 S. Ct. 1817 (1973).

76. Mackowiak v. University Nuclear Systems, Inc., 735 F.2d 1159, 1163–64 (9th Cir. 1984).

77. 97 S. Ct. 568.

78. 97 S. Ct. at 575.

79. Mackowiak v. University Nuclear Systems, 735 F.2d 1159, 1164 (9th Cir. 1984), quoting from Transportation Management, 462 U.S. at 403. In Transportation Management the court spelled out the policy reasons for shifting the burden: "the employer is a wrongdoer; he has acted out of a motive that is declared illegitimate by the statute. It is fair that he bear the risk that the influence of legal and illegal motives cannot be separated because . . . the risk was created by his own wrongdoing." NLRB v. Transportation Management Corp., 462 U.S. 393, 403 (1983).

80. The concept of disparate treatment was defined in the Title VII context in *McDonnell Douglas Corp. v. Green*, 411 U.S. 792, 804 (1973); in an NLRA context in *Wright Line*, 251 N.L.R.B. 1083, 1089 (1980), aff'd sub non. *NLRB v. Wright Line*, 662 F.2d 899 (1st Cir. 1981); in a First Amendment context in *Mount Healthy City School Dist. v. Doyle*, 429 U.S. 274, 287 (1977).

81. *Donovan on Behalf of Chacon v. Phelps Dodge Corp.*, 709 F.2d 86, 93 (D.C. Cir. 1983).

82. See *NLRB v. Faulkner Hospital*, 691 F.2d 51, 56 (1st Cir. 1982); *NLRB v. Clark Manor Nursing Home Corp.*, 671 F.2d 657, 661–663 (1st Cir. 1982). For some cases where the court failed to find disparate treatment, see *Airborne Freight Corp. v. NLRB*, 728 F.2d 357, 358 (6th Cir. 1984); *Viracon, Inc. v. NLRB*, 736 F.2d 1188, 1193 (7th Cir. 1984).

83. *Tameny v. Atlantic Richfield Co.*, 27 Ca.3d 167, 610 P.2d 1330 (1980); *Beasley v. Affiliated Hosp. Products*, 713 S.W.2d 557 (Mo. App. 1986); *Winther v. DEC Intern., Inc.*, 625 F. Supp. 100, 104 (D.C. Col. 1985).

84. *Whirlpool Corp. v. Marshall*, 445 U.S. 1, 10–11 (1980); *Gateway Coal v. U.M.W.A. et al.*, 414 U.S. 368 (1974); *Miller v. Fed. Mine Safety and Health Review Comm'n.*, 687 F.2d 194 (7th Cir. 1982); *Phillips v. Int. Bd. of Mn. Op. App.*, 500 F.2d 772 (D.C. Cir. 1974), cert. denied, 420 U.S. 938 (1975), *Blocker v. Dept. of the Army*, 6 MSPB 395 (1981); OSHA Regulation 29 C.F.R. 1977, 12(b)(2); *Wheeler v. Caterpillar Tractor Co.*, 485 N.E.2d 372 (Ill. 1985).

85. *Whirlpool Corp. v. Marshall*, 100 S. Ct. 883, 889–90 (1980).

86. See *Miller v. Federal Mine Safety and Health Act*, 687 F.2d 194 (7th Cir. 1982); *Blocker v. Dept. of the Army*, 6 MSPB 395 (1981); *Pennsyl. v. Catalytic, Inc.*, 1983 Energy Reorganization Act case No. 2, Decision of the U.S. Secretary of Labor (January 13, 1984).

87. *NLRB v. Erie Resister Corp.*, 373 U.S. 221, 228 (1963).

88. *Int'l Ladies Garment Workers Union v. NLRB*, 366 U.S. 731, 738–739 (1961); see also, *Kroger Co. v. NLRB*, 401 F.2d 682, 686 (6th Cir. 1968), cert. denied, 395 U.S. 904 (1969).

89. *Radio Officers v. Labor Board*, 347 U.S. 17, 45 (1954).

90. Title VII, *Womack v. Munson*, 619 F.2d 1292, 1298 (8th Cir. 1980); NLRA, *Interior Alterations, Inc., NLRB*, 738 F.2d 373, 376 (10th Cir. 1984); FLSA, *Love v. RE/MAX of America, Inc.*, 738 F.2d 383, 387 (10th Cir. 1984); OSHA, *Donovan v. Hahner Foreman and Harness, Inc.*, 736 F.2d 1421, 1429 (10th Cir. 1984); FMHSA, *Munsey v. Morton*, 507 F.2d 1292 (D.C. Cir. 1974).

91. See 10 C.F.R. 2206. The NRC also has concurrent jurisdiction with the U.S. DOL to investigate whistleblower wrongful discharge allegations. See 10 C.F.R. 50.7 and Memorandum of Understanding Between NRC and Department of Labor, Employee Protection, 47 Fed. Reg. 54585 (1982).

92. See generally Thomas Devine and Don Aplin, "Abuse of Authority: The Office of the Special Counsel and Whistleblower Protection," 4 *Antioch Law Journal* 5 (summer 1986).

93. *Silkwood v. Kerr-McGee Corp.*, 104 S. Ct. 615 (1984).

94. 5 U.S.C. 552.

6

PROTECTED WHISTLEBLOWER ACTIVITY

One of the most hotly contested issues in whistleblower law is the exact definition of protected whistleblower activity. The three main unresolved areas of law regarding the scope of protected activity are: the method of making a disclosure, the manner in which a disclosure is made, and the context of the whistleblower disclosure.

As the law develops, one factor becomes clear—when highly technical definitions of protected activity are applied to whistleblower cases the employee is often left without a remedy. For example, an employee at a nuclear power plant disclosed a violation of Nuclear Regulatory Commission regulations to his supervisor. A Department of Labor judge held that this disclosure caused his termination. The employee, however, was denied protection under the nuclear whistleblower protection law because he made the disclosure to his supervisor—not to the NRC.[1] Conversely, the state of New York passed a whistleblower protection act which requires that employees first report potential violations of law to their supervisors. They are not protected under the law if they make their disclosure directly to the government.[2]

This type of contradiction in basic definitions of protected activity undermines whistleblower protection. It is simply not realistic to assume that the typical employee desiring to make a disclosure will be cognizant of such hypertechnical legal distinctions.

SCOPE OF PROTECTED ACTIVITY

Whistleblower protection laws are designed to ensure that certain types of information can be freely transmitted by an employee to the appropriate corrective agency. One of the first questions a whistleblower faces is who should he or she communicate the disclosure to. This issue, which concerns the proper scope of protected activity, remains unresolved. In some jurisdictions the scope of protected activity is broadly defined—and encompasses disclosures made to the press, to a supervisor and to governmental agencies. In other jurisdictions, only complaints raised with governmental agencies are protected—other jurisdictions have more convoluted approaches, such as the state of New York, which requires whistleblowers to first communicate with their supervisor and give management an opportunity to correct the problem. Such contradictory definitions of protected activity have caused hardships for whistleblowers. Most employee whistleblowers are completely unfamiliar with the laws protecting their conduct. Consequently, such employees tend to follow their own common sense in how to make a disclosure and have been subsequently stripped of clearly needed protection.

Employees tend to make their disclosure to those whom they feel the most comfortable talking with—or to the person or agency they feel will competently address their underlying allegations. These decisions are generally made on a case-by-case basis, and are completely determined by the specific conditions found in the workplace, what governmental agencies regulate the industry or have jurisdiction over the wrong-doing, and the subject understanding and knowledge of the specific whistleblower.

One of the first Supreme Court decisions analyzing the scope of protected activity arose under Section 8(a)(4) of the National Labor Relations Act, which prohibits discrimination of employees who have "filed charges or given testimony" before the NLRB.[3] In *NLRB v. Scrivener*, the Supreme Court held that an employee who provided information to a NLRB field examiner was protected from retaliation, although the employee had not "filed charges or given testimony."[4] The court urged a "broad interpretation" of the statutory prohibition against retaliation in order "to prevent the Board's channels of information from being dried up by employer intimidation."[5] The critical concern was to provide coverage under the law for employees who had a "need for protection" and not to deny coverage on the basis of the "vagaries of the selection process" an employee utilized to provide information to the government.[6] For the most part, the U.S. Courts of Appeal have applied the *Scrivener* analysis to other whistleblower statutes and broadly defined the scope of protected activity.

An extremely significant post-*Scrivener* case addressing the scope of protected activity was *Phillips v. Interior Board of Mine Operators*.[7] *Phillips* arose under the 1969 Mine Health and Safety Act which prohibited employment discrimination against any employee who:

(A) has notified the Secretary or his authorized representative of any alleged violation or danger;

(B) has filed, instituted, or caused to be filed or instituted any proceeding under this chapter; or

(C) has testified or is about to testify in any proceeding resulting from the administration or enforcement of the provisions of this chapter.[8]

Based upon that limited statutory definition the *Phillips* court decided whether a complaint made internally to management—by a miner to a foreman—was protected under the act. Such protection was not explicitly granted under the statute.

In a 2–1 decision, Justice Wilkey of the District of Columbia Court of Appeals held that internal whistleblowing was protected. The court looked at the underlying purpose of the act and the "practicalities" which confront employees, management and government in attempting to enforce health and safety regulations.[9] Simply put, it is realistic to assume that an employee who discovers a potential problem will first report it to management—and that such a disclosure could result in discrimination or possible termination.[10]

The *Phillips* holding has been widely followed by other courts.[11] It was endorsed by congressional committees when the 1969 Mine Health and Safety law was amended,[12] and has been upheld by various administrative agencies of the U.S. government.[13]

The *Phillips* decision was a landmark holding, as it recognized two basic principles which underly whistleblower cases. First, that "safety" (or legality) "costs money." There exists a tension in many regulated industries to cut costs—and safety or quality control regulations are often sacrificed in order to meet production needs. Industries—such as mining, atomic energy, and defense or NASA contractors—have all been plagued with the consequences of allowing production or profit pressures to outweigh the public's safety. Employees whose safety activity slows down production have been fired or retaliated against for these activities. Employee complaints—such as the conditions of a specific weld at a nuclear power plant, or the strength of "O-Rings" in the space shuttle, or wiring problems in the B-1 Bomber—if adequately addressed by management, could slow up production and cost a corporation millions of dollars.

For this reason employees who attempt to aggressively follow safety or quality control requirements—and who report such violations to management—have been ostracized at the workplace. Judge Wilkey, in the *Phillips* decision, recognized the phenomena that such employees are "not likely to be popular" with "management." Whistleblowing can cause tension or hostility at the workplace.

Second, the *Phillips* decision did not apply a rigid or static definition of protected activity, but instead recognized the need to protect conduct that "realistically" afforded an employee with the opportunity to effectively communicate his or her concern. Once again the *Phillips* court applied a common sense analysis. To whom an employee will report a possible safety violation will depend upon the circumstances of a particular work environment.[14]

At least one U.S. Court of Appeals has rejected the *Phillips* rule in a case under Section 210 of the Energy Reorganization Act—the nuclear whistleblower protection law.[15] In *Brown & Root v. Donovan*,[16] the U.S. Court of Appeals for the Fifth Circuit refused to apply Section 210 coverage to purely internal whistleblowing, and interpreted the nuclear whistleblower law as requiring direct employee contact with a "competent organ of government."

The fifth circuit justified their narrow interpretation, reasoning that the nuclear whistleblower protection law was not intended to "restructure" the employer–employee relationship:

The Secretary's reading (the U.S. Secretary of Labor adopted the *Phillips* rule and upheld the protection of purely internal whistleblowing) of the statute would appear to prohibit the discipline or discharge of such people for any disagreement with their employers on any matters which involve plant safety. Moreover, the same would appear to be true for *every employee*. Since a wide range of decisions in a nuclear company will have *some* bearing on plant safety, the Secretary asks us to adopt an interpretation that would radically restructure the employee–employer relationship in all nuclear corporations.[17]

The *Brown & Root* decision has been widely criticized.[18] The U.S. Secretary of Labor has refused to follow the decision, as has the U.S. Court of Appeals for the Tenth Circuit.[19]

THE MANNER OF ENGAGING IN PROTECTED ACTIVITY

Protected whistleblowing activity, whether based on statutes or common law, is a narrow exception to the at-will doctrine. It is now well accepted in federal employment discrimination law that employers maintain the right to terminate employees even if part of the motivation for termination was caused by the employee's engagement in protected activity.[20] If the manner an employee utilizes to engage in protected activity is outrageous or improper, the employee can lose protection. Outrageous activity by employees constitutes an independent justification for discipline. Thus courts have held that where otherwise-protected protest activities interfere with an employee's job performance, discipline against such an employee will be deemed proper.[21]

In analyzing whether the manner in which an employee engages in protected activity is so outrageous as to lose protection, the U.S. Supreme Court has drawn a distinction between protected activity which involves speech, versus protected activity which involves conduct. Alleged misconduct based solely on the content of employee speech is subject to strict scrutiny. If an employee files a charge or complaint against an employer with a government regulatory body, the employee cannot be disciplined, even if the content of the charge is libelous.[22] Disclosures made directly to management or to nongovernmental sources are usually protected.[23] Internal protected speech, whether written or oral, should be protected even if it is "vehement, caustic" or "unpleasantly sharp."[24] In *Linn v. United Plant Guard, Workers of America*, the U.S. Supreme Court applied the *New York Times v. Sullivan* rule to speech issues arising under the NLRA:

The enactment of the NLRA manifests a Congressional intent to encourage free debate on issues dividing labor and management. And, as we stated in another context, cases involving speech are to be considered against the backdrop of a profound . . . commitment to the principle that debate . . . should be uninhibited, robust, and wide-open, and that it may well include vehement, caustic, and sometimes unpleasantly sharp attacks.[25]

The *Linn* rule has been cited to or followed in other contexts—including First Amendment retaliatory discharge cases.[26]

Under the *Linn* analysis, speech was protected so long as it did not contain "deliberate or reckless" untruths,[27] was not "grossly dispropor-tionate" to the goal sought,[28] and did not constitute flagrant miscon-duct.[29] An employee calling the president of the corporation a "son-of-a-bitch,"[30] an employee using words such as "m___f___," "damn lies," and "horse's ass,"[31] and an employee's circulation of Jack Lon-don's statement defining a "scab" as a "two-legged animal with a cork-screw soul, water brain (and) a combination backbone of jelly and glue,"[32] were all found to be protected when they occurred within the context of employee activities covered under the NLRA.

When employee conduct transcends pure speech, a stricter balancing test is applied. The courts, on a case–by–case basis, consider whether the employer's interest in the "smooth functioning of his business" is outweighed by the employee's interest in internally resolving the discrimination dispute.[33] Under this balancing test, unprotected con-duct included dissemination of false and derogatory accounts of an employer's management practices to the press,[34] the interference of a company's business relationship with a customer,[35] misuse of a com-pany telephone to call one's attorney,[36] and other conduct which in-terfered with the employee's job performance or disrupted the workplace.[37]

An employee's refusal to perform work is generally not protected. There are, however, two exceptions to this rule. First, under certain limited circumstances an employee can refuse to perform work that he or she believes, in good faith, to be imminently hazardous to his or her health.[38] Second, some state and federal courts have protected employee whistleblowers who have refused to perform illegal work.[39]

As a rule, employee whistleblowers must always be careful about the method and manner they choose to utilize when making a disclosure. Regardless of how significant the disclosure, or how illegal the corporate practices are, insubordination or misconduct in the manner an employee chooses to oppose the illegal practice can result in a legal discharge.

CONTENT OF WHISTLEBLOWER SPEECH OR DISCLOSURE

The content of whistleblower speech or conduct is protected from two basic sources—state or federal statutes, or state common law. If the speech is protected by statute, the scope of protected whistleblowing is limited by and defined by the statute. If an employee files a complaint under a state or federal whistleblower protection statute, the statute itself generally defines the type of complaints or disclosure covered under the law.

A far more difficult question of interpretation arises under state common law. Common law historically is judicially constructed, and as such develops on a case-by-case basis. As various states adopt the public policy exception, each state court has been creating its own definition of public policy. Consequently, states have significantly differed in what types of employee disclosures are covered under the definition of public policy.

Of the states which have adopted the public policy exception there is a clear consensus to protect from discharge employees who refuse to perform an illegal act (such as giving an illegal commercial bribe),[40] or who perform an act which they are statutorily entitled to (such as applying for worker's compensation).[41] Some courts appear to have limited the public policy exception only to these situations.[42] Whether these states will expand their definition of protected activity under the public policy exception is unclear.

A second group of states define public policy as any right, duty, or safety standard codified by a state (or sometimes federal) statute, Executive Order, the Constitution, or other legally binding regulations. In these states the courts have adopted a legislatively defined definition of public policy.[43] Some states also include court decisions, in addition to statutes or regulation articulating the public policy of the state.[44]

In both of the circumstances outlined above, the state courts have limited the public policy exception to circumstances where the whistleblower's or employee's speech or conduct was justifiable under a specific prior statute or legal principle. The courts have essentially looked to the legislature to define the public policy of the state.

A third group of states have not confined themselves to statutory sources for public policy, but have developed their own definition of public policy.[45] The Supreme Court of Vermont in *Payne v. Rozendaal* held that the "absence of a statutory directive" was not "dispositive" as to "whether a public policy against such practices" exists.[46] The Vermont court cited to a 1916 Ohio Supreme Court decision defining public policy:

In substance, [public policy] may be said to be the community common sense and common conscience, extended and applied throughout the state to matters of public morals, public health, public safety, public welfare, and the like. It is that general and well-settled public opinion relating to man's plain, palpable duty to his fellow men, having due regard to all the circumstances of each particular relation and situation.

Sometimes such public policy is declared by Constitution; sometimes by statute; sometimes by judicial decision. More often, however, it abides only in the customs and conventions of the people—in their clear consciousness and conviction of what is naturally and inherently just and right between man and man. It regards the primary principles of equity and justice and is sometimes expressed under the title of social and industrial justice, as it is conceived by our body politic. When a course of conduct is cruel or shocking to the average man's conception of justice, such course of conduct must be held to be obviously contrary to public policy, though such policy has never been so written in the bond, whether it be Constitution, statute, or decree of court. It has frequently been said that such public policy, is a composite of constitutional provisions, statutes, and judicial decisions, and some courts have gone so far as to hold that it is limited to these. The obvious fallacy of such a conclusion is quite apparent from the most superficial examination. When a contract is contrary to some provision of the Constitution, we say it is prohibited by the Constitution, not by public policy. When a contract is contrary to a statute, we say it is prohibited by a statute, not by a public policy. When a contract is contrary to a settled line of judicial decisions, we say it is prohibited by the law of the land, but we do not say it is contrary to public policy. Public policy is the cornerstone—the foundation—of all Constitutions, statutes, and judicial decisions; and its latitude and longitude, its height and its depth, greater than any or all of them. If this be not true, whence came the first judicial decision on matter of public policy? There was no precedent for it, else it would not have been the first.[47]

Under the Vermont court's definition of public policy, the courts are not necessarily bound by statutes or definitions of public policy. Although such an approach may seem to justify broad and potentially abusive judicial powers, in practice only narrow applications of the general public policy definitions have been utilized, such as the use of professional ethical standards to judge conduct, or, as in the *Payne* case, terminations which occurred solely due to a person's age.[48] If only private or personal interests are at stake, or the dispute is over purely internal company procedures, public policy torts have not been upheld.

CONCLUSION

The underlying purpose of whistleblower protection laws is to allow employees to stop, report, or testify about employer actions which are illegal, unhealthy, or violate specific public policies. In passing whistleblower protection provisions, Congress has repeatedly recognized the importance of encouraging such speech: "The best source of information about what a company is actually doing or not doing is often its own employees."[49] Only a broad definition of protecting activity and speech can achieve this goal. An employee, at the factory or shop level, must feel comfortable in bringing allegations of misconduct to the attention of either management or governmental regulatory bodies. Likewise, management must fully understand that employees who make such disclosures cannot be terminated because they complained about or reported alleged wrongdoing. Society will not obtain the full benefits of "whistleblowing" until such a change occurs on the local level.

NOTES

1. See *Brown & Root v. Donovan*, 747 F.2d 1029 (5th Cir. 1984).

2. New York State Labor Law Section 740.

3. *NLRB v. Scrivener*, 405 U.S. 117 (1972).

4. Ibid.

5. 405 U.S. at 122, quoting from *John Hancock Mut. Life Ins. Co. v. NLRB*, 191 F.2d 483, 485 (D.C. Cir. 1951).

6. 405 U.S. at 124.

7. 500 F.2d 772 (D.C. Cir. 1974).

8. 30 U.S.C. 820(b)(1); Federal Coal Mine Health and Safety Act of 1969, Section 110(b)(1).

9. Ibid, at 779.

10. *Phillips*, 500 F.2d at 778.

11. See *Mackowiak v. University Nuclear Systems*, 735 F.2d 1159 (9th Cir. 1984); *Kansas Gas & Electric v. Brock*, 780 F.2d 1505 (10th Cir. 1985); Fair Labor Act cases: *Love v. Re/Max of America Inc.*, 738 F.2d 383, 387 (10th Cir. 1984); *Marshall v. Parking Co. of America Denver, Inc.*, 670 F.2d 141 (10th Cir. 1982); (per curiam); *Brennan v. Maxey's Yamaha, Inc.*, 513 F.2d 179, 180 (8th Cir. 1975); *Hodgson v. Yinger*, 20 Lab. Real. Rep. (BNA) 78 (S.D. 1971); *Goldberg v. Zenger*, 43 Lab. Cas. (CCH) Para. 31, 155 (Utah 1961). 1969 Federal Mine Safety Act cases: *Phillips v. Board of Mine Operations Appeals*, 500 F.2d 772, 781–782 (D.C. Cir. 1974) cert. denied, 420 U.S. 939 (1974); *Munsey v. Morton*, 507 F.2d 1202 (D.C. Cir. 1974); *Baker v. Board of Mine Operations Appeals*, 595 F.2d 746 (D.C. Cir. 1978). OSHA cases: *Donovan v. Peter Zimmer America, Inc.*, 557 F. Supp. 642 (D.S.C. 1982). NLRA cases: *NLRB v. Retail Store Employees' Union*, 570 F.2d 586 (6th Cir. 1978), cert. denied, 439 U.S. 819 (1978). Also see *Givhan v. Western Line Consolidated School District*, 439 U.S. 410 (1979).

12. Senate Report No. 848, 1978 U.S. Code Cong. & Admin. News p. 7303; *Kansas Gas & Electric v. Brock*, 780 F.2d 1505, 1511 (10th Cir. 1985).

13. U.S. Secretary of Labor, see Decision of the Secretary of Labor, *Lockert v. Pullman Power*, 84–ERA–15 (August 19, 1985); Nuclear Regulatory Commission, see Brief of the U.S. Nuclear Regulatory Commission of Americus Curiae in *Kansas Gas & Electric Co. v. Brock*, 780 F.2d 1505 (10th Cir. 1985).

14. A "common sense" approach to defining the scope of protected activity was adopted by a Federal District Court in an OSHA case. The court categorically rejected management's argument that employee whistleblowers must bring their complaints to a government body to be protected:

In the ordinary course of events, an employee who notices a health hazard will begin by bringing the matter to the attention of those with whom he deals directly in his daily worklife, such as the employer, supervisors, co-workers, or union officials. This is simple common sense. These persons are the ones most likely to be in a position to obtain information regarding the alleged hazard and to take appropriate action. It would be foolish to invoke the ponderous mechanisms of government to remedy a problem without first attempting to resolve the problem through voluntary means. If employers have a right to fire an employee who complains to his union or other nongovernmental entity but have no right to fire an employee who complains to a governmental entity, many absurd results will follow. *Donovan v. Diplomat Envelope Corp.*, 587 F. Supp. 1417, 1424 (E.D. N.Y. 1984).

15. 42 U.S.C. 5851(a) defines protected activity as when an employee:

1. commenced, caused to be commenced, or is about to commence or cause to be commenced a proceeding under this Act or the Atomic Energy Act of 1954, as amended, or a proceeding for the administration or enforcement of any requirement imposed under this Act or the Atomic Energy Act of 1954 as amended;
2. testified or is about to testify in any such proceeding, or;
3. assisted or participated or is about to assist or participate in any manner in such a proceeding or in any other manner in such a proceeding or in any other action to carry out the purposes of this Act or the Atomic Energy Act of 1954 as amended.

16. 747 F.2d 1029, 1036 (5th Cir. 1984).

17. 747 F.2d at 1035.

18. See Stephen M. Kohn and Thomas Carpenter, "Nuclear Whistleblower Protection and the Scope of Protected Activity Under Section 210 of the Energy Reorganization Act, 4 *Antioch Law Journal* 73 (summer 1986).

19. *Kansas Gas & Electric Co. v. Brock*, 780 F.2d 1505 (10th Cir. 1985).

20. See *Mt. Healthy City School District Board of Education v. Doyle*, 429 U.S. 274, 287 (1977). In *Mt. Healthy*, Justice Rehnquist held that employees who engage in protected activity should not be placed in a "better position" *viz a viz* other employees who have not engaged in protected conduct. 429 U.S. at 285. Consequently, even if discriminatory animus played a "substantial factor" in an employer's decision to terminate an employee, the employer's termination decision will be upheld *if* the employer can demonstrate that he "would have reached the same decision" even in the absence of protected conduct. 429 U.S. at 287.

21. *Hochstadt v. Worcester Foundation for Experimental Biology*, 545 F.2d 222 (1st Cir. 1976); *EEOC v. Crown Zellerbach Corp.*, 720 F.2d 1008 (9th Cir. 1983); *Wrighten v. Metropolitan Hospitals, Inc.*, 726 F.2d 1346 (9th Cir. 1984).

22. *Pettway v. American Cast Iron Pipe Co.*, 411 F.2d 998 (5th Cir. 1969).

23. *Parker v. Baltimore and O.R. Co.*, 652 F.2d 1012, 1020 (D.C. Cir. 1981).

24. See *Linn v. United Plant Guard, Workers of America*, 383 U.S. 53, 62 (1966); *Montefiore Hospital and Medical Center v. NLRB*, 621 F.2d 510, 517 (2nd Cir. 1980).

25. Linn, 383 U.S. at 62, quoting from *New York Times v. Sullivan*, 376 U.S. 254 (1964).

26. See *Pickering v. Board of Education*, 391 U.S. 563, 573 (1968).

27. *NLRB v. Owners Maintenance Corp.*, 581 F.2d 44, 50 (2nd Cir. 1978).

28. *NLRB v. A. Lasaponarat Sons, Inc.*, 541 F.2d 992, 998 (2nd Cir. 1976).

29. *American Telephone & Telegraph Co. v. NLRB*, 521 F.2d 1159, 1161 (2nd Cir. 1975).

30. *NLRB v. Cement Transport, Inc.*, 490 F.2d 1024, 1030 (6th Cir. 1974), cert. denied, 419 U.S. 828 (1974).

31. *NLRB v. Thor Power Tool Co.*, 351 F.2d 584, 587 (7th Cir. 1965); *Crown Central v. NLRB*, 430 F.2d 724, 726 N.3 (5th Cir. 1970); *Coors Container Co. v. NLRB*, 628 F.2d 1283, 1285 (10th Cir. 1980).

32. *Old Dominion, Etc., v. Austin*, 418 U.S. 264, 268 (1974).

33. *Parker v. Baltimore & O.R. Co.*, 652 F.2d 1012, 1020 (D.C. Cir. 1981).

34. *Whatley v. Met. Atlanta Rapid Transit*, 632 F.2d 1325, 1327 (5th Cir. 1980).

35. *Unt v. Aerospace Corp.*, 765 F.2d 1440, 1446 (9th Cir. 1985).

36. *Hochstadt v. Worcester Foundation, Etc.*, 545 F.2d 222, 228 (1st Cir. 1976).

37. *EEOC v. Crown Zellerbach Corp.*, 720 F.2d 1008, 1014–15 (9th Cir. 1983).

38. In *Whirlpool Corp. v. Marshall*, 445 U.S. 1, 10–11 (1980), the U.S. Supreme Court upheld the legality of OSHA regulations which established a right to refuse work in limited situations where the risk of injury or death is imminent:

Such circumstances will probably not often occur, but such a situation may arise when (1) the employee is ordered by his employer to work under conditions that the employee reasonably believes pose an imminent risk of death or serious bodily injury, and (2) the employee has reason to believe that there is not sufficient time or opportunity either to seek effective redress from his employer or to apprise OSHA of the danger. 450 U.S. at 10–11.

See also *Gateway Coal Co. v. United Mine Workers of America, et al.*, 414 U.S. 368 (1974), where the Court held that a work stoppage called solely to protect employees from immediate danger is authorized by Sec. 502 of the Labor Management Relations Act, 29 U.S.C. 143. A right to refuse hazardous work was also recognized under the Federal Mine Safety Act (*Miller v. Fed. Mine Saf. Rev. Comm'n*, 687 F.2d 194 (7th Cir. 1982).

39. Examples of such cases are *Petermann v. International Brotherhood of Teamsters Local 396* (1959), 174 Cal.App.2d 184, 344 P.2d 25 (for refusing to commit perjury); *Tameny v. Atlantic Richfield Co.* (1980), 27 Cal.3d 167, 610 P.2d 1330, 164 Cal.Rptr. 839 (for refusing to engage in price-fixing); *Harless v. First National Bank* (W.Va. 1978), 246 S.E.2d 270 (for refusing to violate a consumer credit code); *O'Sullivan v. Mallon* (1978), 160 N.J.Super. 416, 390 A.2d 149 (for refusing to practice medicine without a license).

40. See *Hansrote v. Amer. Industrial Technologies*, 586 F. Supp. 113, 115 (W.D. Penn 1984), applying Pennsylvania and Delaware law.

41. *Hansome v. Northwestern Cooperage Co.*, 679 S.W.2d 273, 275–76 (Mo. banc. 1984).

42. See *Smith v. Plezo Technology and Prof. Admin.*, 427 S.2d 182 (Fla. 1983), where the Supreme Court of Florida found a limited public policy claim, relying upon a state statute which "clearly" imposed a "duty" not to terminate employees for filing worker compensation claims. 427 S.2d at 184.

43. See *Kovalesky v. A.M.C. Associated Merchandising Corp.*, 551 F. Supp. 544, 547–48 (S.D. N.Y. 1982); *Martin v. Platt*, 386 N.E.2d 1026, 1028 (Ind. App. 1979).

44. See *Wagenseller v. Scottsdale Memorial Hospital*, 147 Ariz. 370, 378–79; 710 P.2d 1025, 1033–34 (Ariz. 1985).

45. See *Palmateer v. International Harvester Co.*, 421 N.E.2d 876, 878–79 (Ill. 1981).

46. *Payne v. Rozendaal*, 520 A.2d 586 (Vt., 1986).

47. *Pittsburgh, Cincinnati, Chicago and St. Louis Railway v. Kinney*, 95 Ohio 64, 68–69, 115 N.E. 505, 507 (1916), cited in *Payne v. Rozendaal*, 520 A.2d at 586.

48. See *Pierce v. Ortho Pharmaceutical*, 417 A.2d 505 (N.J. 1980).

49. Legislative history of the Federal Water Pollution Control Act cited in the Conference Report of the Clear Air Act, 1977 U.S. Code Cong. & Ad. News, 1077, 1404.

7

FEDERAL PREEMPTION
AND PRECLUSION

Fifty years ago there was virtually no recognized protection for any workers who faced employment discrimination. Slowly, with the passage of laws such as the National Labor Relations Act, the Fair Labor Standards Act, Title VII of the Civil Rights Act of 1964, and the Occupational Health and Safety Act, specific statutory prohibitions on certain forms of employment discrimination or retaliation were enacted. Congress acted in areas which were historically marked with gross injustice or in areas which posed significant health or safety danger.

At the time these laws were passed, they were viewed by Congress and the public as important advances in the protection of employee rights. Given the strength of the common law at-will doctrine, these laws were a major advance in the rights of employees—and for the rights of whistleblowers who exposed or gave testimony concerning alleged violations of these laws.

Since the passage of the statutes, state courts and legislatures have deeply criticized the ironclad interpretation of the common law at-will doctrine. Most state courts have carved out a public policy exception to the at-will doctrine that protects employee whistleblowers under state common law. Consequently, terminations that once were prohibited only by federal statutory law are now prohibited by state common law. Thus, a paradox: What happens when a termination is prohibited by both federal and state law? Is there federal preemption? Should a state voluntarily accede to the federal administrative remedy? In short, what is the relationship between these two remedies?

One of the most important questions in this area of law is: Do the federal whistleblower statutes preempt wrongfully discharged whistleblowers from utilizing the state common law remedy?

The federal preemption doctrine has been used in an increasingly aggressive fashion to undermine whistleblower protection. This has been a serious set back for whistleblowers because, on the whole, federal whistleblower protections are far weaker than state common law remedies in those jurisdictions that recognize the public policy exception tort for wrongful discharge. For example, most federal whistleblower statutes set up an administrative scheme for adjudicating whistleblower wrongful discharge cases, whereas under most state common law, these actions are considered torts.[1] Under most federal laws whistleblowers are denied access to a jury trial and are required to present their cases to Article I Administrative Law Judges (ALJs).[2] The ALJs determine both the law and the facts and award damages—usually limited to back pay, reinstatement and attorney's fees.[3] Punitive damage awards are generally never awarded under the federal law. There are no local courthouses where ALJs reside, and the procedural rules of the federal Administrative Law Judges are usually foreign to most local practitioners.[4]

Not only is the federal forum less familiar to the whistleblower's attorney, and the available damage awards far less attractive, the federal whistleblower laws tend to have absurdly short statutes of limitations—most of which are between thirty and 180 days.[5] These short statutes of limitations have been criticitized by such bodies as the U.S. Administrative Conference,[6] and a large number of federal whistleblower cases are regularly dismissed due to failure to file a complaint in a timely fashion.[7] Conversely, state statutes of limitations in this area are almost always one year or longer.

Due to the limitations of the federal statutory remedies, it is not surprising that corporations and employers are frequently utilizing the federal preemption defense in whistleblower cases.[8] For example, the National Labor Relations Act and the Labor Management Relations Act have been widely used to defeat state public policy tort claims.[9] The U.S. Supreme Court has recently granted *certiorari* to determine the scope of federal preemption over state retaliatory discharge torts under the Labor Management Relations Act.[10]

In the environmental and public health and safety area there has been an increasing trend among employers to argue that the federal environmental whistleblower laws preempt state remedies for whistleblowers. For example, the existence of the employee protection provision of the Toxic Substance Control Act was used by a federal district court in Pennsylvania as grounds for dismissing a state public policy tort.[11] Likewise, the federal Mine Health and Safety Act's whistleblower protection provision was cited to by the U.S. Court of Appeals for the Ninth Circuit as a reason to deny an illegal whistleblower protection under a public policy tort.[12] Employers have aggressively pointed to the whistleblower protection clause of the Atomic Energy Act and the Energy Reorganization Act (Section 210 of the Energy Reorganization Act is codified in 42 U.S.C. 5851) as grounds for preempting state wrongful discharge torts.[13]

IS FEDERAL PREEMPTION OF ENVIRONMENTAL AND NUCLEAR WHISTLEBLOWER STATE TORT ACTION JUSTIFIED?

State tort remedies for wrongfully discharged environmental whistleblowers should not be subject to federal preemption. Such preemption is not justified under the federal statutory scheme, the legislative intent behind the environmental whistleblower laws, or the case law interpreting the preemption doctrine.

Federal preemption, which has its roots in the Supremacy Clause of the U.S. Constitution, prohibits states from enacting or enforcing laws which may negate, undermine, or somehow stand as an obstacle to the enforcement of federal law.[14] Congress can explicitly preempt state action, or it can be "implicitly" authorized by a law pursuant to the law's "structure and purpose."[15] State action is implicitly preempted if a federal statutory or regulatory scheme is "so persuasive as to make reasonable the inference that Congress left no room for the states to supplement it."[16] Even if Congress has not "completely displaced" state involvement in a specific area, state laws can be nullified "to the extent that it actually conflicts with federal laws,"[17] or where state law "stands as an obstacle to the accomplishment and execution" of federal law.[18]

None of the federal environmental protection health and safety laws explicitly preempt state involvement. Thus preemption is valid only if the courts find that Congress implicitly intended state involvement in this area be foreclosed.

Environmental protection and labor relations are areas of law traditionally within the sphere of the police power of a state.[19] States possess "broad authority" under the police power to regulate these issues.[20] It is well established that federal preemption of these police powers must be carefully scrutinized. As the U.S. Supreme Court reasoned in *Ray v. Atlantic Richfield Co.*:

> The Court's prior cases indicate that when a State's exercise of its police power is challenged under the Supremacy Clause, we start with the assumption that the historic police powers of the States were not to be superseded by the Federal Act unless that was the clear and manifest purpose of Congress.[21]

In areas traditionally regulated by the states under their inherent police powers, a stricter standard for applying preemption exists than in other areas of federal law.[22] In order to preempt state action in these areas a "clear and manifest purpose of Congress" must be shown.[23]

In fact, there is a "presumption" that state and local laws "related to health and safety" are not to be "invalidated under the Supremacy Clause.[24] In the area of public health and safety the Supreme Court has adopted strict standards concerning when to apply the preemption rule:

[the moving party] thus present a showing of implicit pre-emption of the whole field, or of a conflict between a particular local provision and the federal scheme, that is strong enough to overcome the presumption that state and local regulation of health and safety matters can constitutionally coexist with federal regulation.[25]

An application of these basic principles of analysis to the issue of whether state wrongful discharge law is preempted due to Congress' passage of environmental whistleblower protection statutes demonstrates that state action in this area is not preempted.

The public policy exception to the common law employment at-will rule in no way interferes with, or stands as an obstacle to, the accomplishment of federal environmental policy. There is not one comment in the legislative history of any of the eight environmental whistleblower laws which even hints at a congressional desire to preempt such state protections. Common sense dictates that the state laws complement and enhance both state and federal policies requiring a clear and healthy natural environment.[26]

The Energy Reorganization Act (ERA) and the Atomic Energy Act (AEA) have been interpreted by the Supreme Court to preempt state regulation of nuclear safety issues.[27] In *Silkwood v. Kerr-McGee Corp.*,[28] however, the U.S. Supreme Court held that the Atomic Energy and Energy Reorganization Acts did not preempt a state tort claim for wrongful death arising out of a violation of radiation safety regulations. The court applied black letter preemption law to the case, and held that the state tort (which concerned the wrongful death of a whistleblower-employee) claim did not "frustrate" the purpose of the AEA and ERA, and held that it was undisputably "possible" for Kerr-McGee to pay both an NRC fine and jury-awarded punitive damages for the same incident.[29]

Although *Silkwood* did not interpret the whistleblower protection provisions of the AEA and ERA, it has been used as precedent for rejecting the preemption of state tort actions.[30] In *Berstler v. Hirsh, Arkin, Pinehurst*, the U.S. Dictrict Court for the Eastern District of Pennsylvania rejected the preemption argument in a nuclear whistleblower case.[31] First, the court found that Congress did not intend to "occupy" the entire field of employer–employee relations at nuclear power plant construction sites. Second, the court found that the whistleblower protection law was "not so pervasive" as to make a reasonable inference that "Congress left no room to supplement it." The court also found that such state torts in no way "prevent" the Secretary of Labor from performing his or her job under Section 210 (the federal nuclear whistleblower protection law), and that the tort did "not create an obstacle" to the purpose of the AEA and ERA. The court found that the state tort action "supplements rather than interferes with (Section 210) and is not inconsistent with its objectives."[32] Four other courts have also refused to find preemption under Section 210.[33]

Two courts have broken with this precedent and preempted whistleblower suits under Section 210. In *Snow v. Bechtel*, the U.S. District Court for the Central District of California preempted a nuclear whistleblower claim.[34] The *Snow* court justified preemption on two grounds. The court viewed Section 210 of the Energy Reorganization Act (whistleblower protection provision), as "primarily" a health and safety statute.[35] Section 210 existed to assist the NRC in its statutory role of ensuring safe atomic energy. Protecting the whistleblower was merely a "secondary" aspect of the broader "safety scheme"[36] The court found preemption because federal laws preempted state laws in areas related to nuclear safety.

The federal environmental laws, and health and safety laws, were enacted to protect the nation from the effects of pollution. They were not intended to interfere with the traditional state power to regulate the employee–employer relationship. Although there is overlap between federal environmental and nuclear whistleblower protection laws, and state tort actions for wrongful discharge, state involvement in the area does not conflict in any way with the effectuation of federal laws. The state interest in ensuring that employers do not retaliate against whistleblowers—regardless of what issue an employee blows the whistle on—should not be preempted by federal environmental and nuclear safety laws.

WHISTLEBLOWER PROTECTION AND NATIONAL LABOR LAW PREEMPTION

The National Labor Relations Act (NLRA)[37] and the Labor Management Relations Act (LMRA)[38] set up a federal scheme regulating labor management relations in the area of collective bargaining and unionization. Specifically, employees who engage in union-related activities, or are covered under a collective bargaining agreement, are protected under these two laws. A wrongfully discharged whistleblower in a unionized workplace may have an option of filing a discrimination complaint under a federal or state statute, under a common law tort *and*/or filing a grievance under a collective bargaining agreement, or an unfair labor practice complaint under the NLRA.

The interrelationship between these various causes of action has been affected by the preemptive force the Supreme Court has recognized in NLRA and LMRA. The U.S. Supreme Court has articulated a "general rule" that neither state nor federal courts have initial jurisdiction over unfair labor practice suits under the NLRA.[39] The court interpreted Congress' intent in passing the NLRA as giving the National Labor Relations Board broad power to interpret and enforce the NLRA.

These powers have been interpreted to be preemptive of state court involvement in unfair labor practice issues. As the Supreme Court stated in *Garner v. Teamsters Union:*

Congress did not merely lay down a substantive rule of law to be enforced by any tribunal competent to apply law generally to the parties. It went on to confide primary interpretation and application of its rules to a specific and specially constituted tribunal. . . . Congress evidently considered that centralized administration of specially designed procedures was necessary to obtain uniform application of its substantive rules and to avoid these diversities and conflicts likely to result from a variety of local procedures and attitudes toward labor controversies . . . A multiplicity of tribunals and diversitiy of procedures are quite as apt to produce incompatible or conflicting adjudications as are different rules of substantive law.[40]

Not only has the Supreme Court recognized a general preemptive doctrine for adjudication of unfair labor practice issues, it has also preempted courts from applying state law for interpreting collective bargaining agreements. Instead of applying state contract law or employment law as rules for interpreting and implementing collective bargaining agreements entered into between labor and management, the Supreme Court required the application of a federal common law in order to issue a uniform and consistent national approach in interpreting collective bargaining agreements, prior to being able to file a suit for the enforcement of contractual rights.[41] Likewise, courts were instructed to defer to the interpretation of the contract given by the arbitrator: "so far as the arbitrator's decision concerns construction of the contract, the courts have no business overruling him because their interpretation of the contract is different from his."[42]

Despite the strong federal policy of state preemption under labor law, the U.S. Supreme Court has long recognized that federal preemption is not complete. Federal labor law does not preempt all state law claims. Neither does federal labor law preempt or preclude the protection of employees under other federal statutes. In the landmark case *San Diego Building Trades Council v. Garmon*, the Supreme Court held that state law claims or remedies were not preempted:[43]

where the activity regulated was a merely peripheral concern of the Labor Management Act . . . [or] touched interests so deeply rooted in local feeling and responsibility that, in the absence of compelling congressional direction, we could not infer that Congress has deprived the States of the power to act.

If state law claims did not interfere with the operation of federal labor laws and the state claims involved were unrelated to the central concerns of federal labor statutes, the Supreme Court has not applied the preemption doctrine. For example, the Court has refused to find preemption in a case dealing with union employee trespassing,[44] malicious defamation committed during a labor dispute,[45] intentional infliction of emotional distress,[46] mass picketing accompanied by threats of violence,[47] and employer misrepresentations to replacement workers.[48]

Thus, even though a state tort or statutory remedy may overlap onto areas covered under the NLRA or a collective bargaining agreement, preemption is not necessarily required.[49] For the U.S. Supreme Court, the critical inquiry regarding preemption is not "whether the state is enforcing a law" relating specifically to "labor relations." Instead, the critical issue is whether a state claim would be "identical" to an unfair labor practice charge raised with the NLRB.[50] Preemption occurs when a state court's "exercise of jurisdiction necessarily involves a risk of interference with the unfair labor practice jurisdiction of the Board."[51] Consequently, if the state has a "significant interest" in protecting a citizen from an alleged wrong, and litigation over the subsequent tort entails "little risk" of interfering with the jurisdiction of the NLRB, the state tort is not preempted.[52] This is true even if the tort arose in the context of a labor dispute.[53]

The U.S. Supreme Court has applied the same sort of analysis in analyzing state tort claims and alleged violations of collective bargaining agreements. Specifically, the rights granted federal courts to enforce collective bargaining agreements does not grant the parties to such an agreement "the ability to contract for what is illegal under state law."[54] If a state tort arises from a right granted by the collective bargaining agreement—or is based upon a term of the collective bargaining agreement—the state cause of action would be preempted.[55] But if the state law rights to obligations "exist independently" of the collective bargaining agreement—and cannot be waived or altered by the agreement—those state rights are not preempted by the agreement.[56]

In a similar vein to the court's recognition that important state law principles are not preempted by federal labor law, the Supreme Court has also recognized that federal statutory laws, such as the Fair Labor Standard Act or Title VII, are not preempted by labor law—even if the violations of these laws would constitute an unfair labor practice or a breach of a collective bargaining agreement.

The leading case affirming this principle was *Alexander v. Gardner-Denver Co.*[57] In *Alexander* an employee grieved a termination under a collective bargaining agreement which banned discharge of employees, except if there was "proper cause." The agreement prohibited racial discrimination. Under the labor contract an arbitrator's decision was "final and binding."[58] The employee lost at arbitration—his termination was upheld.[59] Despite his loss under the collective bargaining agreement, the employee filed a Title VII charge alleging wrongful termination on the basis of racial discrimination. Although two lower courts held that the employee's Title VII claim was preempted, the Supreme Court unanimously disagreed:

> In submitting his grievance to arbitration, an employee seeks to vindicate his contractual right under a collective bargaining agreement. By contrast, in filing a lawsuit under Title VII, an employee asserts independent statutory rights accorded by Congress. [60]

There was no preemption, even though both causes of action arose for the same "factual occurrence."[61] The rights protected by Title VII were not subject to bargaining under the union contract, and the policies behind deferring to labor contract arbitration, so forceful in other aspects of the collective bargaining procedure, did not apply in the Title VII context. The Supreme Court recognized that antidiscrimination laws did not concern "majoritarian processes" but codified an "individual's right to equal employment opportunities."[62]

Whistleblower claims are not explicitly covered under the NLRA. In fact, the NLRB has refused to hold that *individual* complaints regarding health and safety issues are covered under the NLRA.[63] Given the present state of labor preemption law, there is no reason to conclude that whistleblower claims should be uniformly preempted by the NLRA or collective bargaining agreements. The Supreme Court rulings that "deeply rooted" local concerns,[64] or claims which raise "significant" state interest,[65] or claims based on local "health and safety" regulations[66] are not preempted lay a solid foundation for the nonpreemption of state whistleblower claims under federal labor law. The *Alexander* case is dispositive on the issue of whether the NLRA preempts or precludes employees from utilizing other federal whistleblower protection statutes.

The leading case, as to whether protections under the NLRA or in a collective bargaining agreement preempt state tort protections for whistleblowers, is the U.S. Court of Appeals for the Ninth Circuit's decision in *Garibaldi v. Lucky Food Stores, Inc.*.[67] In *Garibaldi* an employee, covered under a collective bargaining agreement, filed a public policy wrongful discharge tort under California state law, alleging he was terminated for reporting the shipment of adulterated milk, condemned under local health laws, to state health officials.[68] The Ninth Circuit applied the Supreme Court precedent of *Farmer v. United Brotherhood of Carpenters* and upheld the state cause of action:

> A claim grounded in state law for wrongful termination for public policy reasons poses no significant threat to the collective bargaining process; it does not alter the economic relationship between the employer and employee. The remedy is in tort, distinct from any contractual remedy an employee might have under the collective bargaining contract. It furthers the state's interest in

protecting the general public—an interest which transcends the employment relationship.[69]

The Ninth Circuit also refused to use the fact that the employee had lost at arbitration as grounds for dismissing the claim under an *estoppel* or preemption doctrine. The court simply applied *Alexander* and held that the state tort rights were independent of any rights created by the collective bargaining agreement.[70]

Employees, however, who have attempted to use the NLRA or rights granted by collective bargaining agreement as the *source* of a state public policy barring their termination have uniformly been rejected.[71] For example, in *Olguin v. Inspiration Consol. Copper Co.,*[72] the ninth circuit explicitly held that an employee who based a wrongful discharge tort on the NLRA, and who could not rely upon any "specific" state "statutes or policies" was preempted from filing an independent tort action.[73]

The issue of federal preemption of state whistleblower claims under Section 301 of the Labor Management Relations Act should be resolved by the case of *Lingle v. Norge Division of Magic Chef, Inc.*[74] In *Lingle* the Supreme Court granted *certiorari* in order to decide whether a state wrongful discharge case, under an Illinois statute barring the termination of a unionized employee for filing a state worker's compensation claim, was preempted under Section 301 because the employee's discharge also violated the collective bargaining agreement.

STATE COURT PRECLUSION OF
PUBLIC POLICY TORTS

Even if a court does not preempt a whistleblower claim, there is no guarantee that a state will not defer to a federal statute and voluntarily refuse to uphold an independent wrongful discharge tort. The absence of federal preemption only gives an employee an opportunity to present a cognizable state wrongful termination suit—it does not guarantee that state courts will accept jurisdiction of such claims. Many state courts have refused to allow whistleblowers to file tort claims if there are federal or state statutory, contractual, or administrative remedies available. It is in this area that the conflict between weak statutory remedies, developed during the period when there was no common law remedy, and the public policy tort, is most strongly felt.

State and federal courts—applying or interpreting state law—have dismissed common law based wrongful discharge tort actions if a statutory remedy exists. The most common expression of this policy is applying the rule that statutory remedies are "exclusive" and preclude utilization of a common law remedy. For example, the Court of Appeals of Michigan dismissed a public policy tort based upon an employee's

refusal to perform unsafe work. There was a state OSHA statute that
allowed employees to refuse unsafe work and set up an administrative
remedy prohibiting retaliatory discharge. The employee could not cite
to the Michagan OSHA law as a source of public policy because he was
required to utilize the weaker administrative one for his discharge action:

It is a general rule of law in Michigan that when a statute creates a new right or
imposes a new duty having no counterpart in the common law the remedies
provided in the statute for violation are exclusive.[75]

Courts have also used the existence of federal administrative or
statutory remedies to justify precluding the use of a state common law
tort.[76] Other courts have required the exhaustion of collective bargaining remedies.[77]

In a less drastic approach, federal courts interpreting Illinois state
law found that the Illinois Human Rights Act (IHRA) precluded the filing of a public policy tort on the basis of age discrimination. Instead of
finding a blanket preemption due to the statutory remedies afforded the
employee under the Illinois Human Rights Act, the courts interpreted
the IHRA statutory language as expressing a *legislative intent* to
preempt other remedies:

the remedies provided by the IHRA are exclusive: (citing to the IHRA itself the
court goes on) except as otherwise provided by law, no court of this state shall
have jurisdiction over the subject of an alleged civil rights violation other than
as set forth in this Act.[78]

Where there was, however, no statutory instruction that a statutory
remedy precluded or preempted the administrative remedy, the Illinois
Supreme Court has rejected preclusion. Illinois has allowed independent tort actions despite the existence of a collective bargaining agreement,[79] and despite a federal statutory whistleblower protection provision (i.e. Section 210 of the Energy Reorganization Act).[80]

In *Kilpatrick v. Delaware County Society,*[81] the issue was whether
OSHA preempted a state public policy tort for retaliatory discharge
after the employee complained of an occupational health hazard. The
federal court ruled that there was no explicit federal preemption required under OSHA, consequently the state was free to act:

Plaintiff, however, does not seek to remedy a violation of OSHA. Rather, she
seeks redress for her unlawful termination, a violation of Pennsylvania common law, a common law which I have held seeks to further policies similar to
those announced by Congress when it enacted OSHA. Nothing in OSHA
preempts this type of common law cause of action.[82]

The court also recognized that discrimination against whistleblowers affects *state* public and employment policies—even if *federal* issues are implicated:

The policies and laws at issue in this lawsuit are first and foremost Pennsylvania policies and laws, and there is little reason to think Pennsylvania courts would entrust their enforcement to the Secretary of Labor. If the policies announced by Congress in OSHA are adopted by Pennsylvania courts, then they become as much a part of Pennsylvania law as any other policy promoted by the common law of Pennsylvania. The fact that OSHA gives the Secretary of Labor the discretionary power to promote similar policies would not deter the Pennsylvania Supreme Court from recognizing a cause of action for wrongful termination in this case.[83]

Likewise, courts have used antirace and antisex discrimination laws as sources of state public policy—even when the employee failed to exhaust the Title VII remedy.[84]

There is disagreement among the state and federal courts as to the relationship between a statutory employment remedy and a public policy tort. Even within the same states confusion and conflict have arisen. This confusion is a clear reflection of the inconsistent decisions which courts have handed down regarding the preemption issue in general.

CONCLUSION

Presently, there is no consistency in state and federal approaches to the preemption and preclusion issue. The conflict has arisen primarily because Congress and state legislatures made explicit statutory abridgments to the at-will doctrine prior to state courts altering that common law doctrine in a majority of jurisdictions. The most troubling paradox has developed in labor law: Unfair and discriminatory labor practices, which were so outrageous or troubling as to spark specific legislative actions, are now, in some jurisdictions, subject to *less* protection than unfair or discriminatory labor practices which are not as threatening to the public welfare. The courts should not use statutes designed to shield employees from retaliation as a sword to eliminate such rights. This is not to say the preemption should not exist. But in finding preemption of state remedies, courts should apply the accepted black letter law of preemption, as utilized in other contexts. The basic rule of federal preemption is well settled, and was outlined in *Silkwood v. Kerr–McGee:*

[S]tate law can be preempted in either of two ways. If Congress evidences an intent to occupy a given field, any state law falling within that field is preempted. . . . If Congress has not entirely displaced state regulation over the matter in question, state law is still preempted to the extent it actually conflicts with federal law, that is, when it is impossible to comply with both state and federal law, . . . or where the state law stands as an obstacle to the accomplishment of the full purposes and objectives of Congress.[85]

Only if a federal statute explicitly provides for the preemption of state public policy torts, or such torts would "conflict" or "stand as an obstacle" to the objective of Congress, should preemption be sanctioned. However, state public policy torts rarely, if ever, would conflict with a Congressional purpose. Under this basic rule, federal preemption of such torts should rarely be upheld. State courts should follow this lead and not preclude public policy torts *unless* the state legislature explicitly so provides.

The ultimate goal of the new public policy tort must include, in part, a change of attitude among employers and employees. People must accept that employees who disclose violations of law or public policy cannot be fired. As long as this right not to be so fired is limited by a variety of preemption-related defenses, this goal will be thwarted.

NOTES

1. See 29 C.F.R. Part 24; 29 C.F.R. Part 18; Eugene R. Fidell, *Federal Protection of Private Sector Health and Safety Whistleblowers: A Report to the Administrative Conference of the United States* (Washington, D.C.; March 1987); Stephen M. Kohn, *Protecting Environmental and Nuclear Whistleblowers: A Litigation Manual*, at page 1–8 (Nuclear Information and Resource Service, Washington, D.C., 1985).

2. Idem.

3. Idem. Compensatory damage awards under the environmental and nuclear whistleblower laws have rarely been awarded. Where they have been awarded, they have been very modest in amount. See *DeFord v. Secretary of Labor*, 700 F.2nd 281, 288 (6th Cir. 1983), and remand order of Secretary of Labor in *DeFord v. TVA*, 81–Energy Reorganization Act–1; *Hedden v. Conam Inspection Co.*, 82–Energy Reorganization Act–3, Department of Labor Administrative Law Judge Decision (1982). The U.S. Department of Labor has yet to award exemplary or punitive damages in a whistleblower case. See *Landers v. Commonwealth–Lord Joint Venture*, 83–Energy Reorganization Act–5, Decision of U.S. Department of Labor Administrative Law Judge (1983).

4. 29 C.F.R. Part 24; N. Reynolds, R. Walker, P. Kykema, *Comments on Preliminary Recommmendations of the Administrative Conference of the United States Regarding Private Sector Health and Safety Whistleblower Statutes* (Bishop, Cook, Purcell and Reynolds, April 10, 1987), pp. 25–31. The Testimony of Nicholas Reynolds, et. al., pinpointed some of the basic procedural problems which confront litigators in this area:

[A]dministrative law judges in the Departmant of Labor at least are called on to try a large number of cases in areas far distant from their own offices under a variety of different statutes. . . . [O]ur experience indicates that these ALJs have great difficulty arranging their trial schedules and extensive travel schedules in such a manner as to permit trial of any case of more than two or three days duration. Because of this limitation, trials of Section 210 cases sometimes tend to be artificially truncated. District judges, on the other hand, are quite used to trials that may take a week or more to permit both parties a fair opportunity to present their respective cases. . . . Because administrative hearings are not uncommonly scheduled for trial in a city thousands of miles from the ALJs home base, any request for scheduling modification threatens to wreak havoc with a travel schedule and trial docket carefully planned to permit the trials of several cases in the same general area in the same time period to permit efficient use of the ALJs time and minimize travel expenses to the taxpayers.

Because of the peculiar nature of Section 210 cases and the context in which they arise, Section 210 litigation frequently entails complicated and protracted discovery battles. ALJs experience difficulty in dealing with these disputes for a variety of reasons. They rarely are physically located in the area in which the case is to be tried and therefore can hardly ever be available except through the mails or by telephone to conduct hearings on discovery disputes as district judges frequently do. Moreover, in cases of discovery abuse by a party ALJs appear unable to impose sanctions directly. Indeed, even under the Administrative Conference's recommendations, subpoena enforcement would necessitate commencement of a separate action in district court, thus needlessly proliferating and complicating any proceeding in which such an action was required. Finally, the applicability of the Federal Rules of Procedure to any particular discovery dispute is generally obscure, owing to pecularities in the Department of Labor's own procedural rules. But federal judges suffer no similar confusion as to the applicability of the federal rules to discorery disputes brought before them, and they have the advantage of being able to consult a vast and growing body of case law construing those rules as well as their own experience in resolving such disputes fairly and expeditiously.

Reynolds et al., also pointed out that there may be constitutional problems with administrative judges, as opposed to juries, awarding compensatory or punitive damages in these cases. Idem., at 25–28. See *Curtis v. Leather*, 415 U.S. 189, 194 (1974); *Atlas Roofing Co., Inc. v. Occupational Safety and Health Review Commission*, 430 U.S. 442, 458 (1977).

5. Section 210, the nuclear whistleblower statute, states:

Any employee who believes that he has been discharged or otherwise discriminated against by any person in violation of subsection (a) of this section may, *within thirty days after such violation occurs*, file (or have any person file on his behalf) a complaint with the Secretary of Labor . . . alleging such discharge or discrimination. (emphasis added)

Also see Clean Air Act, 42 U.S.C. 7622(b) (1); Safe Drinking Water Act, 42 U.S.C. 300j–9(i) (2) (A); Solid Waste Disposal Act, 42 U.S.C. 6971(b); Water Pollution Control Act, 33 U.S.C. 1367(b); Comprehensive Environmental Response, Compensation, and Liability Act, 42 U.S.C. 9610(b); Toxic Substances Control Act, 15 U.S.C. 2622(b) (1); Fidell Report at pp. 20–21.

6. See Fidell Report at pp. 20–21, and Administrative Conference of the United States, Recommendation 87–2, 1 CFR 305.87–2.

7. Idem.; *School District of Allentown v. Marshall*, 657 F.2d 16 (3rd Cir. 1981); *Greenwald v. City of North Miami Beach*, 587 F.2d 779 (5th Cir. 1979); *Rose v. Secretary of Dept. of Labor*, 800 F.2d 563 (6th Cir. 1986).

8. This is not to say that the federal remedies have not been successfully used—or that, depending on the circumstances, the federal remedy may be a more advantageous forum than a state court. See Statement of Congressman James J. Florio, 132 Congressional Record No. 19 (February 16, 1987).

9. The following courts have found Section 301 preemption: See *Johnson v. Hussman Corp.*, 805 F.2d 795 (8th Cir. 1986); *Olguin v. Inspiration Consolidated Copper Co.*, 740 F.2d 1468 (9th Cir. 1984); *DeSoto v. Yellow Freight Systems, Inc.*, 820 F.2d 1434 (9th Cir. 1987), rehearing denied, Nos. 85–6608 and 86–5800 (July 20, 1987). The following courts have found no Section 301 preemption: *Baldracchi v. Pratt & Whitney Aircraft Division*, 814 F.2d 102 (2nd Cir. 1987); *Herring v. Prince Macaroni of New Jersey, Inc.*, 799 F.2d 120 (3rd Cir. 1986); *Peabody Galion v. A.V. Dollar*, 666 F.2d 1309 (10th Cir.1981); *Garibaldi v. Lucky Food Stores, Inc.*, 726 F.2d 1367 (9th Cir. l984), cert. denied, 471 U.S. 1099 (1985). Most state courts have found no preemption under Section 301: *Gonzalez v. Prestress Engineering Corp.*, 115 Ill.2d 1, 104 Ill. Dec. 751, 503 N.E.2d 308 (1986), cert. denied, 107 s.Ct. 3248 (1987); *Puchert v. Agsalud*, 67 Haw. 22, 677 P.2d 449 (1984), appeal dismissed sum. *Pan American World Airways v. Puchert*, 472 U.S. 1001 (1985); *MGM Grand Hotel–Reno v. Insley*, 728 P.2d 821 (Nev. 1986); *Brevik v. Kite Painting, Inc.*, 404 N.W.2d 367 (Minn. Ct. App. 1987), review granted (June 26, 1987).

10. *Lingle v. Norse Division of Magic Chef, Inc.*, No. 87–259 (Oct. Term 1987 U.S. Supreme Court). For a general discussion of federal preemption under U.S. labor laws, see: Brooks, "Preemption of Federal Labor Law by Employment–at–Will Doctrine," 387 *Lab. Law Journal* 335 (1987); *Ohio State Law Journal* 277 (1980); Note, "Labor Law Preemption: *Allis Chalmers Corp. v. Lueck*," 60 *Tulane Law Rev.* 1077 (1986); Zimmerman and Martin, "The National Labor Relations Act and Employment–at–Will: The Federal Preemption Doctrine Revisited." 377 *Labor Law Journal* 223 (1986); "State and Local Plant Closing Laws: The Case Against Preemption," 92 *Gonzaga Law Rev.* 603 (1985); Comment, "Labor Law Preemption—Supreme Court Approves Unemployment Compensation for the Benefit of Striking Employees—*New York Telephone Co. v. New York State Department of Labor*," 99 S. Ct. 1328 (1979). 1980 *Creighton Law Review*, 1005; Comment, "Labor Law Preemption Doctrine—State Trespass Laws—Peaceful Picketing—*Sears, Roebuck and Co. v. San Diego County District Council of Carpenters*," 1980 *New York Law School Law Review*, 689; Kaden, "Federal Labor Preemption: The Supreme Court Draws the Lines," 18 *The Urban Lawyer* 607 (1984); Cox, "Recent Developments in Federal Labor Law Preemption," 41 *Ohio State Law Journal* 277 (1980). See Note 85.

11. *Braun v. Kelsey-Hayes*, 635 F. Supp. 75, 79–80 (E.D.Pa. 1986).

12. See *Olguin v. Inspiration Consol. Copper Co.*, 740 F.2d 1468, 1476 (9th Cir. 1984).

13. See *Stokes v. Bechtel North American Power Corp.*, 614 F. Supp. 732 (1985), no preemption; *Snow v. Bechtel Construction Inc., et al.*, 647 F. Supp. 1514 (U.S. Dist. Court, Central District of California, 1986), finding preemption.

14. U.S. Constitution, Art. VI, Cl. 2.

15. *Jones v. Ruth Packing Co.*, 97 S.Ct. 1305, 1309 (1977); *Fidelity Federal Sav. & Loan Ass'n. v. De La Cuesta*, 102 S.Ct. 3014, 3022 (1982).

16. *Rice v. Santa Fe Elevator Corp.*, 67 S.Ct. 1146, 1152 (1947); *Fidelity Federal Sav. & Loan Ass'n. v. De La Cuesta*, 102 S.Ct. 3014, 3022 (1982).

17. *Florida Lime & Avocado Growers, Inc. v. Paul*, 83 S.Ct. 1210, 1217 (1963).

18. *Hines v. Davidowitz*, 61 S.Ct. 399, 404 (1941); *Fidelity Fed. Sav. & Loan Ass'n. v. De La Cuesta*, 102 S.Ct. 3014, 3022 (1982).

19. Renz, "The Effect of Federal Legislation on Historical State Powers of Pollution Control: Has Congress Muddied State Waters?" 43 *Montana Law Review* 197 (1982).

20. *De Canas v. Bica*, 96 S.Ct. 933, 937 (1976).

21. *Ray v. Atlantic Richfield Co.*, 98 S.Ct. 98, 994 (1978), quoting from *Rice v. Santa Fe Elevator Corp.*, 67 S.Ct. 1146, 1159 (1947).

22. *Fort Halifax Packing Co. v. Coyne*, 107 S.Ct. 2211, 2222 (1987).

23. *Ray v. Atlantic Richfield Co.*, 98 S.Ct. 988, 994 (1978).

24. *Hillsborough County, Fla. v. Auto. Med. Labs.*, 105 S.Ct. 2371, 1276 (1985).

25. Idem; in *California Coastal Comm'n v. Granite Rock Co.*, 107 S.Ct. 1419 (1987), the U.S. Supreme Court found no preemption of a state right to "impose reasonable environmental regulation(s)" on *federal* land use even after the corporation obtained federal permission to conduct a mining operation. 107 S.Ct. at 1431. The Court held that the regulations of the California Coastal Commission did not *per se* conflict with the federal law governing land use on federal property. Also see, *Garibaldi v. Lucky Food Stores, Inc.*, 726 F.2d 1367, 1374 (9th Cir. 1984), no preemption under Labor Management Relations Act of whistleblower cases involving disclosures related to the "health" of a state's citizens.

26. The argument against preemption is even stronger for seven of the environmental laws which contain explicit statutory provisions, authorizing state action in the environmental field. For example, the Solid Waste Disposal Act contains a specific provision concerning the "Retention of State Authority" which provides, in part, that: "Nothing in this chapter shall be construed to prohibit any State or political subdivision thereof from imposing any requirements . . . which are more stringent than those imposed by such regulations." Similar nonpreemption provisions are contained in the Water Pollution Control Act, the Safe Drinking Water Act, the Comprehensive Environmental Response, Compensation and Liability Act, the Toxic Substances Control Act, the Surface Mining Control Act, and the Clean Air Act. Court decisions interpreting these statutes have consistently found no general federal preemption.

27. *Pacific Gas & Elec. Co. v. State Energy Resources Conservation & Dev. Comm'n*, 461 U.S. 190 (1983); Case Comment, "Silkwood v. Kerr-McGee Corp.: Preemption of the State Law for Nuclear Torts?" 12 *Envtl. Law* 1059 (1982); Case Comment, "Nuclear Energy—Federal Preemption—State Moratorium on Nuclear Plant Construction Upheld Against Preemption Challenge: Pacific Gas & Elec. Co. v. State Energy Resources Conservation & Dev. Comm'n," 14 *Seton Hall* 1034 (1984); Lyons, "State Regulation of Nuclear Power Production: Facing the Preemption Challenge from a New Perspective," 76 *N.W.U. Law Rev.* (1981); Ojanen, "Preemption—Atomic Energy," 24 *Nat. Resources Journal* 761 (1984); Berkowitz, "California's Nuclear Power Regulations: Federal Preemption?" 9 *Hastings Const. Law Quarterly* 623 (1982).

28. 104 S.Ct. 615 (1984).

29. 104 S.Ct. 615, 626 (1984).

30. 42 U.S.C. 5851.

31. Memorandum Decision, Civil Action No. 83–6122, slip op. at 3–5 (July 10, 1984, E.D. Pa.).

32. Idem.

33. See, *Stokes v. Bechtel et al.*, 614 F. Supp. 732 (N.D. Calif. 1985); *Parks v. Bechtel Corp. et al.*, No. C–84–8037–WHO (N.D. Calif. March 28, 1985); *Wheeler*

v. Caterpillar Tractor Co., 108 Ill.2d 502, 485 N.E.2d 372 (1985); cert. denied 106 S.Ct. 1641 (1985); Zack Co. v. Howard et al., 86 C 7625 (E.C. No. Dist. Ill.) (March 12, 1987).

34. 647 F. Supp. 1514 (C.D. Cal. 1986). Also see English v. General Electric Co., Civ. Action No. 87-31-CIV-7, U.S. District Court for the Eastern Divison of North Carolina, order of Judge Dupree, Feb. 10, 1988.

35. 42 U.S.C. 5851.

36. Snow v. Bechtel Const. Inc., 647 F. Supp. at 1518.

37. 29 U.S.C. 141 et seq.

38. 29 U.S.C. 185.

39. Vaca v. Sipes, 386 U.S. 171, 179 (1967).

40. 346 U.S. 485, 490–91 (1953).

41. See Republic Steel Corp. v. Maddox, 379 U.S. 650 (1965).

42. United Steelworkers of America v. Enterprise Wheel and Car Corp., 363 U.S. 593, 599 (1960).

43. 359 U.S. 236, 243–244 (1959).

44. Sears, Roebuck & Co. v. San Diego County District Council of Carpenters, 436 U.S. 290 (1977).

45. Linn v. United Plant Guard Workers, Local 114, 383 U.S. 53 (1966).

46. Farmer v. United Brotherhood of Carpenters, Local 25, 430 U.S. 290 (1977).

47. International Union, U.A.W. v. Russell, 356 U.S. 634 (1958).

48. Belknap, Inc. v. Hale, 463 U.S. 491 (1983).

49. See Allis-Chalmers Corp. v. Lueck, 471 U.S. 202 (1985).

50. Sears & Roebuck Co. v. Carpenters, 436 U.S. 180, 197 (1978).

51. 436 U.S. at 197.

52. 436 U.S. at 96.

53. Ibid.

54. Allis-Chalmers Corp. v. Lueck, 105 S.Ct. 1904, 1912 (1985).

55. 105 S.Ct. at 1912.

56. Ibid.

57. 415 U.S. 36 (1974).

58. 415 U.S. at 38–42.

59. 415 U.S. at 42.

60. 415 U.S. at 49–50.

61. 415 U.S. at 50.

62. 415 U.S. at 51.

63. Meyers Industries, Inc., 268 NLRB No. 73 (1984).

64. Garmon, 359 U.S. at 244.

65. Carpenter, 436 U.S. at 96.

66. Teamster Union v. Oliver, 358 U.S. 283, 297 (1959); Malone v. White Motor Corp., 435 U.S. 497, 513 n.13 (1978); Farmer, 430 U.S. 290, 303 (1977).

67. 726 F.2d 1367 (9th Cir. 1984).

68. 726 F.2d at 1374.

69. 726 F.2d at 1375.

70. 726 F.2d at 1375.

71. See Olguin v. Inspiration Consol. Copper Co., 740 F.2d 1468, 1475 (9th Cir. 1984); Carter v. Sheet Metal Worker Intern. Ass'n., 724 F.2d 1472, 1477 (11th Cir. 1984).

72. 740 F.2d 1468 (9th Cir. 1984).

73. 740 F.2d at 1475.

74. U.S. Supreme Court, Oct. 1987 Term, Case No. 87–259.

75. *Ohlsen v. Dst Industries, Inc.*, 314 N.W.2d 699, 704 (Mich. App. 1982).

76. *Corbin v. Sinclair Marketing Inc.*, 684 F.2d 265, 267 (Colo. App. 1984); *Braun v. Kelsey-Hayes*, 635 F. Supp. 75, 79–80 (E.D. Pa. 1986).

77. *Herring v. Prince Foods—Canning Div.*, 611 F. Supp. 177, 180 C.D.C. N.J. (1985); *McKinness v. Western Union Telegraph Co.*, 667 S.W.2d 738, 741 (M.App. 1984).

78. *Stoecklein v. Illinois Tool Works, Inc.*, 589 F. Supp. 139, 145 (N.D. Ill. 1984).

79. *Midgett v. Sackett-Chicago, Inc.*, 105 Ill.2d 143, 473 N.E.2d 1280 (1984).

80. *Wheeler v. Caterpillar Tractor Co.*, 485 N.E.2d 372 (Ill. 1985).

81. 632 F. Supp. 542 (E.D. Pa. 1986).

82. 632 F. Supp. at 548.

83. 632 F. Supp. at 549.

84. See *Lucas v. Brown & Root, Inc.*, 736 F.2d 1202 (8th Cir. 1984).

85. *Silkwood*, 104 S.Ct. 615, 621 (1984), citations omitted. On June 6, 1988 the U.S. Supreme Court held that an employee state tort remedy for wrongful discharge was not pre-empted by Section 301 of the Labor Management Relations Act of 1947. *Lingle v. Norge Division of Magic Chef, Inc.*, ___ U.S. ___ (1988). The analysis employed by the Supreme Court in *Lingle* will probably be utilized by other courts in finding no federal pre-emption of state whistleblower claims.

BIBLIOGRAPHY

BOOKS AND REPORTS

American Bar Association, American Law Institute. *Course of Study Materials—Advanced Labor and Employment Law.* Philadelphia: American Law Institute, 1985.

American Bar Association, Section of Labor and Employment Law. *Committee Reports.* Chicago: ABA Press, 1981– .

Beauchamp, Tom L., and Norman E. Bowie, eds. *Ethical Theory and Business.* Englewood Cliffs, NJ: Prentice-Hall, 1979.

Bender's Forms of Discovery, "Employment Suits." New York: Matthew Bender, 1980.

Borowsky, Philip, and Lex Larson. *Unjust Dismissal.* New York: Matthew Bender, 1987.

Bowman, James, Frederick Elliston, and Paula Lockhart. *Professional Dissent, An Annotated Bibliography and Resource Guide.* New York: Garland Publishing, 1984.

Brecher, Jeremy. *Strike!* Boston, MA: 1972.

Connolly, W. *A Practical Guide to Equal Opportunity Law, Principles and Practices.* New York: Law Review Press, 1975.

Connolly, W., and D. Crowell. *A Practical Guide to the Occupational Safety and Health Act: Law, Principles and Practices.* New York: Law Journal Press, 1977.

Connolly, W., D. Peterson, and M. Connolly. *Use of Statistics in Equal Employment Opportunity Litigation.* New York: Law Journal Seminars Press, 1987.

Cotine, B., L. Birrel, and R. Jennings. *Winning at the Occupational Safety and Health Commission, Workers Handbook on Enforcing Safety and Health Standards.* Washington, DC: Public Citizen Health Research Group, 1975.

Dolson, W., ed. *Annual Labor and Employment Law Institute, New Dimensions in Labor and Employment Relations.* Littleton, CO: Fred Rothman, 1985.

Donaldson, Thomas. "Employee Rights." In *Corporations and Morality.* Englewood Cliffs, NJ: Prentice-Hall 1982.

Elliston, Frederick, John Keenan, Paula Lockhart, and Jane Van Schaick, *Whistleblowing Research: Methodological and Moral Issues.* New York: Praeger, 1985.

Ewing David W. *Freedom Inside the Organization.* New York: E. P. Dutton, 1977.

Fairweather, Owen. *Practice and Procedure in Labor Arbitration.* Washington, DC: Bureau of National Affairs, 1973.

Fidell, Eugene. *Federal Protection of Private Sector Health and Safety Whistleblowers: A Report to the Administrative Conference of the United States.* Washington, DC: Administrative Conference of the United States, March 1987.

Fitzgerald, Ernest A. *The High Priests of Waste.* New York: W. W. Norton, 1972.

Government Accountability Project. *A Whistleblower's Guide to the Federal Bureaucracy.* Washington, DC: Institute for Policy Studies, 1977.

Jackson, Dudley. *Unfair Dismissal.* London and New York: Cambridge University Press, 1975.

Jackson, G. *Labor and Employment Law Desk Book.* Englewood Cliffs, NJ: Prentice-Hall, 1986.

Jenkins, J. *Labor Law, Its Evolution and Development from Criminal Conspiracy to Protected Rights and Mandatory Duties for Unions and Management Alike.* Cincinnati, OH: W. H. Anderson, 1968.

Kohn, Stephen M. *Protecting Environmental and Nuclear Whistleblowers: A Litigation Manual.* Washington, DC: Nuclear Information and Resource Service, 1985.

Larson, A., and L. Larson. *Employment Discrimination.* New York: Matthew Bender, 1987.

Maas, Peter. *Serpico.* New York: Basic Books, 1973.

McGovern, K., ed. *Equal Employment Practice Guide.* Washington, DC: Federal Bar Association, 1978.

McLaughlin, D., and A. Schoomaker. *The Landrum-Griffin Act and Union Democracy.* Ann Arbor: University of Michigan Press, 1979.

Mason, A. *Organized Labor and the Law.* Durham, NC: Duke University Press, 1925.

Mintz, B. *OSHA, History, Law and Policy.* Washington, DC: Bureau of National Affairs, 1984.

Mitchell, Greg. *Truth . . . and Consequences: Seven Who Would Not Be Silenced.* New York: Dembner Books, 1982.

Modjeska, L. *NLRB Practice.* Rochester, NY: Lawyers Cooperative Publishing, 1983.

Molander, Earl A. "Case Five: Whistle Blowing at the Trojan Nuclear Plant." In *Responsive Capitalism: Case Studies in Corporate Social Conduct.* New York: McGraw-Hill, 1980.

Moran, Robert. *How to Avoid OSHA.* Houston, TX: Gulf Publishing, 1980.

Nader, Ralph, Peter J. Petkas, and Date Blackwell, eds. *Whistle-Blowing: The Report of the Conference on Professional Responsibility.* New York: Grossman, 1972.

National Labor Law Center of the National Lawyers Guild, Robert Gibbs, and Paul Levey, eds. *Employee and Union Member's Guide to Labor Law: A Manual for Attorneys Representing the Labor Movement.* New York: Clark Boardman, 1987.

Nothstein, Gary. *The Law of Occupational Safety and Health.* New York: Free Press, 1981.

Pepe, Stephen, and Scott Dunham. *Avoiding and Defending Wrongful Discharge Claims.* Wilmette, IL: Callaghan, 1987.

Perritt, Henry, Jr. *Employee Dismissal Law and Practice.* New York: John Wiley and Sons, 1985.

Peters, Charles, and Taylor Branch, eds. *Blowing the Whistle: Dissent in the Public Interest.* New York: Praeger, 1972.

Piven, Francis, and Richard Cloward. *Poor People's Movements.* New York: Pantheon, 1977.

Practicing Law Institute. *Occupational Disease Litigation, 1983.* New York: Practicing Law Institute, 1983.

Practicing Law Institute. *Unjust Dismissal and At-Will Employment.* New York: Practicing Law Institute, 1982.

Rapalje, Stewart. *A Treatise on Contempt.* New York: L. K. Strouse & Co., 1884.

Rashke, Richard. *The Killing of Karen Silkwood: The Story Behind the Kerr-McGee Plutonium Case.* Boston, MA: Houghton Mifflin Co., 1981.

Redeker, J. *Discipline: Policies and Procedures.* Washington, DC: Bureau of National Affairs, 1983.

Reynolds, N., R. Walker and P. Dykema. *Comments on Preliminary Recommendations of the Administrative Conference of the United States Regarding Private Sector Health and Safety Whistleblower Statutes.* Washington, DC: Bishop, Cook, Purcell and Reynolds, April 10, 1987.

Richy, Charles R. *Manual on Employment Discrimination and Civil Rights Actions in the Federal Courts.* NY: Kluwer Law Book Publishers, Inc., 1985.

Ruzicho, A., and L. Jacobs. *Litigating Age Discrimination Cases.* Wilmette, IL: Callaghan, 1986.

U.S. Comptroller General. *First Year Activities of the Merit Systems Protection Board and The Office of Special Counsel.* Washington, DC: General Accounting Office, 1980.

U.S. Comptroller General. *The Office of the Special Counsel Can Improve Its Management of Whistleblower Cases.* Washington, DC: General Accounting Office, 1980.

U.S. Congress. House. Committee on Interstate and Foreign Commerce. Subcommittee on Transportation and Commerce. *Hazardous Waste Disposal Problems at Federal Facilities.* Hearing. 96th Cong. 2d sess., 1980.

U.S. Congress. House. Committee on Post Office and Civil Service. *Civil Service Reform Act of 1978.* Reprint. 95th Cong., 2d sess., 1978.

U.S. Congress. House. Committee on Post Office and Civil Service. *Civil Service Reform Hearings on H.R. 11280.* 95th Cong., 2d sess., 1978.

U.S. Congress. House. Committee on Post Office and Civil Service. *Hearings on the Whistleblower Protection Provision of the Civil Service Reform Act of 1978.* 96th Cong., 2d sess., 1980.

U.S. Congress. House. Committee on Post Office and Civil Service. *Hearings on Whistleblower Protection.* 99th Cong., 1st sess., 1985.

U.S. Congress. House. Committee on Post Office and Civil Service. Subcommittee on the Civil Service. *Civil Service Reform Oversight, Whistle-blower.* 96th Cong., 2d sess., 1980.

U.S. Congress. House. Committee on Post Office and Civil Service. Subcommittee on the Civil Service. *Federal Productivity and Performance Appraisal. Hearings.* 96th Cong., 1st sess., 1979.

U.S. Congress. House. Committee on Post Office and Civil Service. *Final Report on Violations and Abuses of Merit Principles in Federal Employment Together with Minority Views.* 94th Cong., 2d sess., 1976. Committee Print.

U.S. Congress. Joint Economic Committee. *The Dismissal of A. Ernest Fitzgerald by the Department of Defense. Hearings.* 91st Cong., 1st sess., 1969.

U.S. Congress. Senate. Committee on Governmental Affairs. *Civil Service Reform Act of 1978. Conference Report.* 95th Cong., 2d sess., 1978.

U.S. Congress. Senate. Committee on Governmental Affairs. *Civil Service Reform Act of 1978 and Reorganization Plan No. 2 of 1978. Hearings, on S. 2640, S. 2707, and S. 2830.* 95th Cong., 2d sess., 1978. 2 Vols.

U.S. Congress. Senate. Committee on Governmental Affairs. *The Whistleblowers: A Report on Federal Employees Who Disclose Acts of Governmental Waste, Abuse, and Corruption.* 95th Cong., 2d sess., 1978.

U.S. Congress. Senate. Committee on the Judiciary. *Nomination of Otto F. Otepka. Hearings.* 91st Cong., 1st sess., 1969. 2 pts.

U.S. General Accounting Office. *Whistleblower Complaints Rarely Qualify for Office of Special Counsel Protection.* Washington, DC, May 10, 1985.

U.S. Merit Systems Protection Board. *Whistleblowing and the Federal Employee: Blowing the Whistle on Fraud, Waste, and Mismanagement—Who Does It and What Happens.* Washington, DC: The Board, 1981.

Weiner, P., S. Bompey, and M. Brittan. *Wrongful Discharge Claims, A Preventive Approach.* New York: Practicing Law Institute, 1986.

Westin, Alan F., ed. *Whistle-Blowing! Loyalty and Dissent in the Corporation.* New York: McGraw-Hill, 1980.

Westin, Alan F., and Stephan Salisbury, eds. *Individual Rights in the Corporation: A Reader on Employee Rights.* New York: Pantheon Books, 1980.

Zinn, Howard. *A People's History of the United States.* New York: Harper, 1980.

ARTICLES

Abbot, R. Taylor. "Remedies for Employees Discharged for Reporting an Employer's Violation of Federal Law." 12 *Washington and Lee Law Review* (Fall 1985): 1383.

Abramson, G., and S. Silvestri. "Recognition of a Cause of Action for Abusive Discharge in Maryland." 10 *U. Balt. L. R.* 257 (1981).

Adler, James, and Richard Levey. "Preemption of Workers' Compensation Retaliatory Discharge Laws." 12 *Employee Relations L. R.* 630 (1987).

Allen, R., and P. Linenberger. "The Employee's Rights to Refuse Hazardous Work." 9 *Employee Relations L. J.* 251 (1983).

American Bar Association Section of Labor and Employment Law. "Committee Reports Issue." 2 *Labor Lawyer* 351 (1986).

American Jurisprudence, "Proof of Retaliatory Termination," *Proof of Facts* (2d).

9 *American Law Review* 4th 329 (1981), "Liability for Discharging at-Will Employee for Refusing to Participate in, or for Disclosing, Unlawful or Unethical Acts of Employer or Co-Employees."

12 *American Law Review* 4th 544 (1982), "Modern Status of Rule That Employer May Discharge at-Will Employee for Any Reason."

51 *American Law Review* 2d 742 (1957), "Discharge from Private Employment on Ground of Political Views or Conduct."

60 *American Law Review* 3d 1080 (1974), "Libel and Slander: Privileged Nature of Communication to Other Employees or Employees' Union of Reason for Plaintiff's Discharge."

62 *American Law Review* Fed. 790 (1983), "Admiralty: Recovery for Retaliatory Discharge of at-Will Maritime Employee."

63 *American Law Review* 3d 979 (1975), "Workmen's Compensation: Recovery for Discharge in Retaliation for Filing Claim."

64 *American Law Review* Fed. 825 (1983), "Right of Employee, Discharged for Refusal to Participate in Employer's Anticompetitive Practices, to Bring Action under Federal Antitrust Laws Against Employer."

83 *American Law Review* 2d 532 (1962), "Discharge of Employee as Reprisal or Retaliation for Union Organizational Activities."

86 *American Law Review* 3d 454 (1978), "Liability of Employer, Supervisor, or Manager for Intentionally or Recklessly Causing Employee Emotional Distress."

Anglin, Mary K. "Whistleblowers, Nuclear Plant Safety, and Job Discrimination. *Mackowiak v. University Nuclear Systems—*735 F.2d 1159 (9th Cir. 1984)." 117 *Public Utilities Fortnightly* 56(3) (April 17, 1976).

Archer, Edward. "Employment Contracts in Employment at Will." 16 *Indiana Law Review* 225 (1983).

Bakaly, C. "Erosion of the Employment at Will Doctrine." 8 *J. Contemp. L.* 63 (1982).

Baldwin, Charles G. "Meek v. Opp. Cotton Mills: The Alabama Supreme Court Refuses to Modify the Employment at Will Rule." 36 *Alabama Law Review* 1039 (Summer 1985).

Baldwin, S. "Fear of Firing—Is There a Cause of Action for Wrongful Discharge in Texas?" 47 *Tex. B. J.* 11 (1984).

Baran, Andrew. "Federal Employment—The Civil Service Reform Act of 1978—Removing Incompetents and Protecting Whistle Blowers." *Wayne Law Review* (26 November 1979): 97.

Baxter, R., and J. Farrell. "Constructive Discharge—When Quitting Means Getting Fired." 7 *Empl. L. J.* 346 (1982).

Baxter, R., and J. Wohl. "A Special Update: Wrongful Termination Tort Claims." 11 *Employee Rel. L. J.* 124 (1985).

Baxter, R., and J. Wohl. "Wrongful Termination Lawsuits: The Employers Finally Win a Few." 10 *Employee Rel. L. J.* 258 (1984).

Berkovitz, Dan. "California's Nuclear Power Regulations: Federal Preemption?" 9 *Hastings Const. L. Q.* 623 (1982).

Bierman, L., and S. Youngblood. "Employment at Will and the South Carolina Experiment." 7 *Industrial Relations L. J.* 28 (1985).

Blackburn, J. "Restricted Employer Discharge Rights: A Changing Concept of Employment at Will." 17 *Am. Bus. L. J.* 467 (1980).

Blades, Lawrence. "Employment at Will vs. Individual Freedom: On Limiting the Abusive Exercise of Employer Power." 67 *Columbia Law Review* 1404 (December 1967).

Blank, Ira. "Wrongful Discharge Litigation and Employment-at-Will Rule in Missouri." 40 *J. Mo. B.* 161 (1984).

Blodgett, Nancy. "Whistle-blowers Fight Back: More Are Suing Their Former Employers." 73 *American Bar Association Journal* 20(2) (June 1, 1987).

Blumberg, Phillip I. "Corporate Responsibility and the Employee's Duty of Loyalty and Obedience: A Preliminary Inquiry." 24 *Oklahoma Law Review*, 279 (August 1971).

Blumrosen, Alfred. "Worker's Rights Against Employers and Unions: Justice Francis—A Judge for Our Season." 24 *Rutgers L. J.* 480 (1969–70).

Bogen, Kenneth T. "Managing Technical Dissent in Private Industry: Societal and Corporate Strategies for Dealing with the Whistle-blowing Professional." 13 *Industrial and Labor Relations Forum* 3 (1979).

Bok, Sissela. "Whistleblowing and Professional Responsibility." 11 *New York University Education Quarterly* 2 (Summer 1980).

Bowers and Clarke. "Unfair Dismissal and Managerial Prerogative: A Study of Other Substantial Reasons." 10 *Indus. L. J.* 34 (1981).

Bowman, James S. "Whistle-blowing in the Public Service: An Overview of the Issues." 1 *Review of Public Personnel Administration* 15 (Fall 1980).

Boyan, A. Stephen, Jr. "Whistleblowers: 'Auxiliary Precautions' Against Government Abuse." 2 *Ethical Society* 5 (Spring 1979).

Boyette, K. "Terminating Employees in Virginia: A Roundup for the Employer, the Employee, and Their Counsel." 17 *U. Rich. L. R.* 747 (1983).

Broderick, James A., and Daniel Minahan. "Employment Discrimination under the Federal Mine Safety and Health Act." 84 *West Virginia L. R.* 1023 (1982).

Brown, F. "Limiting Your Risks in the New Russian Roulette—Discharging Employees." 8 *Empl. Rel. L. J.* 380 (1983).

Burke, Maureen H. "The Duty of Confidentiality and Disclosing Corporate Misconduct." 36 *Business Lawyer*, 239 (January 1981).

Burton, Steven. "Breach of Contract and the Common Law Duty to Perform in Good Faith." 94 *Harvard L. R.* 369 (December 1980).

Callan, J. Michael, and H. David. "Professional Responsibility and the Duty of Confidentiality: Disclosure of Client Misconduct in an Adversary System." *Rutgers Law Review* 29 (1976): 332.

Caples, Michael, and Kenneth Hanko. "The Doctrine of at-Will Employment in the Public Sector." 13 *Seton Hall L. R.* 21 (1982–83).

Carrol, M. "Protecting Private Employee's Freedom of Political Speech." 18 *Harvard J. on Legis.* 35 (1981).

Catler, S. "The Case Against Proposals to Eliminate the Employment at Will Rule." 5 *Indus. Rel. L. J.* 471 (1983).

Cerbone, Richard. "The Res Judicata Effect of State Fair Employment Practice Commission Decisions." 37 *Labor Law Journal* 780 (1986).

Chalk, Rosemary, and Frank von Hippel. "Due Process for Dissenting Whistle-Blowers." 81 *Technology Review* 49 (June/July 1979).

Chalk, Rosemary, and Frank von Hippel. "Due Process for Whistle-Blowers: Part 1—The Professional's Dilemma." 102 *Mechanical Engineering* 82 (April 1980).

Chalk, Rosemary, and Frank von Hippel. "Due Process For Whistle-Blowers: Part 2—Who Should Protect Dissenters?" 102 *Mechanical Engineering* 762 (May 1980), p. 76.

Chapman, J. "Bad Faith Discharge of an Employee under a Contract Terminable at Will." 10 *Trial Lawyer Guide* 5 (1966).

Chineson, Joel. "The Fate of Whistleblowers." 22 *Trial* 80(3) (December 1986).

Christiansen, Jon P. "A Remedy for the Discharge of Professional Employees Who Refuse to Perform Unethical or Illegal Acts: A Proposal in Aid of Professional Ethics." 28 *Vanderbilt Law Review* 805 (May 1975).

Clark, Louis. "Blowing the Whistle on Corruption: How to Kill a Career in Washington." 5 *Barrister* 10 (Summer 1978).

Clutterbuck, David. "Blowing the Whistle on Corporate Misconduct." 35 *International Management* 14 (January 1980).

Comment, "The at-Will Doctrine: A Proposal to Modify the Texas Employment Relationship." 36 *Baylor L. R.* 667 (1984).

Comment, "Beyond Pierce v. Ortho Pharmaceutical Corp., the Termination-at-Will Doctrine in New Jersey." 37 *Rutgers L. R.* 137 (1984).

Comment, "Employment–at–Will and the Law of Contracts." 23 *Buffalo L. R.* 211 (1973).

Comment, "The Employment–at–Will Rule." 31 *Alabama L. R.* 421 (1981).

Comment, "The Employment–at–Will Sale: The Development of Exceptions and Pennsylvania's Response." 21 *Duq. L. R.* 477.

Comment, "Fire at Will: An Analysis of the Missouri at Will Employment Doctrine." 25 *St. Louis University L. J.* 845 (1982).

Comment, "'Good Cause': California's New 'Exception' to the at-Will Doctrine," 23 *Santa Clara L. R.* 263 (1983).

Comment, "'Just Cause' Termination Rights for at Will Employees." *Det. C.L.R.* 591 (1982).

Comment, "Labor Law Preemption Doctrine—State Trespass Laws—Peaceful Picketing—Sears, Roebuck and Co. v. San Diego County District Council of Carpenters." *New York Law School L. R.* 689 (1980).

Comment, "Labor Law Preemption—Supreme Court Approves Unemployment Compensation for the Benefit of Striking Employees—New York Telephone Co. v. New York State Department of Labor." 99 S.Ct. 1328 (1979), *Creighton Law Review* 1005 (1980).

Comment, "Limiting the Employer's Absolute Right of Discharge: Can Kansas Courts Meet the Challenge?" 29 *Univ. of Kansas L. R.* 267 (1981).

Comment, "Missouri's Employment at Will: Vulnerable to Prima Facie Tort?" 27 *St. Louis University L. J.* 1001 (1983).

Comment, "Nuclear Energy—Federal Preemption—State Moratorium on Nuclear Plant Construction Upheld Against Preemption Challenge: Pacific Gas & Electric Co. v. State Energy Resources Conservation & Dev. Comm'n." 14 *Seton Hall L. R.* 1034 (1984).

Comment, "Silkwood v. Kerr-McGee Corp.: Preemption of State Law for Nuclear Torts?" 12 *Envtl. L.* 1059 (1982).

Comment, "Termination of the at-Will Employee: The General Rule, and the Wisconsin Rule." 65 *Marq. L. R.* 673 (1982).

Comment, "Towards a Property Right in Employment." 22 *Buffalo L. R.* 1081 (1973).

Comment, "Wrongful Discharge of Employees Terminable at Will—A New Theory of Liability in Arkansas." 34 *Arkansas L. R.* 729 (1981).

Connor, Susan Marie. "A Survey of Illinois Employment Discrimination Law." 31 *De Paul L. R.* 323 (Winter 1987).

Cook, Daniel D. "Whistle-Blowers—Friend or Foe." 5 *Industry Week* 50 (October 1981).

Coombe, John. "Employee Handbooks: Asset or Liability." 12 *Employee Relations L. J.* 4 (1986).

Copus, D. and R. Lindsay. "Successfully Defending the Discriminatory/ Wrongful Discharge Case." 10 *Employee Relations L. J.* 456 (1984–85).

Coven, Mark. "The First Amendment Rights of Policymaking Public Employees." 12 *Harvard Civil Rights—Civil Liberties Law Review* 559 (Summer 1977).

Cox, A. "Recent Developments in Federal Labor Law Preemption." 41 *Ohio State Law Journal* 277 (1980).

Crook. "Employment at Will: The 'American Rule' and Its Application in Alaska." 2 *Alaska L. R.* 23 (1985).

DeFranko, James. "Modification of the Employee at Will Doctrine." 30 *Saint Louis University L. J.* 65.

Decker, Kurt. "At-Will Employment: Abolition and Federal Statutory Regulation." 61 *U. Det. J. Urb L.* 351 (1984).

Decker, Kurt. "At-Will Employment in Pennsylvania—A Proposal for Its Abolition and Statutory Regulation." 87 *Dickinson L. R.* 477 (Spring 1983).

De Giuseppe, J. "The Effect of the Employment-at-Will Rule on Employee Rights to Job Security and Fringe Benefits." 10 *Fordham Urb. L. J.* 1 (1981).

De Giuseppe, J. "The Recognition of Public Policy Exceptions to the Employment-at-Will Rule: A Legislative Function?" 11 *Fordham Urb. L. J.* 721 (1983).

Devine, Thomas and Aplin, Donald, "Abuse of Authority: The Office of the Special Counsel and Whistleblower Protection," 1 *Antioch Law Journal* 5 (Summer 1986).

Dorman, Charles. "Justice Brennan: The Individual and Labor Law," 59 *Chicago-Kent L. R.*, 1003 (1982).

Drachssler, David. "Burdens of Proof in Retaliatory Adverse Action Cases under Title VII." 35 *Labor Law Journal* 28 (1984).

Drachaler, David. "Brown & Root v. Donovan: An Exercise in Judicial Myopia." 747 F.2d 1029 (5th Cir. 1984), 38 *Labor Law Journal* 311 (May 1987).

Epstein, Richard. "In Defense of the Contract at Will." 51 *University of Chicago L. R.* 947 (Fall 1984).

Estreicher, Samuel. "At-Will Employment and the Problem of Unjust Dismissal: The Appropriate Judicial Response." 54 *New York State Bar Journal*, 146 (April 1982).

Ewing, David. "The Employee's Right to Speak Out: The Management Perspective." 5 *Civil Liberties Review*, 10 (September/October 1978).

Ewing, David. "What Business Thinks About Employee Rights." 77 *Harvard Business Review*, 81 (September/October 1977).

Feinman, J. "The Development of the Employment at Will Rule." 20 *Am. J. Legal Hist.* 118 (1976).

Forbes, F., and I. Jones. "A Comparative, Attitudinal and Analytical Study of Dismissal of at-Will Employees Without Cause." 37 *Labor Law Journal* 157 (1986).

Furlane, M. "Employment at Will: An Eroding Doctrine." 65 *Chi B. Rec.* 36 (1983).

Gillette, P. "The Implied Covenant of Good Faith and Fair Dealing: Are Employers the Insurers of the Eighties?" 11 *Employee Relations L. J.* 438 (1985–86).

Glazer, Myron, and Penina Glazer. "Whistleblowing." *Psychology Today* (August 1986).

Glendon, Mary Ann, and Edward Lev. "Changes in the Bonding of the Employment Relationship." 20 *Boston College Industrial and Commercial Law Review* 457 (March 1979).

Goetz, Charles and Robert Scott. "Principles of Relational Contracts." 67 *Virginia L. R.* 1089 (September 1981).

Greenbaum, Marc. "Toward a Common Law of Employment Discrimination." 58 *Temple Law Quarterly* 65 (Spring 1985).

Grove, Kalvin, and Paul Garry. "Employment-at-Will in Illinois: Implications and Anticipations for the Practitioner." 31 *De Paul L. R.* 359 (Winter 1982).

Halbert, Terry Ann. "The Cost of Scruples: A Call for Common Law Protection for the Professional Whistleblower." Pierce v. Ortho Pharmaceutical Corp., 339 A.2d 1023 (N.J. 1979), 10 *Nova Law Journal* 1 (Fall 1985).

Harper, C. "Expanding Liability for Employment Termination." 18 *Trial* 60 (December 1982).

Harrison, Jeffrey. "The 'New' Terminable–at–Will Contract: An Interest and Cost Incidence Analysis." 69 *Iowa L. R.* 327 (January 1984).

Harrison, Jeffrey. "Wrongful Discharge: Toward A More Efficient Remedy." 56 *Indiana L. J.* 207.

Heinsz, Timothy. "The Assault on the Employment at Will Doctrine: Management Considerations." 48 *Missouri L. R.* 855 (Fall 1983).

Hentoff, Nat. "Putting the Gag on CIA Whistle Blowers." 5 *Civil Liberties Review* 37 (July/August 1978).

Herman, Donand and Yvonne Sor. "Property Rights in One's Job." 24 *Arizona Law Review* 763 (1982).

Heshizer, B. "The Implied Contract Exception to at-Will Employment." 35 *Lab. L. J.* 131 (1984).

Holkstra. "Palmateer [Palmateer v. International Harvester Co., 421 N.E.2d 876 (Ill.)]: A Further Extension to Retaliatory Discharge in Illinois." 71 *Ill. B. J.* 298 (1983).

Hopkins and Robinson. "Employment at-Will, Wrongful Discharge, and the Covenant of Good Faith and Fair Dealing in Montana, Past, Present and Future." 46 *Montana L. R.* 1 (1985).

Ichinose, S. "Hawaii's Supreme Court Recognizes Tort of Retaliatory Discharge of an at-Will Employee." 17 *Hawaii B. J.* 123 (1982).

Ingram, Timothy. "On Muckrakers and Whistle Blowers." 1 *Business and Society Review* 21 (August 1972).

Isbell-Sirotkin, Eric. "Defending the Abusively Discharged Employee: In Search of a Judicial Solution." 12 *New Mexico L. R.* 711 (Spring 1982).

Kaden, L. "Federal Labor Preemption: The Supreme Court Draws the Lines." 18 *The Urban Lawyer* 607 (1984).

Kinyon, Susan, and Josef Rohlik. "'Deflouring' *Lucas* Through Labored Characterizations: Tort Actions of Unionized Employees." 30 *Saint Louis University L. J.* 1 (October 1985).

Kirschner, R., and M. Walfoort. "The Duty of Fair Representation: Implications of Bowen." 1 *Labor Lawyer* 19 (1985).

Kohn, Stephen, and Thomas Carpenter. "Nuclear Whistleblower Protection and the Scope of Protected Activity Under Section 210 of the Energy Reorganization Act." Brown & Root, Inc. v. Donovan, 747 F.2d 1029 (5th Cir. 1984), 4 *Antioch Law Journal* 75 (Summer 1986).

Kohn, Stephen, and Michael Kohn. "An Overview of Federal and State Whistleblower Protections." 4 *Antioch Law Journal* 99 (Summer 1986).

Krauskopf, Joan. "Employment Discharge: Survey and Critique of the Modern at Will Rule." 51 *University of Missouri-Kansas City L. R.* 189 (Winter 1983).

Kurzman, Dani. "Michigan's Whistleblowers' Protection Act: Job Protection for Citizen Crime Fighters." 5 *Corporation, Finance & Business Law Journal* 43 (Summer 1981).

Lindauer, Mitchell. "Government Employee Disclosures of Agency Wrongdoing: Protecting the Right to Blow the Whistle." 42 *University of Chicago L. R.* 530 (Spring 1975).

Linzer, Peter. "The Decline of Assent: At-Will Employment as a Case Study of the Breakdown of Private Law Theory." 20 *Georgia L. R.* 323 (Winter 1986).

Loomis, Lloyd. "Employee Assistance Programs: Their Impact on Arbitration and Litigation of Termination Cases." 12 *Employee Relations L. J.* 275 (1986).

Love, Jean. "Retaliatory Discharge for Filing a Workers' Compensation Claim: The Development of a Modern Tort Action." 37 *Hastings L. J.* 551 (March 1986).

Lowy, Joan. "Constitutional Limitations on the Dismissal of Public Employees." 43 *Brooklyn Law Review* 1 (Summer 1976).

Ludington, John. "Employer Discrimination Against Employees for Filing Charges or Giving Testimony Under NLRA." 35 *ALR Fed.* 8.

Lyons, W. "State Regulation of Nuclear Power Production: Facing the Preemption Challenge from a New Perspective." 76 *Northwestern Univ. L. Rev.* 134 (1981).

McGowan, William. "The Whistleblowing Game." *New Age* (September 1984).

McKinney, Charles. "Fair Representation of Employees in Unionized Firms." 35 *Labor Law Journal* 693 (1984).

McWeeny, R. "Out of the Fog: A Different View on Retaliatory Employee Discharge." 54 *Conn. B.J.* 235 (1980).

Madison, J. "The Employee's Emerging Right to Sue for Arbitrary or Unfair Discharge." 6 *Employee Rel. L. J.* 422 (1981).

Malin, Martin. "Protecting the Whistleblower from Retaliatory Discharge." 16 *Univ. of Mich. J. L. Reform* 277 (Winter 1983).

Mallur, Jane. "Punitive Damages for Wrongful Discharge of at-Will Employees." 26 *William and Mary L. R.* 449.

Marcotte, Paul. "Blowing Whistle Can Pay Off." 73 *American Bar Association Journal* 31(1) (March 1, 1987).

Marrinan, S. "Employment at-Will: Pandora's Box May Have an Attractive Cover." 7 *Hamline L. R.* 155 (1984).

Marshall, Gary, and Maris Wicker. "The Status of the At-Will Employment Doctrine in Virginia after *Bowman v. State Bank of Keysville*." Bowman v. State Bank, 331 S.E.2d 797 (Va. 1985), 20 *University of Richmond Law Review* 267 (Winter 1986).

Martin, B. Morris. "Contracts." 34 *Mercer L. R.* 71 (Fall 1982).

Martin, D., K. Bartol, and M. Levine. "The Legal Ramifications of Performance Appraisal." 12 *Employee Relations L. J.* 370 (1986–87).

Martin, John. "The Whistleblower Revisited." 8 *George Mason University L. R.* 123 (Fall 1985).

Martucci, W., and J. Utz. "Wrongful Interference with Protected Rights under ERISA." 2 *The Labor Lawyer* 251 (1986).

Mauk, William. "Wrongful Discharge: The Erosion of 100 Years of Employer Privilege." 21 *Idaho L. R.* 201 (Spring 1985).

Mayer, Stephen. "N.J.'s 'Whistleblower Act.'" 119 *New Jersey Law Journal* 1 (March 5, 1987).

Mennemeier, K. "Protection from Unjust Discharges: An Arbitration Scheme." 19 *Harvard J. on Legis.* 49 (1982).

Miller and Estes. "Recent Judicial Limitations on the Right to Discharge: A California Trilogy." 16 *University of California, Davis L. R.* 65 (1982).

Minda, Gary. "The Common Law of Employment at-Will in New York: The Paralysis of Nineteenth Century Doctrine." 36 *Syracuse L. R.* 939 (1985).

Mooney, Thomas, and Jeffrey Pingpank. "Wrongful Discharge: A 'New' Cause of Action?" 54 *Connecticut Bar J.* 213 (June 1980).

Moore, T. "Individual Rights of Employees with the Corporation." 6 *Corp. L. Rev.* 39 (1983).

Murg, G., and C. Seharman. "Employment at Will: Do the Exceptions Overwhelm the Rule?" 23 *Boston Coll. L. R.* 329 (1982).

Nader, Ralph. "No Protection for Outspoken Scientists." *Physics Today* (July 1973): 77.

Naylor, Gregory. "Employment at Will: The Decay of an Anachronistic Shield for Employers." 33 *Drake L. R.* 113 (1983–84).

Near, Janet, and Marcia Niceli. "Retaliation Against Whistle Blowers: Predictors and Effects." 71 *Journal of Applied Psychology* 137 (1986).

Nickel, Henry. "The First Amendment and Public Employees—An Emerging Constitutional Right to be a Policeman?" 37 *George Washington Law Review* 409 (December 1968).

Note, "Employment at Will: A Proposal to Adopt the Public Policy Exception in Florida." 34 *University of Florida L. R.* 614 (1982).

Note, "Labor Law Preemption: *Allis Chalmers Corp. v. Lueck.*" 60 *Tulane L. R.* 1077 (1986).

Note, "The Role of Federal Courts in Changing State Law: The Employment at Will Doctrine in Pennsylvania." 133 *University of Penn. L. R.* 227 (1984).

Nulton, W., H. Jacobs, and C. Craver. "Duty of Fair Representation in Grievance and Arbitration Procedures." 1 *The Labor Lawyer* 321 (1985).

Ojanen, I. "Preemption—Atomic Energy." 24 *Nat. Resources J.* 761 (1984).

Olsen, Theodore. "Wrongful Discharge Claims Raised by at-Will Employees: A New Legal Concern for Employers." 32 *Labor Law Journal* 265 (May 1981).

Parker, J. Wilson. "The Constitutional Status of Public Employee Speech: A Question for the Jury?" 65 *Boston Univ. L. R.*, 483 (May 1985).

Peck, Cornelius. "Some Kind of Hearing for Persons Discharged from Private Employment." 16 *San Diego L. R.* 313 (1979).

Peck, Cornelius. "Unjust Discharges from Employment: A Necessary Change in the Law." 40 *Ohio State Law Journal* 1 (1979).

Pierce, E., R. Mann, and B. Roberts. "Employee Termination at Will: A Principled Approach." 28 *Villanova L. R.* 1 (November 1982).

Pickholz, Marvin. "The Victim and Witness Protection Act of 1982—Implications for the in-House Counsel." 13 *Securities Regulation L. J.* 195 (Fall 1985).

Pilon, Roger. "Corporations and Rights: On Treating Corporate People Justly." 13 *Georgia L. R.* 1245 (Summer 1979).

Platt, L. Steven. "Rethinking the Right of Employers to Terminate at-Will Employees." 15 *John Marshall L. R.* 633 (Summer 1982).

Power, R. "A Defense of the Employment at Will Rule." 27 *St. Louis U. L. J.* 881 (1983).

Raven-Hansen, Peter. "Do's and Don'ts for Whistleblowers: Planning for Trouble." 82 *Technology Review* 34 (May 1980).

Raymond, Bradley, and Donna Nuyen. "Labor Law." 29 *Wayne L. R.* 841 (1983).

Renz, J. "The Effect of Federal Legislation on Historical State Powers of Pollution Control: Has Congress Muddied State Waters?" 43 *Montana L. R.* 197 (1982).

Richards, T. and J. De Franco. "Retaliatory Discharge: Its Applicability to Employees Protected by a Just Cause Provision." 72 *Ill. B. J.* 480 (1984).

Riggs, A. "Legal Principles Applicable to Proper Discharge Procedures." 37 *Labor Law Journal* 204 (1986).

Rishel, G. "Retaliatory Discharge: A Broadened Tort Through Statutory Analogy." 70 *Ill. B. J.* 454 (1982).

Robbins, Albert. "Dissent in the Corporate World: When Does an Employee Have the Right to Speak Out?" 5 *Civil Liberties Review* 6 (September/October 1978).

Robbins, M., N. Norwood, and N. Taldone. "A Symposium: Wrongful Discharge and the Unionized Employee." 12 *Employee Relations L. J.* 19 (1986).

Rohwer, Claude. "Terminable at-Will Employment: New Theories for Job Security." 15 *Pacific L. R.* 766.

Rongine, Nicholas. "Toward a Coherent Legal Response to the Public Policy Dilemma Posed by Whistleblowing." (Special Issue—Business and the First Amendment), 23 *American Business Law Journal* 291 (Summer 1985).

Ryan, T. "Status of Wrongful Discharge in Wisconsin." 56 *Wis. B. Bull.* 22 (April 1983).

Schneier, Mark. "Public Policy Limitations on the Retaliatory Discharge of at-Will Employees in the Private Sector." 14 *Univ. of California, Davis L. R.* 811 (1981).

Schreiber, Mark. "Wrongful Termination of at-Will Employees." 68 *Massachusetts L. R.* 22 (March 1983).

Shapiro, S. "Action for Wrongful Discharge of an Employee." 24 *S. Tex. L. J.* 883 (1983).

Siniscalco, G. "Reductions in Force: Minimizing Exposure to Contract, Tort and Discrimination Claims." 9 *Employee Relations L. J.* 203 (1983).

Smith, Ray, and David Kays. "Preempting State Regulation of Employment Relations: A Model for Analysis." 20 *University of San Francisco L. R.* 35 (Fall 1985).

Soloman, Lewis, and Terry Garcia. "Protecting the Corporate Whistle Blower under Federal Anti-Retaliation Statutes." 5 *The Journal of Corporation Law* 275 (Winter 1980).

Steiner, J., and A. Dabrow. "The Questionable Value of Inclusion of Language Confirming Employment at-Will Status in Company Personnel Documents." 37 *Labor Law Journal* 639 (1986).

Strasser. "Employment at-Will: The Death of a Doctrine?" *National Law Journal* (January 20, 1986).

Summers, Clyde. "Individual Protection Against Unjust Dismissal: Time for a Statute." 62 *Virginia L. R.* 481 (April 1976).

Summers, Clyde. "Protecting All Employees Against Unjust Dismissal." 58 *Harvard Business Review* 132 (January/February 1980).

Summers, Clyde. "The Rights of Individual Workers: The Contract of Employment and the Rights of Individual Employees: Fair Representation and Employment at Will." 52 *Fordham L. R.* 1082 (1984).

Tepker, Harry. "Oklahoma's at-Will Rule: Heeding the Warning of America's Evolving Employment Law?" 39 *Oklahoma L. R.* 373 (Fall 1986).

Vaughn, Robert. "Public Employees and the Right to Disobey." 29 *Hastings Law Journal* 261 (November 1977).

Vaughn, Robert. "Statutory Protection of Whistleblowers in the Federal Executive Branch." 3 *Univ. of Ill. L. R.* 615 (1982).

Vernon and Gray. "Termination at Will—The Employer's Right to Fire." 6 *Employee Rel. L. J.* 25 (1981).

Villemez, Jane. "The First Amendment and the Law Enforcement Agency: Protecting the Employee Who Blows the Whistle." 18 *Land and Water Law Review* 789 (Fall 1983).

Wald, M., and D. Wolf. "Recent Developments in the Law of Employment at Will." 1 *The Labor Lawyer* 533 (1985).

Walters, Kenneth. "Your Employees' Right to Blow the Whistle." 53 *Harvard Business Review* 26 (July/August 1975).

Walterscheid, E. "When Employees Act Contrary to the Interests of Their Employers: Activities Unprotected under Title VII." 12 *Employee Relations L. J.* 609 (1987).

Weeks, Joseph. "NLRA Preemption of State Common Law Wrongful Discharge Claims: The Bhopal Brigade Goes Home." 13 *Pepperdine L. R.* 607 (1986).

Zimmerman, D., and J. Howard-Martin. "The Federal Preemption Doctrine Revisited." 37 *Labor Law Journal* 223 (1986).

TABLE OF CASES

U.S. SUPREME COURT

Pacific Gas & Elec. Co. v. State Energy Resources Conservation & Dev. Comm'n, 461 U.S. 190 (1983)

Pan American World Airways v. Puchert, 472 U.S. 1001

Perry v. Sindermann, 408 U.S. 593 (1972)

Pickering v. Board of Education, 391 U.S. 563 (1968)

Radio Officers v. NLRB, 347 U.S. 17 (1945)

Rankin v. McPherson, ___ U.S. ___ 107 S.Ct. 2891 (1987)

Ray v. Atlantic Rich. Co., 98 S.Ct. 98 (1978)

Republic Steel Corp. v. Maddox, 379 U.S. 650 (1965)

Rice v. Santa Fe Elevator Corp., 331 U.S. 218 (1947)

San Diego Building Trades Council v. Garmon, 354 U.S. 236 (1959)

Sears & Roebuck Co. v. Carpenters, 436 U.S. 180 (1978)

Silkwood v. Kerr-McGee Corp., 464 U.S. 238 (1984)

Steele v. Louisville & N.R. Co., 323 U.S. 192 (1944)

Teamster Union v. Oliver, 358 U.S. 283 (1959)

Texas Dept. of Community Affairs v. Burdine, 450 U.S. 248 (1981)

U.S. v. Price, 383 U.S. 787 (1965)

United Steelworkers of America v. Enterprise Wheel and Car Corp., 363 U.S. 593 (1960)

Vaca v. Sipes, 386 U.S. 171 (1967)

Whirlpool Corp. v. Marshall, 445 U.S. 1 (1980)

Zipes v. Transworld Airlines, Inc., 455 U.S. 385 (1982)

U.S. COURT OF APPEALS

Airborne Freight Corp. v. NLRB, 728 F.2d 357 (6th Cir. 1984)

Alabama v. United States, 304 F.2d 583 (5th Cir. 1962)

American Telephone & Telegraph Co. v. NLRB, 521 F.2d 1159 (2nd Cir. 1975)

Authier v. Ginsberg, 757 F.2d 796 (6th Cir. 1985)

Baker v. Board of Mine Operations Appeals, 595 F.2d 746 (D.C. Cir. 1978)

Baldracchi v. Pratt & Whitney Aircraft Division, 814 F.2d 102 (2nd Cir. 1987)

Bartel v. Federal Aviation Administration, 725 F.2d 1403 (D.C. Cir. 1984)

Bickham v. Miller, 584 F.2d 736 (5th Cir. 1978)

Bonham v. Dresser Industries, Inc., 569 F.2d 187 (3rd Cir. 1977)

Brennan v. Maxey's Yamaha, Inc. 513 F.2d 179 (8th Cir. 1975)

Brockell v. Norton, 688 F.2d 588 (8th Cir. 1982); Brockell v. Norton, (2nd Appeal), 732 F.2d 664 (8th Cir. 1984)

Brown & Root, Inc. v. Donovan, 747 F.2d 1029 (5th Cir. 1984)

Burcanan v. Bolt Brother's Construction Company, Inc., 741 F.2d 750 (5th Cir. 1984)

Buschi v. Kirven, 775 F.2d 1240 (4th Cir. 1985)

FEDERAL DISTRICT COURT

FEDERAL RULES DECISIONS

MISCELLANEOUS AND ADMINISTRATIVE

APPENDIXES: FEDERAL WHISLTLEBLOWER PROTECTION LAWS

Appendix 1
U.S. Constitution, Amendments I and XIV

AMENDMENT I

Congress shall make no law respecting an establishment of religion, or prohibiting the free exercise thereof; or abridging the freedom of speech, or of the press; or the right of the people peaceably to assemble, and to petition the Government for a redress of grievances.

AMENDMENT XIV

SECTION 1. All persons born or naturalized in the United States, and subject to the jurisdiction thereof, are citizens of the United States and of the State wherein they reside. No State shall make or enforce any law which shall abridge the privileges or immunities of citizens of the United States; nor shall any State deprive any person of life, liberty, or property, without due process of law; nor deny to any person within its jurisdiction the equal protection of the laws.

The reader is advised to compare these texts with statutory texts printed in the most recent editions of the U.S. Code.

Appendix 2
Toxic Substances Control Act, 15 U.S.C. 2622

§ 2622 Employee protection
(a) In general

No employer may discharge any employee or otherwise discriminate against any employee with respect to the employee's compensation, terms, conditions, or privileges of employment because the employee (or any person acting pursuant to a request of the employee) has—

(1) commenced, caused to be commenced, or is about to commence or cause to be commenced a proceeding under this chapter;

(2) testified or is about to testify in any such proceeding; or

(3) assisted or participated or is about to assist or participate in any manner in such a proceeding or in any other action to carry out the purposes of this chapter.

(b) Remedy

(1) Any employee who believes that the employee has been discharged or otherwise discriminated against by any person in violation of subsection (a) of this section may, within 30 days after such alleged violation occurs, file (or have any person file on the employee's behalf) a complaint with the Secretary of Labor (hereinafter in this section referred to as the "Secretary") alleging such discharge or discrimination. Upon receipt of such a complaint, the Secretary shall notify the person named in the complaint of the filing of the complaint.

(2)(A) Upon receipt of a complaint filed under paragraph (1), the Secretary shall conduct an investigation of the violation alleged in the complaint. Within 30 days of the receipt of such complaint. Within 30 days of the receipt of such complaint, the Secretary shall complete such investigation and shall notify in writing the complainant (and any person acting on behalf of the complainant) and the person alleged to have committed such violation of the results of the investigation conducted pursuant to this paragraph. Within ninety days of the receipt of such complaint the Secretary shall, unless the proceeding on the complaint is terminated by the Secretary on the basis of a settlement entered into by the Secretary and the person alleged to have committed such violation, issue an order either providing the relief prescribed by subparagraph (B) or denying the complaint. An order of the Secretary shall be made on the record after notice and opportunity for agency hearing. The Secretary may not enter into a settlement terminating a proceeding on a complaint without the participation and consent of the complainant.

(B) If in response to a complaint filed under paragraph (1) the Secretary determines that a violation of subsection (a) of this section has occurred, the Secretary shall order (i) the person who committed such violation to take affirmative action to abate the violation, (ii) such person to reinstate the complainant to the complainant's former position together with the compensation (including back pay), terms, conditions, and privileges of the complainant's employment, (iii) compensatory damages, and (iv) where appropriate, exemplary damages. If such an order issued, the Secretary, at the request of the complainant, shall assess against the person against whom the order is issued a sum equal to the aggregate amount of all costs and expenses (including attorney's fees) reasonably incurred, as determined by the Secretary, by the complianant for, or in connection with, the bringing of the complaint upon which the order was issued.

(c) Review

(1) Any employee or employer adversely affected or aggrieved by an order issued under subsection (b) of this section may obtain review of the order in the United States Court of Appeals for the circuit in which the violation, with respect to which the order was issued, allegedly occurred. The petition for review must be filed within sixty days from the issuance of the Secretary's order. Review shall conform to chapter 7 of title 5.

(2) An order of the Secretary, with respect to which review could have been obtained under paragraph (1), shall not be subject to judicial review in any criminal or other civil proceeding.

(d) Enforcement

Whenever a person has failed to comply with an order issued under subsection (b)(2) of this section the Secretary shall file a civil action in the United States district court for the district in which the violation was found to occur to enforce such order. In actions brought under this subsection, the district courts shall have jurisdiction to grant all appropriate relief, including injunctive relief and compensatory and exemplary damages. Civil actions brought under this subsection shall be heard and decided expeditiously.

(e) Exclusion

Subsection (a) of this section shall not apply with respect to any employee who, acting without direction from the employee's employer (or any agent of the employer), deliberately causes a violation of any requirement of this chapter.

(Pub.L. 94-469. § 23, Oct. 11, 1976, 90 Stat. 2044.)

Appendix 3
Comprehensive Environmental Response, Compensation and Liability Act ("Superfund"), Employee Protection, 42 U.S.C. 9610

§ 9610 Employee Protection

(a) Activities of employee subject to protection

No person shall fire or in any other way discriminate against, or cause to be fired or dicriminated against, any employee or any authorized representative of employees by reason of the fact that such employee or representative has provided information to a State or to the Federal Government, filed, instituted, or caused to be filed or instituted any proceeding under this chapter, or has testified or is about to testify in any proceeding resulting from the administration or enforcement of the provisions of this chapter.

(b) Administrative grievance procedure in cases of alleged violations

Any employee or a representative of employees who believes that he has been fired or otherwise discriminated against by any person in violation of subsection (a) of this section may, within thirty days after such alleged violation occurs, apply to the Secretary of Labor for a review of such firing or alleged discrimination. A copy of the application shall be sent to such person, who shall be the respondent. Upon receipt of such application, the Secretary of Labor shall cause such investigation to be made as he deems appropriate. Such investigation shall provide an opportunity for a public hearing at the request of any party to such review to enable the parties to present information relating to such alleged violation. The parties shall be given written notice of the time and place of the hearing at least five days prior to the hearing. Any such hearing shall be of record and shall be subject to section 554 of title 5. Upon receiving the report of such investigation, the Secretary of Labor shall make findings of fact. If he finds that such violation did occur, he shall issue a decision, incorporating an order therein and his findings, requiring the party committing such violation to take such affirmative action to abate the violation as the Secretary of Labor deems appropriate, including, but not limited to, the rehiring or reinstatement of the employee or representative of employees to his former position with compensation. If he finds that there was no such violation, he shall issue an order denying the application. Such order issued by the Secretary of Labor under this subparagraph shall be subject to judicial review in the same manner as orders and decisions are subject to judicial review under this chapter.

(c) Assessment of costs and expenses against violator subsequent to issuance of order of abatement

Whenever an order is issued under this section to abate such violation, at the request of the applicant of a sum equal to the aggregate amount of all costs and expenses (including the attorney's fees) determined by the Secretary of Labor to have been reasonably incurred by the applicant for, or in connection with, the institution and prosecution of such proceedings, shall be assessed against the person committing such violation.

(d) Defenses

This section shall have no application to any employee who acting without discretion from his employer (or his agent) deliberately violates any requirement of this chapter.

(e) Presidential evaluations of potential loss of shifts of employment resulting from administration or enforcement of provisions; investigations; procedures applicable, etc.

The President shall conduct continuing evaluations of potential loss of shifts of employment which may result from the administration or enforcement of the provisions of this chapter, including, where appropriate, investigating threatened plant closures or reductions in employment allegedly resulting from such administration or enforcement. Any employee who is discharged, or laid off, threatened with discharge or layoff, or otherwise discriminated against by any person because of the alleged results of such administration or enforcement, or any representative of such employee, may request the President to conduct a full investigation of the matter and at the request of any party, shall hold public hearings, require the parties, including the employer involved, to present information relating to the actual or potential effect of such administration or enforcement on employment and any alleged discharge, layoff or other discrimination, and the detailed reasons or justification therefore. Any such hearing shall be of record and shall be subject to section 554 of title 5. Upon receiving the report of such investigation, the President shall make findings of fact as to the effect of such administration or enforcement on employment and on the alleged discharge, layoff, or discrimination and shall make such recommendations as he deems appropriate. Such report, findings, and recommendations shall be available to the public. Nothing in this subsection shall be construed to require or authorize the President or any State to modify or withdraw any action, standard, limitation, or any other requirement of this chapter.

(Pub. L. 96-510, title I, § 110, Dec. 11, 1980, 94 Stat. 2787.)

Appendix 4
Water Pollution Control Act, 33 U.S.C. 1367

§ 1367 Employee protection

(a) Discrimination against persons filing, instituting, or testifying in proceedings under this chapter prohibited

No person shall fire, or in any other way discriminate against, or cause to be fired or discriminated against, any employee or any authorized representative of employees by reason of the fact that such employee or representative has filed, instituted, or caused to be filed or instituted any proceeding under this chapter, or has testified or is about to testify in any proceeding resulting from the administration or enforcement of the provisions of this chapter.

(b) Application for review; investigation; hearing; review

Any employee or a representative of employees who believes that he has been fired or otherwise discriminated against by any person in violation of subsection (a) of this section may, within thirty days after such alleged violation occurs, apply to the Secretary of Labor for a review of such firing or alleged discrimination. A copy of the application shall be sent to such person who shall be the respondent. Upon receipt of such application, the Secretary of Labor shall cause such investigation to be made as he deems appropriate. Such investigation shall provide an opportunity for a public hearing at the request of any party to such review to enable the parties to present information relating to such alleged violation. The parties shall be given written notice of the time and place of the hearing at least five days prior to the hearing. Any such hearing shall be of record and shall be subject to section 554 of title 5. Upon receiving the report of such investigation, the Secretary of Labor shall make findings of fact. If he finds that such violation did occur, he shall issue a decision, incorporating an order therein and his findings, requiring the party committing such violation to take such affirmative action to abate the violation as the Secretary of Labor deems appropriate, including, but not limited to, the rehiring or reinstatement of the employee or representative of employees to his former position with compensation. If he finds that there was no such violation, he shall issue an order denying the application. Such order issued by the Secretary of Labor under this subparagraph shall be subject to judicial review in the same manner as orders and decisions of the Administrator are subject to judicial review under this chapter.

(c) Costs and expenses

Whenever an order is issued under this section to abate such violation, at the request of the applicant, a sum equal to the aggregate amount of all costs and expenses (including the attorney's fees), as determined by the Secretary of Labor, to have been reasonably incurred by the applicant for, or in connection with, the institution and prosecution of such proceedings, shall be assessed against the person committing such violation.

(d) Deliberate violations by employee acting without direction from his employer or his agent

This section shall have no application to any employee who, acting without direction from his employer (or his agent) deliberately violates any prohibition of effluent limitation or other limitation under section 1311 or 1312 of this title, standards of performance under section 1316 of this title, effluent standard, prohibition or pretreatment standard under section 1317 of this title, or any other prohibition or limitation established under this chapter.

(e) Investigations of employment reductions

The Administrator shall conduct continuing evaluations of potential loss or shifts of employment which may result from the issuance of any effluent limitation or order under this chapter, including, where appropriate, investigating threatened plant closures or reductions in employment allegedly resulting from such limitation or order. Any employee who is discharged or laid-off, threatened with discharge or lay-off, or otherwise discriminated against by any person because of the alleged results of any effluent limitation or order issued under this chapter, or any representative of such employee, may request the Administrator to conduct a full investigation of the matter. The Administrator shall thereupon investigate the matter and, at the request of any party, shall hold public hearings on not less than five days notice, and shall at such hearings require the parties, including the employer involved, to present information relating to the actual or potential effect of such limitation or order on employment and on any alleged discharge, lay-off, or other discrimination and the detailed reasons or justification therefor. Any such hearing shall be of record and shall be subject to section 554 of title 5. Upon receiving the report of such investigation, the Administrator shall make findings of fact as to the effect of such effluent limitation or order or employment and on the alleged discharge, lay-off, or discrimination and shall make such recommendations as he deems appropriate. Such report, findings, and recommendations shall be available to the public. Nothing in this subsection shall be construed to require or authorize the Administrator to modify or withdraw any effluent limitation or order issued under this chapter.

(June 30, 1948, ch. 758, title V, § 507, as added Oct. 18, 1972, Pub. L. 92-500, § 2, 86 Stat. 890.)

§ 6971 Employee protection

(a) General

No person shall fire, or in any other way discriminate against, or cause to be fired or discriminated against, any employee or any authorized representative of employees by reason of the fact that such employee or representative has filed, instituted, or caused to be filed or instituted any proceeding under this chapter or under any applicable implementation plan, or has testified or is about to testify in any proceeding resulting from the administration or enforcement of the provisions of this chapter or of any applicable implementation plan.

(b) Remedy

Any employee or a representative of employees who believes that he has been fired or otherwise discriminated against by any person in violation of subsection (a) of this section may, within thirty days after such alleged violation occurs, apply to the Secretary of Labor for a review of such firing or alleged discrimination. A copy of the application shall be sent to such person who shall be the respondent. Upon receipt of such application, the Secretary of Labor shall cause such investigation to be made as he deems appropriate. Such investigation shall provide an opportunity for a public hearing at the request of any party to such review to enable the parties to present information relating to such alleged violation. The parties shall be given written notice of the time and place of the hearing at least five days prior to the hearing. Any such hearing shall be of record and shall be subject to section 554 of title 5. Upon receiving the report of such investigation, the Secretary of Labor shall make findings of fact. If he finds that such violation did occur, he shall issue a decision, incorporating an order therein and his findings, requiring the party committing such violation to take such affirmative action to abate the violation as the Secretary of Labor deems appropriate, including, but not limited to, the rehiring or reinstatement of the employee or representative of employees to his former position with compensation. If he finds that there was no such violation, he shall issue an order denying the application. Such order issued by the Secretary of Labor under this subparagraph shall be subject to judicial review in the same manner as orders and decisions of the Administrator or subject to judicial review under this chapter.

(c) Costs

Whenever an order is issued under this section to abate such violation, at the request of the applicant, a sum equal to the aggregate amount of all costs and expenses (including the attorney's fees) as determined by the Secretary of Labor, to have been reasonably incurred by the applicant for, or in connection with, the institution and prosecution of such proceedings, shall be assessed against the person committing such violation.

(d) Exception

This section shall have no application to any employee who, acting without direction from his employer (or his agent) deliberately violates any requirement of this chapter.

(e) Employment shifts and loss

The Administrator shall conduct continuing evaluations of potential loss or shifts of employment which may result from the administration or enforcement of the provisions of this chapter and applicable implementation plans, including, where appropriate, investigating threatened plant closures or reductions in employment allegedly resulting from such administration or enforcement. Any employee who is discharged, or laid off, threatened with discharge or layoff, or otherwise discriminated against by any person because of the alleged results of such administration or enforcement, or any representative of such employee, may request the Administrator to conduct a full investigation of the matter. The Administrator shall thereupon investigate the matter and, at the request of any party, shall hold public hearings on not less than five days notice, and shall at such hearings require the parties, including the employer involved, to present information relating to the actual or potential effect of such administration or enforcement on employment and on any alleged discharge, layoff, or other discrimination and the detailed reasons or justification therefor. Any such hearing shall be of record and shall be subject to section 554 of title 5. Upon receiving the report of such investigation, the Administrator shall make findings of fact as to the effect of such administration or enforcement on employment and on the alleged discharge, layoff, or discrimination and shall make such recommendations as he deems appropriate. Such report, findings, and recommendations shall be available to the public. Nothing in this subsection shall be construed to require or authorize the Administrator or any State to modify or withdraw any standard, limitation, or any other requirement of this chapter or any applicable implementation plan.

(Pub. L. 89-272, title II, § 7001, as added Pub. L. 94-580, § 2 Oct. 21, 1976, 90 Stat. 2824.)

Appendix 6
Clean Air Act, 42 U.S.C. 7622

§ 7622 Employee protection

(a) Discharge or discrimination prohibited

No employer may discharge any employee or otherwise discriminate against any employee with respect to his compensation, terms, conditions, or privileges of employment because the employee (or any person acting pursuant to a request of the employee)—

> (1) commenced, caused to be commenced, or is about to commence or cause to be commenced a proceeding under this chapter or a proceeding for the administration or enforcement of any requirment imposed under this chapter or under any applicable implementation plan,

> (2) testified or is about to testify in any such proceeding, or

> (3) assisted or participated or is about to assist or participate in any manner in such a proceeding or in any other action to carry out the purposes of this chapter.

(b) Complaint charging unlawful discharge or discrimination; investigation; order

(1) Any employee who believes that he has been discharged or otherwise discriminated against by any person in violation of subsection (a) of this section may, within thirty days after such violation occurs, file (or have any person file on his behalf) a complaint with the Secretary of Labor (hereinafter in this subsection referred to as the "Secretary") alleging such discharge or discrimination. Upon receipt of such a complaint, the Secretary shall notify the person named in the complaint of the filing of the complaint.

(2)(A) Upon receipt of a complaint filed under paragraph (1), the Secretary shall conduct an investigation of the violation alleged in the complaint. Within thirty days of the receipt of such complaint, the Secretary shall complete such investigation and shall notify in writing the complainant (and any person acting in his behalf) and the person alleged to have committed such violation of the results of the investigation conducted pursuant to this subparagraph. Within ninety days of the receipt of such complaint the Secretary shall, unless the proceeding on the complaint is terminated by the Secretary on the basis of a settlement entered into by the Secretary and the person alleged to have committed such violation, issue an order either providing the relief prescribed by subparagraph (B) or denying the complaint. An order of the Secretary shall be made on the record after notice and opportunity for public hearing. The Secretary may not enter into a settlement terminating a proceeding on a complaint without the participation and consent of the complaint.

(B) If, in response to a complaint filed under paragraph (1), the Secretary determines that a violation of subsection (a) of this section has occurred, the Secretary shall order the person who committed such violation to (i) take affirmative action to abate the violation, and (ii) reinstate the complainant to his former position together with the compensation (including back pay), terms, conditions, and privileges of his employment, and the Secretary may order such person to provide compensatory damages to the complainant. If an order is issued under this paragraph, the Secretary, at the request of the complainant, shall assess against the person against whom the order is issued a sum equal to the aggregate amount of all costs and expenses (including attorney's and expert witness' fees) reasonably incurred, as determined by the Secretary, by the complainant for, or in connection with, the bringing of the complaint upon which the order was issued.

(c) Review

(1) Any person adversely affected or aggrieved by an order issued under subsection (b) of this section may obtain review of the order in the United States court of appeals for the circuit in which the violation, with respect to which the order was issued, allegedly occured. The petition for review must be filed within sixty days from the issuance of the Secretary's order. Review shall conform to chapter 7 of title 5. The commencement of proceedings under this subparagraph shall not, unless ordered by the court, operate as a stay of the Secretary's order.

(2) An order of the Secretary with respect to which review could have been obtained under paragraph (1) shall not be subject to judicial review in any criminal or other civil proceeding.

(d) Enforcement of order by Secretary

Whenever a person has failed to comply with an order issued under subsection (b)(2) of this section, the Secretary may file a civil action in the United States district court for the district in which the violation was found to occur to enforce such order. In actions brought under this subsection, the district courts shall have jurisdiction to grant all appropriate relief including, but not limited to, injunctive relief, compensatory, and exemplary damages.

(e) Enforcement of order by person on whose behalf order was issued

(1) Any person on whose behalf an order was issued under paragraph (2) of subsection (b) of this section may commence a civil action against the person to whom such order was issued to require compliance with such order. The appropriate United States district court shall have

jurisdiction, without regard to the amount in controversy or the citizenship of the parties, to enforce such order.

(2) The court, in issuing any final order under this subsection, may award costs of litigation (including reasonable attorney and expert witness fees) to any party whenever the court determines such award is appropriate.

(f) Mandamus

Any nondiscretionary duty imposed by this section shall be enforceable in a mandamus proceeding brought under section 1361 of title 28.

(g) Deliberate violation by employee

Subsection (a) of this section shall not apply with respect to any employee who, acting without direction from his employer (or the employer's agent), deliberately causes a violation of any requirement of this chapter.

(July 14, 1955, ch. 360, title III, § 322, as added Aug. 7, 1977, Pub. L. 95-95, title III, § 312, 91 Stat. 783.)

§ 5851 Employee protection
(a) Discrimination against employee

No employer, including a Commission licensee, an applicant for a Commission license, or a contractor or a subcontractor of a Commission licensee or applicant, may discharge any employee or otherwise discriminate against any employee with respect to his compensation, terms, conditions, or privileges of employment because the employee (or any person acting pursuant to a request of the employee)—

(1) commenced, caused to be commenced, or is about to commence or cause to be commenced a proceeding under this chapter or the Atomic Energy Act of 1954, as amended [42 U.S.C. 2011 et seq.], or a proceeding for the administration or enforcement of any requirement imposed under this chapter or the Atomic Energy Act of 1954, as amended;

(2) testified or is about to testify in any such proceeding or;

(3) assisted or participated or is about to assist or participate in any manner in such a proceeding or in any other manner in such a proceeding or in any other action to carry out the purposes of this chapter of the Atomic Energy Act of 1954, as amended [42 U.S.C 2011 et seq.].

(b) Complaint, filing and notification

(1) Any employee who believes that he has been discharged or otherwise discriminated against by any person in violation of subsection (a) of this section may, within thirty days after such violation occurs, file (or have any person file on his behalf) a complaint with the Secretary of Labor (hereinafter in the subsection referred to as the "Secretary") alleging such discharge or discrimination. Upon receipt of such a complaint, the Secretary shall notify the person named in the complaint of the filing of the complaint and the Commission.

(2)(A) Upon receipt of a complaint filed under paragraph (1), the Secretary shall conduct an investigation of the violation alleged in the complaint. Within thirty days of the receipt of such complaint, the Secretary shall complete such investigation and shall notify in writing the complaint, the Secretary shall complete such investigation and shall notify in writing the complaint (and any person acting in his behalf) and the person alleged to have committed such violation, of the results of the investigation conducted pursuant to this subparagraph. Within ninety days of the receipt of such complaint the Secretary shall, unless the proceeding on the complaint is terminated by the Secretary on the basis of a settlement entered into by the Secretary and the person alleged to have committed such violation, issue an order either providing the relief prescribed by subparagraph (B) or denying the complaint. An order of the Secretary shall be made on the record after notice and opportunity for public hearing. The Secretary may not enter into a settlement terminating a proceeding on a complaint without the participation and consent of the complainant.

(B) If, in response to a complaint filed under paragraph (1), the Secretary determines that a violation of subsection (a) of this section has occurred, the Secretary shall order the person who committed such violation to (i) take affirmative action to abate the violation, and (ii) reinstate the complainant to his former position together with the compensation (including back pay), terms, conditions, and privileges of his employment, and the Secretary may order such person to provide compensatory damages to the complainant. If an order is issued under this paragraph, the Secretary, at the request of the complainant shall assess against the person against who the order is issued a sum equal to the aggregate amount of all costs and expenses (including attorney's and expert witness' fees) reasonably incurred, as determined by the Secretary, by the complainant for, or in connection with, the bringing of the complaint upon which the order was issued.

(c) Review

(1) Any person adversely affected or aggrieved by an order issued under subsection (b) of this section may obtain review of the order in the United States court of appeals for the circuit in which the violation, with respect to which the violation, with respect to which the order was issued, allegedly occurred. The petition for review must be filed within sixty days from the issuance of the Secretary's order. Review shall conform to chapter 7 of title 5. The commencement of proceedings under this subparagraph shall not, unless ordered by the court, operate as a stay of the Secretary's order.

(2) An order of the Secretary with respect to which review could have been obtained under paragraph (1) shall not be subject to judicial review in any criminal or other civil proceeding.

(d) Jurisdiction

Whenever a person has failed to comply with an order issued under subsection (b)(2) of this section, the Secretary may file a civil action in the United States district court for the district in which the violation was found to occur to enforce such order. In actions brought under this subsection, the district courts shall have jurisdiction to grant all appropriate relief including, but not limited to, injunctive relief, compensatory, and exemplary damages.

(e) Commencement of action

(1) Any person on whose behalf an order was issued under paragraph (2) of subsection (b) of this section may commence a civil action against the person to whom such order was issued to require compliance with such order. The appropriate United States district court shall have jurisdiction, without regard to the amount in controversy or the citizenship of the parties, to enforce such order.

(2) The court, in issuing any final order under this subsection, may award costs of litigation (including reasonable attorney and expert witness fees) to any party whenever the court determines such award is appropriate.

(f) Enforcement

Any nondiscretionary duty imposed by this section shall be enforceable in a mandamus proceeding brought under section 1361 of title 28.

(g) Deliberate violations

Subsection (a) of this section shall not apply with respect to any employee who, acting without direction from his or her employer (or the employer's agent), deliberately causes a violation of any requirement of this chapter or of the Atomic Energy Act of 1954, as amended [42 U.S.C. 2011 et seq.].

(Pub. L. 93-438, title II, § 210, as added Pub. L. 95-601, § 10, Nov. 6, 1978, 92 Stat. 2951.)

Appendix 8
Safe Drinking Water Act, 42 U.S.C. 300j-9

(i) Discrimination prohibition: filing of complaint; investigation; order of Secretary; notice and hearing; settlements; attorneys' fees; judicial review; filing of petition; procedural requirments; stay of orders; exclusiveness of remedy; civil actions for enforcement of orders; appropriate relief; expedition of proceedings; mandamus proceedings; prohibition inapplicable to undirected but deliberate violations

(1) No employer may discharge any employee or otherwise discriminate against any employee with respect to his compensation, terms, conditions, or privileges of employment because the employee (or any person acting pursuant to a request of the employee) has—

(A) commenced, caused to be commenced, or is about to commence or cause to be commenced a proceeding under this subchapter or a proceeding for the administration or enforcement of drinking water regulations or underground injection control programs of State,

(B) testified or is about to testify in any such proceeding, or

(C) assisted or participated or is about to assist or participate in any manner in such a proceeding or in any other action to carry out the purposes of this subchapter.

(2)(A) Any employee who believes that he has been discharged or otherwise discriminated against by any person in violation of paragraph (1) may, within 30 days after such violation occurs, file (or have any person file on his behalf) a complaint with the Secretary of Labor (hereinafter in this subsection referred to as the "Secretary") alleging such discharge or discrimination. Upon receipt of such a complaint, the Secretary shall notify the person named in the complaint of the filing of the complaint.

(B)(i) Upon receipt of a complaint filed under subparagraph (A), the Secretary shall conduct an investigation of the violation alleged in the complaint. Within 30 days of the receipt of such complaint, the Secretary shall complete such investigation and shall notify in writing the complainant (and any person acting in his behalf) and the person alleged to have committed such violation, of the results of the investigation conducted pursuant to this subparagraph. Within 90 days of the receipt of such complaint the Secretary shall, unless the proceeding on the complaint is terminated by the Secretary on the basis of a settlement entered into by the Secretary and the person alleged to have committed such violation, issue an order either providing the relief prescribed by clause

(ii) or denying the complaint. An order of the Secretary shall be made on the record after notice and opportunity for agency hearing. The Secretary may not enter into a settlement terminating a proceeding on a complaint without the participation and consent of the complainant.

(ii) If in response to a complaint filed under subparagraph (A) the Secretary determines that a violation of paragraph (1) has occurred, the Secretary shall order (I) the person who committed such violation to take affirmative action to abate the violation, (II) such person to reinstate the complainant to his former position together with the compensation (including back pay), terms, conditions, and privileges of his employment, (III) compensatory damages, and (IV) where appropriate, exemplary damages. If such an order is issued, the Secretary, at the request of the complainant, shall assess against the person against whom the order is issued a sum equal to the aggregate amount of all costs and expenses (including attorney's fees) reasonably incurred, as determined by the Secretary, by the complainant for, or in connection with, the bringing of the complaint upon which the order was issued.   (3)(A) Any person adversely affected or aggrieved by an order issued under paragraph (2) may obtain review of the order in the United States Court of Appeals for the circuit in which the violation, with respect to which the order was issued, allegedly occurred. The petition for review must be filed within sixty days from the issuance of the Secretary's order. Review shall conform to chapter 7 of title 5. The commencement of proceedings under this subparagraph shall not, unless ordered by the court, operate as a stay of the Secretary's order.

(B) An order of the Secretary with respect to which review could have been obtained under subparagraph (A) shall not be subject to judicial review in any criminal or other civil proceeding.

(4) Whenever a person has failed to comply with an order issued under paragraph (2)(B), the Secretary shall file a civil action in the United States District Court for the district in which the violation was found to occur to enforce such order. In actions brought under this paragraph, the district courts shall have jurisdiction to grant all appropriate relief including, but not limited to, injunctive relief, compensatory, and exemplary damages. Civil actions filed under this paragraph shall be heard and decided expeditiously.

(5) Any nondiscretionary duty imposed by this section is enforceable in mandamus proceeding brought under section 1361 of title 28.

(6) Paragraph (1) shall not apply with respect to any employee who, acting without direction from his employer (or the employer's agent), deliberately causes a violation of any requirement of this subchapter.
(July 1, 1944, ch. 373, title XIV, § 1450, as added Dec. 16, 1974, Pub. L. 93-523, § 2(a), 88 Stat. 1691, and amended S. Res. 4, Feb. 4, 1977.)

(c) Discrimination or interference prohibited; complaint; investigation; determination; hearing

(1) No person shall discharge or in any manner discriminate against or cause to be discharged or cause discrimination against or otherwise interfere with the exercise of the statutory rights of any miner, representative of miners or applicant for employment in any coal or other mine subject to this chapter because such miner, representative of miners or applicant for employment has filed or made a complaint under or related to this chapter, including a complaint notifying the operator or the operator's agent, or the representative of the miners at the coal or other mine of an alleged danger or safety or health violation in a coal or other mine, or because such miner, representative of miners or applicant for employment is the subject of medical evaluations and potential transfer under a standard published pursuant to section 811 of this title or because such miner, representative of miners or applicant for employment has instituted or caused to be instituted any proceeding under or related to this chapter or has testified or is about to testify in any such proceeding, or because of the exercise by such miner, representative of miners or applicant for employment on behalf of himself or others of any statutory right afforded by this chapter.

(2) Any miner or applicant for employment or representative of miners who believes that he has been discharged, interfered with, or otherwise discriminated against by any person in violation of this subsection may, within 60 days after such violation occurs, file a complaint with the Secretary alleging such discrimination. Upon receipt of such complaint, the Secretary shall forward a copy of the complaint to the respondent and shall cause such investigation to be made as he deems appropriate. Such investigation shall commence within 15 days of the Secretary's receipt of the complaint, and if the Secretary finds that such complaint was not frivolously brought, the Commission, on an expedited basis upon application of the Secretary, shall order the immediate reinstatement of the miner pending final order on the complaint. If upon such investigation, the Secretary determines that the provisions of this subsection have been violated, he shall immediately file a complaint with the Commission, with service upon the alleged violator and the miner, applicant for employment, or representative of miners alleging such discrimination or interference and propose an order granting appropriate relief. The Commission shall afford an opportunity for a hearing (in accordance with section 554 of title 5 but without regard to subsection

(a)(3) of such section) and thereafter shall issue an order, based upon findings of fact, affirming, modifying, or vacating the Secretary's proposed order, or directing other appropriate relief. Such order shall become final 30 days after its issuance. The Commission shall have authority in such proceedings to require a person committing a violation of this subsection to take such affirmative action to abate the violation as the Commission deems appropriate, including, but not limited to, the rehiring or reinstatement of the miner to his former position with back pay and interest. The complaining miner, applicant, or representative of miners may present additional evidence on his own behalf during any hearing held pursuant to his paragraph.

(3) Within 90 days of the receipt of a complaint filed under paragraph (2), the Secretary shall notify, in writing, the miner, applicant for employment, or representative of miners of his determination whether a violation has occurred. If the Secretary, upon investigation, determines that the provisions of this subsection have not been violated, the complainant shall have the right, within 30 days of notice of the Secretary's determination, to file an action in his own behalf before the Commission, charging discrimination or interference in violation of paragraph (1). The Commission shall afford an opportunity for a hearing (in accordance with section 554 of title 5 but without regard to subsection (a)(3) of such section), and thereafter shall issue an order, based upon findings of fact, dismissing or sustaining the complainant's charges and, if the charges are sustained, granting such relief as it deems appropriate, including, but not limited to, an order requiring the rehiring or reinstatement of the miner to his former position with back pay and interest or such remedy as may be appropriate. Such order shall become final 30 days after its issuance. Whenever an order is issued sustaining the complainant's charges under this subsection, a sum equal to the aggregate amount of all costs and expenses (including attorney's fees) as determined by the Commission to have been reasonably incurred by the miner, applicant for employment or representative of miners for, or in connection with, the institution and prosecution of such proceedings shall be assessed against the person committing such violation. Proceeding under this section shall be expedited by the Secretary and the Commission. Any order issued by the Commission under this paragraph shall be subject to judicial review in accordance with section 816 of this title. Violations by any person of paragraph (1) shall be subject to the provisions of sections 818 and 820(a) of this title.

Appendix 10
Fair Labor Standard Act, 29 U.S.C. 215(a)(3)

(a) After the expiration of one hundred and twenty days from June 25, 1938, it shall be unlawful for any person. . .

(3) to discharge or in any other manner discriminate against any employee because such employee has filed any complaint or instituted or caused to be instituted any proceeding under or related to this chapter, or has testified or is about to testify in any such proceeding, or has served or is about to serve on an industry committee.

Appendix 11
Occupational Safety and Health Act, 29 U.S.C. 660(c)

(c) Discharge or discrimination against employee for exercise of rights under this chapter; prohibition; procedure for relief

(1) No person shall discharge or in any manner discriminate against any employee because such employee has filed any complaint or instituted or caused to be instituted any proceeding under or related to this chapter or has testified or is about to testify in any such proceeding or because of the exercise by such employee on behalf of himself or others of any right afforded by this chapter.

(2) Any employee who believes that he has been discharged or otherwise discriminated against by any person in violation of this subsection may, within thirty days after such violation occurs, file a complaint with the Secretary alleging such discrimination. Upon receipt of such complaint, the Secretary shall cause such investigation to be made as he deems appropriate. If upon such investigation, the Secretary determines that the provisions of this subsection have been violated, he shall bring an action in any appropriate United States district court against such person. In any such action the United States district courts shall have jurisdiction, for cause shown to restrain violations of paragraph (1) of this subsection and order all appropriate relief including rehiring or reinstatement of the employee to his former position with back pay.

(3) Within 90 days of the receipt of a complaint filed under this subsection the Secretary shall notify the complainant of his determination under paragraph (2) of this subsection.

Appendix 12
National Labor Relations Act, 29 U.S.C. 158(a)(4)

(a) Unfair labor practices by employer

It shall be an unfair labor practice for an employer. . .

(4) to discharge or otherwise discriminate against an employee because he has filed charges or given testimony under this subchapter.

(c) Complaint for unlawful discharge, discipline, etc,; notification; investigation into merits of complaint; preliminary order for relief; objections to findings or order; hearing; final order; order of abatement, reinstatement, and damages; costs and expenses

(1) Any employee who believes he has been discharged, disciplined, or otherwise discriminated against by any person in violation of subsection (a) or (b) of this section may, within one hundred and eighty days after such alleged violation occurs, file (or have filed by any person on the employee's behalf) a complaint with the Secretary of Labor alleging such discharge, discipline, or discrimination. Upon receipt of such a complaint, the Secretary of Labor shall notify the person named in the complaint of the filing of the complaint.

(2)(A) Within sixty days of the receipt of a complaint filed under paragraph (1) of this subsection, the Secretary of Labor shall conduct an investigation and determine whether there is reasonable cause to believe that the complaint has merit and notify the complainant and the person alleged to have committed a violation of this section of his findings. Where the Secretary of Labor has concluded that there is reasonable cause to believe that a violation has occurred, he shall accompany his findings with a preliminary order providing the relief prescribed by subparagraph (B) of this paragraph. Thereafter, either the person alleged to have committed the violation or the complainant may, within thirty days, file objections to the findings or preliminary order, or both, and request a hearing on the record, except that the filing of such objections shall not operate to stay any reinstatement remedy contained in the preliminary order. Such hearings shall be expeditiously conducted. Where a hearing is not timely requested, the preliminary order shall be deemed a final order which is not subject to judicial review. Upon the conclusion of such hearing, the Secretary of Labor shall issue a final order within one hundred and twenty days. In the interim, such proceedings may be terminated at any time on the basis of a settlement agreement entered into by the Secretary of Labor, the complainant, and the person alleged to have committed the violation.

(B) If, in response to a complaint filed under paragraph (1) of this subsection, the Secretary of Labor determines that a violation of subsection (a) or (b) of this section has occurred, the Secretary of Labor shall order (i) the person who committed such violation to take affirmative action to abate the violation, (ii) such person to reinstate the complainant to the complainant's former position together with the compensation (including back pay), terms, conditions, and privileges of the complainant's employment, and (iii) compensatory damages. If such an order is issued, the Secretary of Labor, at the request of the complainant may assess against the person against whom the order is issued a sum equal to the aggregate amount of all costs and expenses (including attorney's fees) reasonably incurred, as determined by the Secretary of Labor, by the complainant for, or in connection with, the bringing of the complaint upon which the order was issued.

(d) Judicial review of order; waiver

(1) Any person adversely affected or aggrieved by an order issued after a hearing under subsection (c) of this section may obtain review of the order in the United States Court of Appeals for the circuit in which the violation, with respect to which the order was issued, allegedly occurred, or the circuit in which such person resided on the date of such violation. The petition for review must be filed within sixty days from the issuance of the Secretary of Labor's order. Such review shall be in accordance with the provisions of chapter 7 of title 5 and shall be heard and decided expeditiously.

(2) An order of the Secretary of Labor, with respect to which review could have been obtained under this section, shall not be subject to judicial review in any criminal or other civil proceeding.

(e) Civil action to enforce order; relief granted

Whenever a person has failed to comply with an order issued under subsection (c)(2) of this section, the Secretary of Labor shall file a civil action in the United States district court for the district in which the violation was found to occur in order to enforce such order. In actions brought under this subsection, the district courts shall have jurisdiction to grant all appropriate relief, including injunctive relief, reinstatement, and compensatory damages. Civil actions brought under this subsection shall be heard and decided expeditiously.

Appendix 14
Longshoreman's and Harbor Worker's Compensation Act,
33 U.S.C. 948(a)

§ 948a Discrimination against employees who bring proceedings; penalties; deposit of payments in special fund; civil actions, entitlement to restoration of employment and compensation, qualifications requirement; liability of employer for penalties and payments; insurance policy exemption from liability. . .

It shall be unlawful for any employer or his duly authorized agent to discharge or in any other manner discriminate against an employee as to his employment because such employee has claimed or attempted to claim compensation from such employer, or because he has testified or is about to testify in a proceeding under this chapter. The discharge or refusal to employ a person who has been adjudicated to have filed a fraudulent claim for compensation is not a violation of this section. Any employer who violates this section shall be liable to a penalty of not less than $1,000 or more than $5,000, as may be determined by the deputy commissioner. All such penalties shall be paid to the deputy commissioner for deposit in the special fund as described in section 944 of this title, and if not paid may be recovered in a civil action brought in the appropriate United States district court. Any employee so discriminated against shall be restored to his employment and shall be compensated by his employer for any loss of wages arising out of such discrimination: Provided, That if such employee shall cease to be qualified to perform the duties of his employment, he shall no be entitled to such restoration and compensation. The employer alone and not his carrier shall be liable for such penalties and payments. Any provision in and insurance policy undertaking to relieve the employer from the liability for such penalties and payments shall be void.

Appendix 15
Civil Service Reform Act, 5 U.S.C. 2302

Prohibited personnel practices

(a)(1) For the purpose of this title, "prohibited personnel practice" means any action described in subsection (b) of this section.

(2) For the purpose of this section—

(A) "personnel action" means—

(i) An appointment;

(ii) A promotion;

(iii) an action under chapter 75 of this title or other disciplinary or corrective action;

(iv) a detail, transfer, or reassignment;

(v) a reinstatement;

(vi) a restoration;

(vii) a reemployment;

(viii) a performance evaluation under chapter 43 of this title;

(ix) a decision concerning pay, benefits, or awards, or concerning education or training if the education or training may reasonably be expected to lead to an appointment, promotion, performance evaluation, or other action described in this subparagraph; and

(x) any other significant change in duties or responsibilities which is inconsistent with the employee's salary or grade level;

with respect to an employee in, or applicant for, a covered position in an agency;

(B) "covered position" means any position in the competitive service, a career appointee position in the Senior Executive Service, or a position in the excepted service, but does not include—

(i) a position which is excepted from the competitive service because of its confidential, policy-determining, policy-making, or policy-advocating character; or

(ii) any position excluded from the coverage of this section by the President based on a determination by the President that it is necessary and warranted by conditions of good administration.

(C) "agency" means an Executive agency, the Administrative Office of the United States Courts, and the Government Printing Office, but does not include—

(i) a Government corporation;

(ii) the Federal Bureau of Investigation, the Central Intelligence Agency, the Defense Intelligence Agency, the National Security Agency, and, as determined by the President, any Executive agency or unit thereof the principal function of which is the conduct of foreign intelligence or counterintelligence activities; or

(iii) the General Accounting Office.

(b) Any employee who has authority to take, direct others to take, recommend, or approve any personnel action, shall not, with respect to such authority—

(1) discriminate for or against any employee or applicant for employment—

(A) on the basis of race, color, religion, sex, or national origin, as prohibited under section 717 of the Civil Rights Act of 1964 (42 U.S.C. 2000e-16);

(B) on the basis of age, as prohibited under sections 12 and 15 of the Age Discrimination in Employment Act of 1967 (29 U.S.C. 631, 633a);

(C) on the basis of sex, as prohibited under section 6(d) of the Fair Labor Standards Act of 1938 (29 U.S.C. 206(d));

(D) on the basis of handicapping condition, as prohibited under section 501 of the Rehabilitation Act of 1973 (29 U.S.C. 791); or

(E) on the basis of marital status or political affiliation, as prohibited under any law, rule, or regulation;

(2) solicit or consider any recommendation or statement, oral or written, with respect to any individual who requests or is under consideration for any personnel action unless such recommendation or statement is based on the personal knowledge or records of the person furnishing it and consists of—

(A) an evaluation of the work performance, ability, aptitude, or general qualifications of such individual; or

(B) an evaluation of the character, loyalty, or suitability of such individual;

(3) coerce the political activity of any person (including the providing of any political contribution or service), or take any action against any employee or applicant for employment as a reprisal for the refusal of any person to engage in such political activity;

(4) deceive or willfully obstruct any person with respect to such person's right to compete for employment;

(5) influence any person to withdraw from competition for any position for the purpose of improving or injuring the prospects of any other person for employment;

(6) grant any preference or advantage not authorized by law, rule, or regulation to any employee or applicant for employment (including defining the scope or manner of competition or the requirements for any position) for the purpose of improving or injuring the prospects of any particular person for employment:

(7) appoint, employ, promote, advance, or advocate for appointment, employment, promotion, or advancement, in or to a civilian position any individual who is a relative (as defined in section 3110(a)(3) of this title) of such employee if such position is in the agency in which such employee is serving as a public official (as defined in section 3110(a)(2) of this title) or over which such employee exercises jurisdiction or control as such an official;

(8) take or fail to take a personnel action with respect to any employee or applicant for employment as a reprisal for—

(A) a disclosure of information by an employee or applicant which the employee or applicant reasonably believes evidences—

(i) a violation of any law, rule, or regulation, or

(ii) mismanagement, a gross waste of funds, an abuse of authority, or a substantial and specific danger to public health or safety,

if such disclosure is not specifically prohibited by law and if such information is not specifically required by Executive order to be kept secret in the interest of national defense of the conduct of foreign affairs; or

(B) a disclosure to the Special Counsel of the Merit Systems Protection Board, or to the Inspector General of any agency or another employee designated by the head of the agency to receive such disclosures, of information which the employee or applicant reasonably believes evidences—

(i) a violation of any law, rule, or regulation, or

(ii) mismanagement, a gross waste of funds, an abuse of authority, or a substantial and specific danger to public health or safety;

(9) take or fail to take any personnel action against any employee or applicant for employment as a reprisal for the exercise of any appeal right granted by any law, rule, or regulation;

(10) discriminate for or against any employee or applicant for employment on the basis of conduct which does not adversely affect the performance of the employee or applicant or the performance of others; except that nothing in this paragraph shall prohibit an agency from taking into account in determining suitability or fitness any conviction of the employee or applicant for any crime under the laws of any State, of the District of Columbia, or of the United States; or

(11) take or fail to take any other personnel action if the taking of or failue to take such action violates any law, rule, or regulation implementing, or directly concerning, the merit system principles contained in section 2301 of this title.

This subsection shall not be construed to authorize the withholding of information from the Congress or the taking of any personnel action against an employee who discloses information to the Congress.

(c) The head of each agency shall be responsible for the prevention of prohibited personnel practices, for the compliance with and enforcement of applicable civil service laws, rules, and regulations, and other aspects of personnel management. Any individual to whom the head of an agency delegates authority for personnel management, or for any aspect thereof, shall be similarly responsible within the limits of the delegation.

(d) This section shall not be construed to extinguish or lessen any effort to achieve equal employment opportunity through affirmative action or any right or remedy available to any employee or applicant for employment in the civil service under—

(1) section 717 of the Civil Rights Act of 1964 (42 U.S.C 2000e-16), prohibiting discrimination on the basis of race, color, religion, sex, or national origin;

(2) sections 12 and 15 of the Age Discrimination in Employment Act of 1967 (29 U.S.C. 631, 633a), prohibiting discrimination on the basis of age;

(3) under section 6(d) of the Fair Labor Standards Act of 1938 (29 U.S.C. 206(d)), prohibiting discrimination on the basis of sex;

(4) section 501 of the Rehabilitation Act of 1973 (29 U.S.C. 791), prohibiting discrimination on the basis of handicapping condition; or

(5) the provisions of any law, rule, or regulation prohibiting discrimination on the basis of marital status or political affiliation.

Appendix 16
Employee Retirement Income Act, 29 U.S.C. 1132(a)

(a) Persons empowered to bring a civil action
A civil action may be brought—

(1) by a participant or beneficiary—

(A) for the relief provided for in subsection (c) of this section, or

(B) to recover benefits due to him under the terms of his plan, to enforce his rights under the terms of the plan, or to clarify his rights to future benefits under the terms of the plan;

(2) by the Secretary, or by a participant, beneficiary or fiduciary for appropriate relief under section 1109 of this title;

(3) by a participant, beneficiary, or fiduciary (A) to enjoin any act or practice which violates any provision of this subchapter or the terms of the plan, or (B) to obtain other appropriate equitable relief (i) to redress such violations or (ii) to enforce any provisions of this subchapter or the terms of the plan;

(4) by the Secretary, or by a participant, or beneficiary for appropriate relief in the case of a violation of 1025(c) of this title;

(5) except as otherwise provided in subsection (b) of this section, by the Secretary (A) to enjoin any act or practice which violates any provision of this subchapter, or (B) to obtain other appropriate equitable relief (i) to redress such violation or (ii) to enforce any provision of this subchapter; or

(6) by the Secretary to collect any civil penalty under subsection (i) of this section.

Appendix 17
Federal Surface Mining Act, 30 U.S.C. 1293

§ 1291 Employee protection

(a) Retaliatory practices prohibited

No person shall discharge, or in any other way discriminate against, or cause to be fired or discriminated against, any employee or any authorized representative of employees by reason of the fact that such employee or representative has filed, instituted, or caused to be filed or instituted any proceeding under this chapter, or has testified or is about to testify in any proceeding resulting from the administration or enforcement of the provisions of this chapter.

(b) Review by Secretary; investigation; notice; hearing; findings of fact; judicial review

Any employee or a representative of employees who believes that he has been fired or otherwise discriminated against by any person in violation of subsection (a) of this section may, within thirty days after such alleged violation occurs, apply to the Secretary for a review of such firing or alleged discrimination. A copy of the application shall be sent to the person or operator who will be the respondent. Upon receipt of such application, the Secretary shall cause such investigation to be made as he deems appropriate. Such investigation shall provide an opportunity for a public hearing at the request of any party to such review to enable the parties to present information relating to the alleged violation. The parties shall be given written notice of the time and place of the hearing at least five days prior to the hearing. Any such hearing shall be of record and shall be subject to section 554 of title 5. Upon receiving the report of such investigation the Secretary shall make findings of fact. If he finds that a violation did occur, he shall issue a decision incorporating therein his findings and an order requiring the party committing the violation to take such affirmative action to abate the violation as the Secretary deems appropriate, including, but not limited to, the rehiring or reinstatement of the employee or representative of employees to his former position with compensation. If he finds that there was no violation, he will issue a finding. Orders issued by the Secretary under this subsection shall be sucject to judicial review in the same manner as orders and decisions of the Secretary are subject to judicial review under this chapter.

(c) Costs

Whenever an order is issued under this section to abate any violation, at the request of the applicant a sum equal to the aggregate amount of all costs and expenses (including attorney's fees) to have been reasonably incurred by the applicant for, or in connection with, the institution and prosecution of such proceedings, shall be assessed against the persons committing the violaton.

(Pub. L. 95-87, title VII, § 703, Aug. 3, 1977, 91 Stat. 520.)

Appendix 18
False Claims Act, 31 U.S.C. 3730(h)

Any employee who is discharged, demoted, suspended, threatened, harassed, or in any other manner discriminated against in the terms and conditions of employment by his or her employer because of lawful acts done by the employee on behalf of the employee or others in furtherance of an action under this section, including investigation for, initiation of, testimony for, or assistance in an action filed or to be filed under this section, shall be entitled to all relief necessary to make the employee whole. Such relief shall include reinstatement with the same seniority status such employee would have had but for the discrimination, 2 times the amount of back pay, interest on the back pay, and compensation for any special damages sustained as a result of the discrimination, including litigation costs and reasonable attorneys' fees. An employee may bring an action in the appropriate district court of the United States for the relief provided in this subsection.

Appendix 19
Title VII, 42 U.S.C. 2000e-4(a)

Sec. 704. (a) It shall be an unlawful employment practice for an employer to discriminate against any of his employees or applicants for employment, for an employment agency, or joint labor-management committee controlling apprenticeship or other training or retraining, including on-the-job training programs, to discriminate against any individual, or for a labor organization to discriminate against any member thereof or applicant for membership, because he has opposed any practice made an unlawful employment practice by this title, or because he has made a charge, testified, assisted, or participated in any manner in an investigation, proceeding, or hearing under this title.

Appendix 20
Age Discrimination in Employment Act, 29 U.S.C. 623(d)

(d) It shall be unlawful for an employer to discriminate against any of his employees or applicants for employment, for an employment agency to discriminate against any individual, or for a labor organization to discriminate against any member thereof, or applicant for membership because such individual, member or applicant for membership has opposed any practice made unlawful by this section, or because such individual, member or applicant for membership has made a charge, testified, assisted, or participated in any manner in an investigation, proceeding, or litigation under this Act.

Appendix 21
Job Training and Partnership Act, 29 U.S.C. 1574(g)

(g) Secretary's action against harassment of complainants

If the Secretary determines that any recipient under this chapter has discharged or in any other manner discriminated against a participant or against any individual in connection with the administration of the program involved, or against any individual because such individual has filed any complaint or instituted or caused to be instituted any proceeding under or related to this chapter, or has testified or is about to testify in any such proceeding or investigation under or related to this chapter, or otherwise unlawfully denied to any individual a benefit to which that individual is entitled under the provisions of this chapter or the Secretary's regulations, the Secretary shall, within thirty days, take such action or order such corrective measures, as necessary, with respect to the recipient or the aggrieved individual, or both.

Appendix 22
Migrant & Seasonal Agricultural Workers Protection Act, 29 U.S.C. 1855

(a) Prohibited activies

No person shall intimidate, threaten, restrain, coerce, blacklist, discharge, or in any manner discriminate against any migrant or seasonal agricultural worker because such worker has, with just cause, filed any complaint or instituted, or caused to be instituted, any proceeding under or related to this chapter, or has testified or is about to testify in any such proceedings, or because of the exercise, with just cause, by such worker on behalf of himself or others of any right or protection afforded by this chapter.

(b) Proceedings for redress of violations

A migrant or seasonal agricultural worker who believes, with just cause, that he has been discriminated against by any person in violation of this section may, within 180 days after such violation occurs, file a complaint with the Secretary alleging such discrimination. Upon receipt of such complaint, the Secretary shall cause such investigation to be made as he deems appropriate. If upon such investigation, the Secretary determines that the provisions of this section have been violated, the Secretary shall bring an action in any appropriate United States district court against such person. In any such action the United States district courts shall have jurisdiction, for cause shown, to restrain violation of subsection (a) of this section and order all appropriate relief, including rehiring or reinstatement of the worker, with back pay, or damages.

Appendix 23
Safe Containers for International Cargo Act, 46 U.S.C. 1506

(a) Discrimination against a reporting employee prohibited

No person shall discharge or in any manner discriminate against an employee because the employee has reported the existence of or reported a violation of this chapter to the Secretary or his agents.

(b) Complaint alleging discrimination

An employee who believes that he has been discharged or discriminated against in violation of this section may, with 60 days after the violation occurs, file a complaint alleging discrimination with the Secretary of Labor.

(c) Investigation by Secretary of Labor; judicial relief

The Secretary of Labor may investigate the complaint and, if he determines that this section has been violated, bring an action in an appropriate United States district court. The district court shall have jurisdiction to restrain violations of subsection (a) of this section and to order appropriate relief, including rehiring and reinstatement of the employee to his former position with back pay.

(d) Notification to complainant of intended action

Within 30 days after the receipt of a complaint filed under this section the Secretary of Labor shall notify the complainant of his intended action regarding the complaint.

§1985.   Suits   by   and   against   labor
        organizations

Venue, amount, and citizenship

(a)   Suits for violation of contracts between an employer and a labor organization representing employees in an industry affecting commerce as defined in this chapter, or between any such labor organizations, may be brought in any district court of the United States having jurisdiction of the parties, without respect to the amount in controversy or without regard to the citizenship of the parties.

§ 1981.   Equal rights under the law

All persons within the jurisdiction of the United States shall have the same right in every State and Territory to make and enforce contracts, to sue, be parties, give evidence, and to the full and equal benefit of all laws and proceedings for the security of persons and property as is enjoyed by white citizens, and shall be subject to like punishment, pains, penalties, taxes, licenses, and exactions of every kind, and to no other.

Appendix 26
Civil Rights Act of 1871, 42 U.S.C. 1983

Civil action for deprivation of rights

Every person who, under color of any statute, ordinance, regulation, custom, or usage, of any State or Territory or the District of Columbia, subjects, or causes to be subjected, any citizen of the United States or other person within the jurisdiction thereof to the deprivation of any rights, privileges, or immunities secured by the Constitution and laws, shall be liable to the party injured in an action at law, suit in equity, or other proper proceeding for redress. For the purposes of this section, any Act of Congress applicable exclusively to the District of Columbia shall be considered to be a statute of the District of Columbia.

Appendix 27
Civil Rights Act of 1871, 42 U.S.C. 1985

§ 1985.   Conspiracy to interfere with civil
            rights

Preventing officers from performing duties

(1)   If two or more persons in any State
or Territory conspire to prevent, by force,
intimidation, or threat, any person from
accepting or holding any office, trust or
place of confidence under the United States,
or from discharging any duties thereof; or to
induce by like means any officer of the United
States to leave any State, district, or place,
where his duties as an officer are required to
be performed, or to injure him in his person
or property on account of his lawful discharge
of the duties of his office, or while engaged
in the lawful discharge thereof, or to injure
his property so as to molest, interrupt,
hinder or impede him in the discharge of his
official duties;

Obstructing justice; intimidating party,
witness, or juror

(2)   If two or more persons in any State
or Territory conspire to deter, by force,
intimidation, or threat, any party or witness
in any court of the United States from
attending such court, or from testifying to
any matter pending therein, freely, fully, and
truthfully, or to injure such party or witness
in his person or property on account of his
having so attended or testified, or to
influence the verdict, presentment, or
indictment of any grand or petit juror in any
such court, or to injure such juror in his
person or property on account of any verdict,
presentment, or indictment lawfully assented
to by him, or of his being or having been such
juror; or if two or more persons conspire for
the purpose of impeding, hindering,
obstructing, or defeating, in any manner, the
due course of justice in any State or
Territory, with intent to deny to any citizen
the equal protection of the laws, or to injure
him or his property for lawfully enforcing, or

attempting to enforce, the right of any person, or class of persons, to the equal protection of the laws;

Depriving persons of rights or privileges

(3) If two or more persons in any State or Territory conspire or go in disguise on the highway or on the premises of another, for the purpose of depriving, either directly or indirectly, any person or class of persons of the equal protection of the laws, or of equal privileges and immunities under the laws; or for the purpose of preventing or hindering the constituted authorities of any State or Territory from giving or securing to all persons within such State or Territory the equal protection of the laws; or if two or more persons conspire to prevent by force, intimidation, or threat, any citizen who is lawfully entitled to vote, from giving his support or advocacy in a legal manner, toward or in favor of the election of any lawfully qualified person as an elector for President or Vice President, or as a Member of Congress of the United States; or to injure any citizen in person or property on account of such support or advocacy; in any case of conspiracy set forth in this section, if one or more persons engaged therein do, or cause to be done, any act in furtherance of the object of such conspiracy, whereby another is injured in his person or property, or deprived of having and exercising any right or privilege of a citizen of the United States, the party so injured or deprived may have an action for the recovery of damages occasioned by such injury or deprivation, against any one or more of the conspirators.

Appendix 28
Civil Rights Act of 1871, 42 U.S.C. 1986

§1986. Action for neglect to prevent

Every person who, having knowledge that any of the wrongs conspired to be done, and mentioned in section 1985 of this title, are about to be committed, and having power to prevent or aid in preventing the commission of the same, neglects or refuses to do so, if such wrongful act be committed, shall be liable to the party injured, or his legal representatives, for all damages caused by such wrongful act, which such person by legal diligence could have prevented; and such damages may be recovered in an action on the case; and any number of persons guilty of such wrongful neglect or refusal may be joined as defendants in the action; and if the death of any party be caused by any such wrongful act and neglect, the legal representatives of the deceased shall have such action therefor, and may recover not exceeding $5,000 damages therein, for the benefit of the widow of the deceased, if there be one, and if there be no widow, then for the benefit of the next of kin of the deceased. But no action under the provisions of this section shall be sustained which is not commenced within one year after the cause of action has accrued.

Appendix 29
Civil Rights Attorney's Fee Act, 42 U.S.C. 1988

§ 1988.   Proceedings in vindication of civil
                rights; attorney's fees

        In any action or proceeding to enforce a
provision of sections 1981, 1982, 1983, 1985,
and 1986 of this title, title IX of Public Law
92-318, or title VI of the Civil Rights Act of
1964, the court, in its discretion, may allow
the prevailing party, other than the United
States, a reasonable attorney's fee as part of
the costs.

Appendix 30
Civil Rights Act of 1870, 18 U.S.C. 241

§ 241. Conspiracy against rights of citizens

If two or more persons conspire to injure, oppress, threaten, or intimidate any citizen in the free exercise or enjoyment of any right or privilege secured to him by the Constitution or laws of the United States, or because of his having so exercised the same; or

If two or more persons go in disguise on the highway, or on the premises of another, with intent to prevent or hinder his free exercise or enjoyment of any right or privilege so secured--

They shall be fined not more than $10,000 or imprisoned not more than ten years, or both; and if death results, they shall be subject to imprisonment for any term of years or for life.

INDEX

Age Discrimination in Employment Act, 30. *See also* Civil rights laws

Alabama, 40

Alaska, 41

Animus, 77–78

Arizona, 41–42

Arkansas, 7, 41

Atomic Energy Act. *See* Energy Reorganization Act

Attorney ethics, 1

At-will doctrine, 8–14; general, 39–40; state-by-state analysis, 40–59

Blacklisting, 21

Breach of contract, 40. *See also names of specific states*

Burden of proof, 18, 21, 81

California, 2, 39, 42–43

Causes of Action: blacklisting, 21; breach of contract, 40; civil rights laws, 20–21, 27–28, 30–31; conspiracy, 20–21, 28, 31; contempt, 5–8; covenant of good faith and fair dealing, 40; criminal sanctions, 31, 42; defamation, 40; Duty of Fair Representation doctrine, 25–26; fraud, 40; implied cause of action, 26, 27; implied contract, 40; intentional infliction of emotional distress, 40; interference with contract, 40; invasion of privacy, 40; libel, 44–45; protection of parties to litigation, 6–8

Choice of remedies, 73–74, 75–76. *See also* pre-emption

Circumstantial evidence, 77–78

Civil Rights Act of 1870 (42 U.S.C. 1981), 31. *See also* Civil rights laws

Civil rights laws, 20–21, 27–28, 30–31. *See also* U.S. Constitution, development of whistleblower protection

Civil Service Reform Act, 13, 18, 28–29, 73

Clean Air Act, 13, 19–20, 74

Colorado, 43

Columbia Law Journal, 2

Connecticut, 43–44

Conspiracy, 20–21, 28, 31

Consumer Credit Protection Act, 27

Contempt, 5–8

Covenant of good faith and fair dealing, 40. *See also names of specific states*

Criminal sanctions, 31, 42. *See also* Civil rights laws

Defamation, 40. *See also names of specific states*

Delaware, 44
Department of Interior, 27
Disclosure, role of, 83
Discovery, 78–80
Discriminatory motive, 77–78
Disparate treatment, 80, 81–82
District of Columbia, 29, 44–45
Dual motive, 81–82
Duty of Fair Representation doctrine, 25–26

Employee Retirement Income Security Act, 28
Energy Reorganization Act, 19–20, 25, 74, 75, 94, 106–107
Equal Pay Act, 30. *See also* Civil Rights laws
Equitable tolling, 74–75

Fair labor standards, 13, 28, 109
False Claims Act, 21–22, 31
Federal Aviation Act, 27
Federal Employers Liability Act, 27
Federal Mine Health and Safety Act, 13, 24–25, 92–94
Federal pre-emption, 18, 75, 103–114
Federal protection for whistle-blowers, 17–31. *See also specfic states*; U.S. Constitution, development of whistleblower protection
Federal statutes: Age Discrimination in Employment Act, 30; Civil Rights Act of 1870 (42 U.S.C.), 31; Civil Service Reform Act, 13, 18, 28–29, 73; Clean Air Act, 13, 19–20, 74; Consumer Credit Protection Act, 27; Employee Retirement Income Security Act, 28; Energy Reorganization Act, 19–20, 25, 74, 75, 94, 106–107; Equal Pay Act, 30; Fair Labor Standards Act, 13, 28, 109; False Claims Act, 21–22, 31; Federal Aviation Act, 27; Federal Employers Liability Act, 27; Federal Mine Health and Safety Act, 13, 24–25, 92–94; Freedom of Information Act, 80, 84; Job Training and Partnership Act, 27; Labor Management

Disclosure Act, 26; Longshoremans and Harbor Workers Compensation Act, 29; Migrant and Seasonal Worker Protection Act, 29–30; National Labor Relations Act (NLRA), 12–13, 25, 82–83, 92, 95, 107–111; Nevada, 52; OSHA, 13, 23–24, 74, 82; Racketeer Influenced and Corrupt Organization Act, 31; Railway Labor Act, 27; Safe Containers for International Cargo Act, 30; Safe Drinking Water Act, 19–20, 74; Section 301 of the LMRA, 25–26, 107–111; Solid Waste Disposal Act, 19–20, 74; Superfund, 19–20, 74; Surface Mining Control and Reclamation Act, 27; Surface Transportation Assistance Act, 22–23; Title VII of the Civil Rights Act of 1964, 30, 109; Toxic Substance Control Act, 13, 19–20, 73; U.S. Constitution, development of whistleblower protection, 5–14 (First Amendment, 13–14, 18–19; Fourteenth Amendment, 18–19); Water Pollution Control Act, 19–20, 73, 74; Welfare and Pension Plans Disclosure Act, 28
First Amendment. *See* U.S. Constitution, development of whistleblower protection
Florida, 45
Fraud, 40. *See also names of specific states*
Freedom of Information Act, 80, 84

Georgia, 45
Good faith whistleblowing, 7, 83
Government employees, 18–19, 28–29. *See also* Civil Service Reform Act; U.S. Constitution, development of whistleblower protection
Government investigation, 83–85

Hawaii, 45

Idaho, 45–46
Illinois, 46, 112

About the Authors

STEPHEN M. KOHN was born on September 6, 1956, in Greenbrook, New Jersey. He received a B.S. degree from Boston University, a Masters degree from Brown University, and a J.D. degree from the Northeastern University School of Law. A former Adjunct Professor of Law at Antioch School of Law, Stephen Kohn has authored two additional books: *Protecting Environmental and Nuclear Whistleblowers: A Litigation Manual* and *Jailed for Peace: The History of American Draft Law Violators, 1658–1985* (Greenwood Press, 1985). He has also authored numerous law review articles on labor law and civil liberties.

MICHAEL D. KOHN was born on December 28, 1954, in Plainfield, New Jersey. He received a B.S. degree from Rutgers University and a J.D. degree from the Antioch School of Law, where he served as articles editor to the *Antioch Law Journal*. Michael Kohn has coauthored numerous law review articles on labor law and civil liberties, as well as coauthoring a forthcoming book on the deportation trial of exiled South African activist Dennis Brutus.

Both are in private practice and can be contacted at Kohn, Kohn and Colapinto, 517 Florida Ave, N.W., Washington, D.C. 20001.